The Two Faces of Fear

RECENT TITLES IN

Global and Comparative Ethnography
Edited by Javier Auyero

Violence at the Urban Margins
Edited by Javier Auyero, Philippe Bourgois, and Nancy Scheper-Hughes

Concrete Jungles
By Rivke Jaffe

Soybeans and Power
By Pablo Lapegna

Occupying Schools, Occupying Land
By Rebecca Tarlau

Privilege at Play
By Hugo Cerón-Anaya

Narrow Fairways
By Patrick Inglis

Lives on the Line
By Jeffrey J. Sallaz

The Ambivalent State
By Javier Auyero and Katherine Sobering

Beyond the Case
By Corey M. Abramson and Neil Gong

Burning Matters
By Peter C. Little

Delivery as Dispossession
By Zachary Levenson

Activism under Fire
By Anjuli Fahlberg

The Two Faces of Fear
By Ana Villarreal

The Two Faces of Fear

*Violence and Inequality in the
Mexican Metropolis*

ANA VILLARREAL

OXFORD
UNIVERSITY PRESS

Oxford University Press is a department of the University of Oxford. It furthers the University's objective of excellence in research, scholarship, and education by publishing worldwide. Oxford is a registered trade mark of Oxford University Press in the UK and certain other countries.

Published in the United States of America by Oxford University Press 198 Madison Avenue, New York, NY 10016, United States of America.

© Oxford University Press 2024

All rights reserved. No part of this publication may be reproduced, stored in a retrieval system, or transmitted, in any form or by any means, without the prior permission in writing of Oxford University Press, or as expressly permitted by law, by license, or under terms agreed with the appropriate reproduction rights organization. Inquiries concerning reproduction outside the scope of the above should be sent to the Rights Department, Oxford University Press, at the address above.

You must not circulate this work in any other form and you must impose this same condition on any acquirer.

Library of Congress Cataloging-in-Publication Data
Names: Villarreal, Ana, author.
Title: The two faces of fear : violence and inequality in the Mexican metropolis / Ana Villarreal.
Description: New York, NY : Oxford University Press, [2024] |
Series: Global and comparative ethnography |
Includes bibliographical references and index.
Identifiers: LCCN 2023057464 (print) | LCCN 2023057465 (ebook) |
ISBN 9780197688014 (paperback) | ISBN 9780197688007 (hardback) |
ISBN 9780197688038 (epub) | ISBN 9780197688021 | ISBN 9780197688045
Subjects: LCSH: Fear—Social aspects—Mexico—Monterey. |
Emotions—Social aspects—Mexico—Monterey. | Income distribution—Mexico—Monterey
Classification: LCC BF575.F2 V545 2024 (print) | LCC BF575.F2 (ebook) |
DDC 972/.13—dc23/eng/20231221
LC record available at https://lccn.loc.gov/2023057464
LC ebook record available at https://lccn.loc.gov/2023057465

DOI: 10.1093/oso/9780197688007.001.0001

¿Dónde están?
To the disappeared in Mexico, their families, and
to all forging civic fronts to demand an accountable state.

Contents

1. Fear as an Everyday Problem	1
2. Ubiquitous Violence	26
3. The Logistics of Fear	44
4. Defending San Pedro	60
5. Restructuring Nightlife	83
6. An Oasis from War	101
7. Fear and Inequality at the Onset of Crises	125
Acknowledgments	135
Appendix: Gaining Distance	139
Notes	145
Bibliography	159
Index	177

1

Fear as an Everyday Problem

June 8, 2013

We meet in her two-bedroom house with bars on every window and two locks on the front door. She is a public schoolteacher, fifty-nine, divorced, and living on her own. Her two daughters abroad beg her to leave Guadalupe (a working-class municipality of the Monterrey Metropolitan Area). There have been multiple kidnappings in her neighborhood—including of people she knows locked up in a casa de seguridad (safety house) four blocks away. Her sense of safety stems from living close to relatives and work. "My brother lives two blocks away, my sister lives four blocks in the other direction. If I were to move, I wouldn't feel safer. My school is five minutes away. I feel safe here," she explains, though she takes certain precautions. She is home by 9:30 p.m., watches out for suspicious individuals and vehicles when leaving her house, calls out "Who is it?" when someone knocks, and does not open the door to strangers no matter what they're selling.

This is the first time we sit down to talk, though she remembers my face. Her daughter and I were coworkers, and I once dropped her off at their previous home a decade before. I had just seen her daughter in the United States, where she now lives. Her daughter suggested the interview, established email contact between us, and asked me to deliver an envelope full of pictures of the schoolteacher's only grandson. With such a treasure in my hands, the doors open wide. I am greeted with a smile, a hug, and a full meal before sitting down for coffee and a two-hour interview in her living room. I start with some basic questions—place of birth, education, work—and learn that while originally trained as a schoolteacher, she did not teach for seventeen years. Only recently had she resumed teaching. "When did you start teaching again?" I ask. She breaks down—tears, trembling voice. I turn off my audio recorder and tell her that we do not have to continue. "I don't want to talk about how I went back to teaching," she says. I nod. I won't mention it again. "You can continue taping the interview." I insist we do not need to continue. "I'm fine, I just had a moment," she assures me. We continue. Some thirty minutes later, she recalls the moment that triggered this reaction: surviving a shooting at her previous job,

The Two Faces of Fear. Ana Villarreal, Oxford University Press. © Oxford University Press 2024.
DOI: 10.1093/oso/9780197688007.003.0001

2 THE TWO FACES OF FEAR

which prompted her to take a public teaching job that paid less but was closer to home. Throughout the interview, she returned to the shooting multiple times with details she had left out and its deep impact on her everyday life.

She used to be "audacious," going "everywhere," and "at all times," or at least that is how her previous life seemed now. She did not change her ways at first. "I refused to accept violence was escalating, even if I had suffered a car chase . . . and a detour when they threw a head on a street . . . and then a bomb." She did not watch the news. "I did not want to start the morning with such negativity." At work, she silenced coworkers asking if she had heard what she did not want to hear. "I refused to accept Monterrey was in such a cycle of violence and that at any moment I could be next . . . and then it happened to me." She was in her office finishing a report over the weekend when she thought she heard fireworks. Looking out the window, she saw the military shooting at a group of men taking refuge behind her car. She sheltered in a corner of her office, dialing every number she knew, but nobody picked up. The military came in moments later and asked what she had seen. "I saw you shooting at the car." "No," they told her, reframing what she had seen. "It was los malos (the evil ones) who were shooting." Who would be responsible for the damage? She wanted to file a report. A soldier handed her a school notebook and suggested she write up her report then and there. How would she get back home? Her car had bullet holes from the shooting. She feared other soldiers on the streets might mistake her for a criminal running away and shoot at her. "Nothing's going to happen to you," they assured her, taking packs of water bottles from her office on their way out. "That is when I realized I now lived in a very violent city, me cayó el veinte." (I got it.) Everything changed after the shooting.

She used to go grocery shopping and to the movies late at night. Now she buys groceries during the day and has started knitting. She used to visit her friends in their homes in the nearby municipality of San Nicolás and La Independencia, a prominent working-class neighborhood in Monterrey. Now she has coffee with them once a week in a shopping mall—a central location to all—and makes sure to be home by 9:30 p.m., though a curfew is not a guarantee. "I know something can happen day or night, to anyone, not only to me, but anyone; we can all get caught in crossfire." Still, she lives by her curfew. If gathering with friends later, she hosts at home, and they bring their husbands for added protection. She used to visit her parents' tombs in a nearby town. Now the plastic flowers she buys for them every year are piling up in her closet. "It took me two years, but I've built a bubble I can live in," she says, though livability came at a cost, which she experienced as rapid aging. As she curtails her *activities, she has become a fearful old lady:* "Me volví una viejita, me volví una viejita miedosa." *She prays she can "find herself again." Once I had packed up my audio recorder, she added, "I have never let my daughters see this side I have just shown to you. I don't want to worry them. They can't do anything. If you heard me talking to them on the phone, you would hear me say 'nothing happened,' but talking to you right now, I become aware of the many things that have changed."*

Fear is most often approached as a paradox. Noting wide discrepancies between reported fear and the likelihood of being harmed, scholars of fear have long asked, "why are people so afraid?" This question, compelling and nuanced in many contexts, falls apart in the face of a large-scale threat. As a major turf war between multiple factions of organized crime, the police, and the military disrupted the lives of all in the Monterrey Metropolitan Area in northeastern Mexico in the 2010s, this public schoolteacher feared getting caught in crossfire because her car was caught in crossfire. She feared kidnapping after her neighbors were kidnapped just blocks away from her home. Marginalized youth feared forced recruitment into organized crime because their friends had been abducted. Business owners feared extortion and kidnapping, for they were systematically extorted and kidnapped. Fears varied greatly in this metropolis at this time, but fear in this book is no paradox. Rather, fear is a problem: Where to live? Where to work? How to get around the city? Where and when to organize a social gathering safely or as safely as possible? How to advertise a business? These are the questions people ask themselves every day in places where fear has become a pervasive problem in their lives.

This book provides a new framework to approach fear as an everyday problem, focusing on the experience, practices, and resources of those who fear. Through closely examining its far-reaching impact on social ties, daily practices, and urban spaces, the book brings two seemingly contradictory faces of fear into focus: its ability to simultaneously isolate and to concentrate people and resources, deepening existing inequalities in places of severe societal disruption. The schoolteacher's narrative exemplifies common logistical patterns I observed across social classes: relocating work and leisure closer to home, to occur earlier in the day, and to fall within self-imposed curfews. Fear isolates as individuals curtail their activities and retreat behind locked doors; yet fear also concentrates people and resources, exacerbating class, racial, and spatial divides.

4   THE TWO FACES OF FEAR

In 2011, as metropolitan homicides peaked, ten thousand people came out of their homes and onto a major avenue where they gathered on a weekly basis with their children. They brought private practices into public space, volunteering to teach each other how to do things they loved: practicing yoga and tai chi, playing chess, using a hula hoop, selling homemade snacks and handmade crafts. They exchanged books and offered each other plant seedlings. They reconnected with acquaintances they had not seen in decades. "People are bonding," one said. Indeed, a surprising aspect of this war for some was that neighbors were becoming more aware of public space and the importance of the neighborhood scale. How did a turf war spur the rise of one of the largest public spaces this metropolis has ever seen?

A turf war like the one that took Monterrey hostage in the 2010s may disrupt the lives of all, but some had far more resources to deal with its new problems. As the business elite in this metropolis—one of the wealthiest in Latin America—pooled their resources, they created unexpected outcomes. They called to "defend" the metropolis through new public-private partnerships to revamp the state police and were particularly successful in securing one of its nine municipalities: San Pedro Garza García, or San Pedro for short. San Pedro was already the preferred place of residence for the wealthy. As violence and fear rose, all other aspects of upper-class and upper-middle-class life were reorganized within San Pedro. Major businesses and wealthy families residing elsewhere relocated to this municipality where land values increased as they plummeted elsewhere. Within San Pedro, nightlife clubbing options expanded as metropolitan nightlife was temporarily destroyed downtown. Most surprisingly, a massive public space arose in San Pedro as public parks fell into disuse elsewhere in the metropolis. Walls have long been associated with urban privilege, yet in the midst of this turf war, only the most privileged could be unwalled.

This is a book about how fear and violence exacerbated inequality in the Monterrey Metropolitan Area in the early 2010s, but the problems fear raised for its urban residents are far from exclusive. At the turn of the twenty-first century, Latin America became the most violent region in the world.[1] Violence is pervasive in its cities, and particularly, as Auyero notes, at its urban margins.[2] Fear of falling victim to recurrent criminal and state violence permeates the structures of everyday life, with a deep impact on how citizens engage with each other and with their urban environments.[3] There are certainly differences in the forms and levels of violence across the region. Nonetheless, Carrión leveraged surveys to reveal common patterns across countries: fear restricts schedules, destroys public space, and decreases urbanites' ability to socialize.[4] Fear has a profound impact on the most basic temporal, spatial, and social components of urban life in contemporary Latin America.

Drawing on and extending this line of work, this book takes a closer qualitative look at how people re-create their lives in the face of these restrictions. Whatever fear destroys, people will seek to re-create so that life can go on. Approaching fear as a problem reveals that fear also reschedules, relocates, recalibrates, and regroups in ways that profoundly transform housing, work, leisure, consumption, and presentations of self, with consequences for others. People may confront similar problems when all is disrupted, but they have unequal resources. As the most privileged bind fear to the extent that they can, they widen the gaps. In brief, the central finding of this book is that fear is a powerful polarizer. It deepens classism and racism in everyday relations. It also rapidly exacerbates multiple forms of inequality, including urban inequality, through further isolating and concentrating the resources of the privileged. These two faces of fear provide a novel way to examine widening gaps in other metropoles and at the onset of other crises.

Binding Fear through Everyday Logistics

The study of fear has been marginal to the sociology of emotions, yet establishing its aggravating impact on inequality makes it a matter of general sociological interest.[5] Within the field of sociology, sociologists of crime have been most concerned with understanding fear. Since the 1960s, a rich interdisciplinary literature around the concept of "fear of crime" closely scrutinizes variations of reported fear across class, gender, race, age, and space, revealing how and why those who report being most afraid of crime are often those who are least likely to be victimized.[6] Since the 2000s, this disjuncture between reported fear and actual crime or some other threat has also been theorized as a "culture of fear," "liquid fear," and a "society of fear," attributing fear to manipulative media, state policies, a precarious economy, and modernity, among other factors.[7] While the most prominent concepts in the literature are designed to answer the question of why people fear, fear needs no explanation in some contexts. In such places, sociologists can raise new questions and closely scrutinize the polarizing power of fear on social relations and structures.

6 THE TWO FACES OF FEAR

What do people do when they are afraid, and how do their actions matter for broader inequalities? Sociologists have primarily worked on understanding emotion in face-to-face interactions.[8] For example, from a micro and pragmatist perspective, Tavory considers emotion as a component of everyday problem-solving practices.[9] Emotion is central to the everyday. In the last two decades, sociologists of emotion have called for more work at a macro and structural level. Barbalet, for instance, argues that explaining emotion requires showing what emotions do in structural relationships, for "emotion arises from or inheres in the structural relations of society."[10] Little work has been done within the sociology of emotions to link the micro and the macro and thus reveal how central emotions are to explain what people do and their impact on the broader structures that we live in. Elias is a unique exception, for he considers close interrelations between large-scale processes of pacification of violence, shifts in social relations, and individual emotion.[11] Welding elements from these distinct approaches, I approach fear as a problem and conceptualize the "logistics of fear" as the ensemble of strategies people employ to bind fear on an everyday basis with relational and structural outcomes. As people leverage uneven resources, however, they transform their experience of fear, their relationships with others and with the broader urban structures in which they live.

The logistics of fear encompass a wide set of practices, ranging from reinforcing everyday spaces to relocating residence, work, and leisure, to rescheduling activities within self-imposed curfews, to recalibrating status markers, and regrouping in both public and private spaces. The term "logistics," military in origin, is particularly fitting to encompass this broad range of practices, given that several are military strategies downscaled and extended into civilian life, as in "armoring" spaces and vehicles and traveling in "convoys" and "caravans." Moreover, this is the language locals used to describe their strategies: *blindar* (to armor), *bajar el perfil* (to lower ones profile), *ir en caravana* (to caravan), *viajar en convoy* (to travel in a convoy). While highly individualized, and dynamic, these strategies are nonetheless patterned. Attention to these practices over time reveals two seemingly contradictory faces of fear: (1) fear isolates, fragments, and destroys as individuals curtail their activities, retreat into physically and symbolically fortified perimeters, and strip themselves from self-identifiers; and (2) fear concentrates; it regroups people as they lean into the safety of numbers, strengthening in-class social relations and reinforcing traditional male protective roles. To bind fear, people regrouped in their homes, on the streets, and on highways, in cars and in buses, in pairs and in larger groups. All tried to regroup, although these strategies were not available to all. Young, poor, dark-skinned men were discouraged from gathering in public spaces and targeted when they did. Moreover, they could not lower their profile, for they were racially profiled. Their inability to regroup and recalibrate in a high-violence context attests to fear deepening their preexisting criminalization, making the most basic strategies unavailable to those who needed them the most.

Over time, and through practice, the logistics of fear bind fear amid an ongoing threat. In the case of the public schoolteacher, it "took two years," but it was through relocating her work and leisure practices closer to and inside of her home (already close to relatives, for others sought to relocate closer to relatives), rescheduling everyday activities within a self-imposed curfew, and regrouping with friends at home that she was able to "build a bubble" she could live in. The interview itself allowed her, as others, to "become aware of the many things that had changed," which she had taken for granted. Her narrative reveals that new logistics had an impact on her lived experience of fear. She felt "safe" in a context where she knew "things could happen" because she had redesigned her life to bind fear to the extent that she could, both materially and symbolically. Beyond the physical locks on her doors and the bars on her windows, she created "symbolic security" by imposing a curfew on her life. She most likely did not go out "at all times" before the shooting, but her life did not have a 9:30 p.m. curfew either. Aware it might not protect her from crime, she lived by it because curfews bind fear to certain times of day, enabling activities that might not be carried out otherwise. Symbolic security, which I conceptualize as a sense of security that stems from symbolically reordering the world into a safer place through the creation of symbols and the drawing of symbolic boundaries, was constructed in other realms of life as well.[12] Through rescheduling, relocating, and recalibrating their social practices, locals bound fear temporally, spatially, and in relation to their consumption practices and presentations of self. Spatial patterns in these varied and dynamic logistics on a metropolitan scale reveal widening and deepening socio-spatial divides as the privileged regrouped and spatially reconcentrated uneven resources.

8 THE TWO FACES OF FEAR

Unwalled within a Defended City

What do the privileged do when they are in peril? How do their fears shape their relations to others, their city, and the state in high-violence contexts? While sociologists tend to study the privileged and the periled separately, much can be gained, as Patillo shows, from examining those who are "cushioned" with more resources but nonetheless confronting the perils common to their group.[13] All may have feared in the Monterrey Metropolitan Area at this time, yet the fears of the privileged carried more weight in accelerating ongoing processes of urban segregation. Fear is an established driving force of urban inequality. In urban Brazil, Caldeira finds that "fear of crime" underlies the rise of "fortified enclaves" where walls and private security are used to forge areas of social homogeneity that fragment urban space.[14] In high-violence contexts, however, where the privileged fear violence and are targeted—in this case, kidnapped, extorted, and killed—walls, video, and private security guards may fall short of the threat. The privileged may continue to opt out of public education, public health institutions, and public transportation, as many do in Latin America, but they need a minimum of public security to work—at least where they work.

Increasing evidence shows that the most privileged in Mexico are relying on private security as well as the private use of public security. With regard to Mexico City, Davis, Müller, and Zamorano Villarreal all reveal how private interests merge with policing initiatives, calling into question the very existence of "public" security in the nation's capital.[15] In Central Mexico, Capron finds upper-class and upper-middle-class residents utilizing neighborhood associations as a mechanism to "co-produce" public security through direct financing of police equipment and hiring of police. Such initiatives raise important equity issues, for "beyond gates and walls, in the poor neighborhoods and towns . . . local police are not treated in the same way, they are fewer."[16] Moreover, the police do not treat marginal residents in the same way.[17] San Pedro is similar, though distinct in scale.

As a major turf war erupted, the local business elite established new public-private partnerships with the state government to revamp the state police force.[18] Their marketing teams suggested avoiding the word "police," however, given the rampant distrust in state authorities.[19] They created the *Fuerza Civil* (the civic force), although "civic" here stands primarily for the business elite who funneled the necessary resources to create it. Human rights defenders noted its primary beneficiaries "were the local, national and foreign investors who saw their operations protected . . . and their upper-class neighborhoods sealed."[20] In San Pedro, a member of the business elite took office and sought to "armor" this municipality, revamping the local police and employing paramilitary forces to defend it.[21] Through a period of heightened violence, San Pedro maintained significantly lower homicide rates than the rest of the metropolis. The difference was salient at its borders. In a meticulous eight-year analysis of the spatial distribution of reported homicides in the metropolis, Dorantes-Gilardi and colleagues noted that "safe neighborhoods seem to be located around the municipality boundaries."[22] The securing of this municipal border calls attention to defensive tactics employed at a city level, as well as to its socio-spatial consequences.

In the 1970s, Suttles conceptualized the "defended neighborhood" as one in which residents deploy mechanisms of territorial defense to bind an area within which they feel safe—a concept that has been widely used to think about the creation of local orders, particularly among gangs.[23] Rescaling Suttles's concept to a city scale, I conceptualize San Pedro as a "defended city" where the most privileged concentrate and leverage the state to protect themselves and their interests at a city level. To further clarify what a defended city is and is not, San Pedro is not Santa Fe—an iconic luxurious district in Mexico City that epitomizes what an elite enclave can look like in Mexico.[24] San Pedro is a municipality. It has a mayor, a municipal budget, a legal administrative border to enclose these resources within, and its own police forces to defend it (more numerous, better paid, and better equipped than the rest in the metropolis). San Pedro is closer to Marcuse's citadel, "created by a dominant group to protect or enhance its superior position," which in this case includes protection from rampant violence.[25] Through defending one city and concentrating within, San Pedro became increasingly "disembedded" from the metropolitan area, a more extreme version of a process Rodgers also observed in Managua, Nicaragua.[26]

Suttles argued the defense of a territory may prompt social cohesion among its residents. He was focused on theoretical concerns about how urbanites can fulfill their "desire for community" in a city of strangers.[27] San Pedro provides an extreme case to test this assumption—a common one running through the literature on gated communities. Even within tightly secured and socially homogenous spaces, the upper and upper-middle classes were not at ease. They were suspicious of strangers who could afford to live in their exclusive neighborhoods, attend their private schools, as well as shop and dine in the same high-end stores and restaurants—for "you do not know who they are," they explained. That is the definition of a stranger, but in high-fear contexts, there are only friends and enemies. Strangers were suspect until a common tie was established, reinforcing in-network relations among *los conocidos* (acquaintances), yet another means of defense deployed within the most exclusive spaces in the defended city.

To defend is to exclude. San Pedro brings into focus how violence, fear, and territorial defense leveraged by its most privileged residents can prompt simultaneous urban fragmentation—as in the rapid rise of gated communities—and spatial concentration of privilege, capital, and public security within one city to the detriment of a broader metropolitan area. As violence rose, wealthy individuals and businesses from elsewhere moved into San Pedro, furthering the spatial concentration of capital and all economic opportunities that come with it—for service providers, for small businesses, for shops and restaurants—to the detriment of those outside. While not a physical wall, the municipal border enwalled social relations and practices and further split insiders and outsiders. Within San Pedro, existing class and racial divides were further exacerbated. The working poor were already suspect before the war. As Camus, Cerón-Anaya, and Ramos-Zayas argue, the privileged tend to blame the working poor for all kinds of problems in their everyday lives.[28] Fear deepened preexisting classism and racism. Inside the homes of the privileged, Durin found violence and fear heightening employers' surveillance of domestic workers.[29] On the streets, Hernández-León, among others, documented marginalized dark-skinned youth were already criminalized as *pandilleros* (gang members) before the war (a pervasive pattern many have observed elsewhere).[30] As violence and fear rose, they were charged with more and treated as *sicarios* (killers).

Considering all these consequences, contemporary San Pedro also calls for a classed socio-spatial analysis of civic engagement in violent contexts.[31] While civic engagement is desirable for a strong democracy, it is important to examine which citizens are mobilizing for which city. In Brazil, González and Mayka note civic engagement in policing produces "asymmetric citizenship," identifying some citizens as "virtuous" while further criminalizing others as "security threats."[32] In Monterey, Ramírez Atilano found business-led civic engagement programs in and around a private university called for "all" citizens to participate, yet filtered a "desirable" from an "unwanted" citizenry in practice.[33] When the privileged fear and organize to revamp public institutions to defend themselves at the city level, their ability to privately leverage public security might translate into a successful case, but it is successful only for some. Contemporary San Pedro ultimately reveals that when one municipality is defended, the rest of a metropolis—its most marginalized sectors especially—is further disadvantaged.

The Battle for Monterrey and San Pedro

"If we lose Monterrey, everything will be lost." In 2011, a local business leader captured the disbelief of Monterrey's business elite facing a major turf war over Mexico's "business jewel."[34] Multiple and major turf wars had been underway since Mexican President Calderón declared a "war on drug traffickers" following a contested election in 2006. For the business elite in Monterrey, however, the war had been taking place elsewhere—in border towns like Ciudad Juárez or Tijuana. Home to prestigious universities, thriving industries, and multinational corporations, Monterrey seemed exempt at first from the violence engulfing northern Mexico. As the first bodies were hung from its pedestrian bridges in 2010, the *Wall Street Journal* reported an "exodus" of wealthy Mexicans, US citizens, and other foreigners, delivering "a blow to a city, which for some time was proud to be one of the wealthiest and safest in Latin America."[35]

"We thought it would be temporary," this business leader continued. "That it was related to minor arrangements between mafias. We heard there were drug traffickers living here, but at the time we did not request that they leave the city. I'll be honest, in Monterrey, we became a bit arrogant." He publicly called for measures to defend the city, such as remaking the state police and building a sense of citizenship to increase citizen demands on the state. Above all, he called for a fight when other businessmen were leaving. "I was enraged to see them drop in the towel, that they did not stay to defend what their parents and grandparents had built."[36] Understanding the deep origins of this massive turf war over industrial and wealthy Monterrey requires considering the conditions that favored its industrialization in the first place: namely, its proximity to US industry and markets and the historic centrality of contraband in the region, which provided the initial capital for its industrial success.

There is an origins story locals like to share at family gatherings, passed down from generation to generation, to explain how a small arid town in the middle of nowhere became one of the wealthiest cities in Latin America. "In the beginning, there was beer," the story goes. "Beer needed a bottle. The

12   THE TWO FACES OF FEAR

bottle needed a cap, a label, ink, and so the great industries of Monterrey were born."[37] Beer, glass, and steel manufacturing are all central to the industrialization of Monterrey, yet in the "beginning," every industry needs capital and labor. Two wars in the mid-nineteenth century created unique conditions for industry, commerce, and contraband to thrive. When the US-Mexico border was redrawn as an outcome of the *Intervención Estadounidense*, or US-Mexican War (1846–1848), Monterrey became a border town. Its proximity to the US border is fundamental to its political economy—licit and illicit. Shortly after, the American Civil War (1861–1865) broke out, with significant consequences for the Mexican northeastern states bordering the Confederate states. The Union sought to strangle the Confederate slave-picked cotton economy by blocking all its ports. Desperate to trade, the Confederate states found an alternate route to the Atlantic via northeastern Mexico.[38]

In these four monumental years of the American Civil War, a massive trade of southern slave-picked cotton for gunpowder rushed northeastern Mexico into the global economy with Monterrey, Nuevo León, as its regional administrative capital.[39] Union officials alerted the US secretary of state that this trade provided Confederates with resources equivalent to an army of ten thousand men, for "all gunpowder that the rebels received west of the Mississippi came from Mexico."[40] On the Mexican side, this juncture provided significant capital for the industrial city to come and for the transformation of Monterrey into *La Sultana del Norte* (the Sultan of the North)— that is, the national destination for rural migrants looking for work in its steel, glass, and beer factories at the turn of the twentieth century.

Over the course of the twentieth century, the prohibition of alcohol, marijuana, opiates, and cocaine created the incentives for powerful groups of organized crime to emerge and consolidate in the United States and in Mexico.[41] For much of the twentieth century, the Mexican drug trade provided US consumers with desired drugs without significant violence. As discussed in Chapter 2, "Ubiquitous Violence," escalating binational drug-prohibition policies, shifts in Mexican state-criminal relations, the restructuring of the global cocaine market, the widespread availability of US-manufactured guns at the border, and new and more-brutal groups of organized crime like the Zetas all contributed to spawn devastating turf wars. While many of these factors preceded Calderón's presidency (2006–2012), his "war on drug trafficking" marked a definitive escalation in ongoing criminal and state violence impacting the general population.

Regional and local dynamics are at play in these turf wars as old and new groups of organized crime dispute long-standing contraband routes. For northeastern Mexico, the *Cartel del Golfo* (Gulf Cartel) and the Zetas are of central importance to the period covered in this book. The Gulf Cartel takes its name from the Gulf of Mexico and has its origins smuggling liquor across the US border during Prohibition. In the late 1990s, the Gulf Cartel hired the Zetas as an armed wing—a newly formed criminal group of US-trained elite Mexican army deserters. In 2010, the Zetas and the Gulf Cartel split.[42] Their turf war over northeastern Mexico reverberated across the region. In 2010 and 2011, homicides in all three northeastern states of Tamaulipas, Nuevo León, and Coahuila—the old cotton-turned-cocaine corridor—skyrocketed, as depicted in Figure 1.1. In the state of Nuevo León, homicide rates increased from around 5 to 45 homicides per 100,000 inhabitants between 2009 and 2011.

The Zetas turned to terror as a means of asserting territory over their rivals. Moreover, they diversified their criminal ventures, turning to, among other things, the systematic kidnapping and extortion of the general population, wealthy and poor, big business and small.[43] Unlike drug traffickers in the northwest, where drug trafficking originated in Mexico decades before,

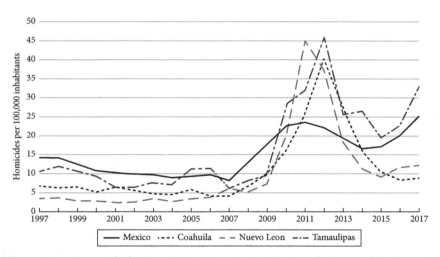

Figure 1.1 The Battle for Northeastern Mexico in Homicide Rates, 1997-2017

Figure 1.1 depicts the simultaneous rise of homicide rates in the three northeastern Mexican states of Coahuila, Nuevo León, and Tamaulipas between 2009 and 2012 almost doubling national homicide rates for Mexico. Source: *Estadísticas de mortalidad, defunciones por homicidio* (Instituto Nacional de Estadística y Geografía 2018); *Indicadores demográficos 1950-2050 – población a mitad de año* (Consejo Nacional de Población 2018).

they were not embedded in drug-cultivating peasant communities.[44] It is perhaps for this reason that no group was spared. Thousands were displaced, and thousands more disappeared.[45] The depth and scope of the violence unleashed by the Zetas and state forces colluding with them was proportional only to the profits at stake in controlling one of the world's most lucrative contraband regions. Ultimately, what a massive battle for industrial, wealthy, low-crime Monterrey revealed to surprised local entrepreneurs and fleeing foreigners in the 2010s is how deeply Monterrey and northeastern Mexico have long been embedded in licit and illicit commodity flows worth fighting for.

Though invested in defending Monterrey, a large metropolis of over five million inhabitants, the business elite were particularly successful in defending San Pedro, the wealthiest of its nine municipalities, shown in Figure 1.2. In San Pedro, the survival of capital and the literal survival of a business elite were simultaneously secured. Locally and internationally, San Pedro was recognized as the safest municipality in the metropolis. Some of its residents never left its borders; others imposed curfews on their families and themselves, requiring them to be within city borders by dusk. Even the US Department of State established a curfew for US consular personnel that

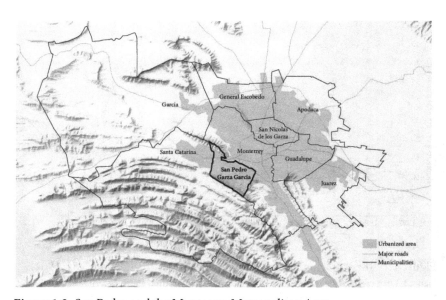

Figure 1.2 San Pedro and the Monterrey Metropolitan Area

Figure 1.2 maps nine municipalities comprising the Monterrey Metropolitan Area, including the wealthy municipality of San Pedro Garza García in bold lines. Map drawn by Sahoko Yui.

did not allow them to "travel outside the San Pedro Garza Garcia municipal boundaries between midnight and 6 a.m."[46]

The battle for Monterrey and the defense of San Pedro provide a compelling example of the logistics of fear and the rise of a defended city, given the ubiquity of violence and fear at the onset of this turf war as well as the collision of extreme violence and extreme inequality. Prior to this war, the Metropolitan Area of Monterrey was already a very unequal metropolis. Rapid industrialization in the twentieth century created wealth for some at the expense of the majority living at the margins of a rapidly expanding metropolis.[47] Those employed in major industries had access to housing, services, and healthcare, though the vast majority were left to build their own homes in precarious conditions and deprived of basic services and government support.[48] Fear and violence built on and exacerbated these preexisting inequalities.

As stated, at the beginning of this section, members of the business elite called on each other to stay and defend the city, reproaching those moving across the border to Texas. One said during an interview: "*O sea* (I mean), there are people, and I told them, 'we need to stay and defend what is ours.'" He referenced a 2010 shootout outside an elite school that the *Wall Street Journal* reported as one that stoked "fears among Mexico's elite that no area of the country is safe."[49] He leaned over and lowered his voice so that two domestic workers in his kitchen would not hear his next comment. "That incident . . . was a fight amongst maids." The shootout involved former bodyguards, which he referred to as domestic workers—a classist move putting the blame of gun violence on low-income workers. "Do I leave my house? No, you stay, and you defend it."

Echoing the call of the business leader mentioned earlier, this businessman would stay and defend his city, which he referred to as his "house," but the metropolis was unequally defended. As the wealthiest further concentrated in a defended San Pedro, marginalized youth were further scattered and socially disbanded. Young and poor dark-skinned men were the worst hit. Their music, their fashion, their way of walking and dancing, and even their forms of leisure were already reasons to call the police on them and to not hire them. Through this turf war, they were detained at higher rates, systematically extorted, forcibly recruited into organized crime, and killed. When examining "successful" security policies in response to violence and fear, it is thus essential to ask: defending whom and at whose expense?

16 THE TWO FACES OF FEAR

Researching Fear in Times of War

I was not planning to write a book about fear. When this war erupted, I was abroad studying to become a sociologist of work. I had trained as a city bus driver to better understand the making of public transportation in this metropolis and its role in the reproduction of inequality through an ethnography of a bus line in Guadalupe (not far from where the public schoolteacher introduced at the beginning of this chapter lived). This was an unlikely choice for a woman raised in private schools in San Pedro. Like many of my classmates, I had never stepped foot inside a bus. I drove everywhere, including to the private college I attended in San Pedro in my early twenties. One day after class, I saw a bus stop behind the parking lot, walked past my car, and boarded the bus.

There were no maps, but everybody knew where they were going. There were no posted schedules, but I later learned drivers were keeping close track of time to get more passengers and thus increase their profit. I got off downtown where all radial bus lines meet and wondered how I would get back. I approached people waiting in line at unmarked street corners and asked for directions. "Where do you come from?" they asked, as I looked for a corner and a bus to take me back. "Not far," I said, quickly realizing how little I knew my hometown. A bus driver was headed "in that direction" and dropped me off on the other side of the Santa Catarina River, a little more than a mile from my university. Walking back, I noticed the distances bus passengers walk to access their places of employment in San Pedro, where residents have long advocated to keep bus service at a bare minimum. Every morning, at multiple bus stops, workers who have been riding the bus for one or two hours, depending on their level of marginality, walk miles more uphill. Alternatively, employers might pick them up from the bus stop. In such cases, it is common to see women drive domestic workers in the backseats of their cars. Those who do are stating that while willing to drive workers between their homes and bus stops, the workers are not equal. They will further signal and enforce class and racial differences in their homes, which workers often access through separate entrances.

Over the next few years, I interviewed bus drivers, bus line owners, union leaders, and state officials and carried out my first ethnography as a bus driver trainee. I was significantly taller and lighter skinned than my classmates at the public bus driving school and my coworkers at the bus line. Their most frequent question was where I lived. I rented a house in a middle-class neighborhood downtown to take the bus everywhere and be able to reply, "I live

FEAR AS AN EVERYDAY PROBLEM   17

downtown." I was confident "San Pedro" would be a far tougher gap to bridge than my height or skin tone, already a synonym for wealth before the war. "Downtown Monterrey" got a pass. For bus drivers in Guadalupe, I was a well-off student living downtown. For the families of my classmates in San Pedro, downtown had long ceased to be a place to live in. As the war erupted, it would become a place to avidly avoid.

In 2007, during one of my rounds as a trainee, there was a shooting in Guadalupe that caused an almost two-hour traffic delay. A bus driver was almost caught in the crossfire when a bullet traversed the window to his left and the front glass before his eyes. Other bus drivers began calling him *el sicario* (the killer) to laugh off the scare. The war was starting in the streets of working-class neighborhoods and even in San Pedro, where a high-ranking public official was shot outside a church long frequented by the business elite. The violence was still sporadic. I left to continue training as a sociologist abroad. Over the next three years, the stories I heard during brief visits kept getting worse. The war was escalating and rapidly engulfed the entire metropolis. *La inseguridad* (the insecurity) was all people talked about. At that point, any other topic seemed off-topic. If sociology could not help me understand why this was happening, what people were doing, and what can be done, then what was I training for?

The war abruptly put me in the position of an ethnographer conducting a "revisit," collecting updates from previously established trust networks.[50] "Everything changed," said the bus line secretary at her baby shower. Mass graves were found in her municipality of Juárez, one of the most marginalized in the metropolis. She did not want to have a baby shower. Her husband convinced her to, so she chose a fast-food restaurant in Monterrey she perceived as a safer location for her guests. One of my neighbors downtown sold hot dogs to locals partying in the Barrio Antiguo, a metropolitan nightlife center that was gravely hit by gun violence—discussed in detail in Chapter 5, "Restructuring Nightlife." He now commuted to San Pedro to clean pools. A bus line owner had transformed his office into a windowless, bulletproof panic room; he feared an armed robbery because bus lines handle a lot of cash. Pictures of his children that used to hang from the walls were gone (an indicator that he feared their kidnapping). Revisiting fieldwork relations and locations provided such data on relocated leisure, reconverted jobs, and reinforced everyday spaces. My revisit, however, was not limited to previous fieldwork ties and everyday spaces. As a local, I had a life of social ties, practices, and spaces to draw on, all disrupted by the war.

THE TWO FACES OF FEAR

I chose fear because it was everywhere. During the summer of 2011, I took my first notes on how others updated me on what I could and could no longer do, where I could and could no longer go, providing the first data to conceptualize the logistics of fear. Over 2012 and 2013, I sought to systematically document these responses to violence and fear across the class spectrum. Access included reencounters with acquaintances from two decades of attending elementary school, high school, and college. Access also included previous work and fieldwork acquaintances from across the class spectrum as well as relatives and their networks. I drew on all these ties to conduct a twenty-four-month ethnography, beginning in the summer of 2011, through most of 2012 and 2013 and early 2014, and with short revisits in 2015 and 2017. Traditional stages of "entering" and "exiting" the field, however, do not map onto this project neatly.

As mentioned before, I was "in the field" prior to taking field notes. Being local also meant that some of the savvy advice I received from top scholars about how to conduct fieldwork in high-violence environments—like scheduling the most dangerous interviews right before catching a flight out—did not apply to me. As a socially embedded local, I cannot leave. I moved slowly through trust networks to build a sample of 154 residents from across the class spectrum, including residents of working-class, middle-class, upper-middle-class, and upper-class neighborhoods, human rights activists, journalists, academics, community organizers, young professionals, college students, and one priest. I sought to stretch my observations as far as possible in both directions to seize, as broadly as possible, the classed repercussions of increased violence and fear. As a local ethnographer, gaining access was easier than gaining distance, further detailed in the Appendix, "Gaining Distance."

Every invitation to reconnect with old friends and acquaintances became fieldwork, including my first reunion with an elementary school cohort I hadn't seen in fifteen years. The gathering took place in a home perched high in the Sierra Madre Mountains in San Pedro. I drove past two security gates to park behind several dozen cars lining the wall of my classmate's property. It would have been a short walk to the main entrance, but I did not have to walk. In San Pedro, class is measured in steps taken in everyday life. A shuttle van ferried guests back and forth to the entrance half a block away. It was also an added safety precaution. Even within a doubly secured gated neighborhood, upper-class and upper-middle-class residents were wary of walking on a street at night.

FEAR AS AN EVERYDAY PROBLEM   19

I boarded the shuttle van and sat next to a classmate I had not seen in over a decade. She was visibly shaken and whispered in my ear that a man had approached her as she was getting out of her car. "I told him, 'Take the keys.' " She quietly replayed the experience, extending her shaking hand holding invisible keys at the shuttle driver, keeping her hand low where he would not see it. "*Wey, no mames, casi me orino*," she added in local jargon. (She thought she would pee her pants.) Minutes earlier, the shuttle driver had approached her to offer a ride down the block; she thought he wanted to steal her car. This type of interaction became typical during the war. As discussed throughout this book, while the privileged had greater resources to defend themselves and their everyday spaces, their unease remained pervasive. Upper-middle-class residents, including my classmate, saw danger in the simplest interaction with someone from a lower-class position and a darker skin tone. This was also true in middle-class neighborhoods, where lower-class, and especially dark-skinned, pedestrians walking by were more likely to be seen as intruders posing danger.

Two uniformed domestic workers greeted us at the entrance and directed us through the main hallway toward the garden. Every door to our right and left was open. Every space was lit. Every empty and laboriously furnished room was on display. Walking out a door to the garden revealed a cliff with a stunning panoramic view of the metropolitan area. It was a clear night. Behind us, the city lit the rocks at the top of the Sierra Madre. Before us, urban lights stretched deep into the horizon, up and over the hill of the Loma Larga marking one of the boundaries between San Pedro and Monterrey, looking minuscule from this height—high-rises on one side, La Independencia on the other. Farther north, and on the other side of the Santa Catarina River, they lit downtown Monterrey—although the Barrio Antiguo was no longer as brightly lit. Beyond they lit middle-class and upper-middle-class neighborhoods in San Nicolás, including those close to the largest public university in the metropolis. Farther out, stretching to the left and right, up and around the base of more mountains and hills, were the municipalities of Santa Catarina, Guadalupe, Escobedo, García, Juárez, and Apodaca, not all as visible, where multiple factories run twenty-four hours a day.[51] Thousands of cars rushed through major avenues and highways, though fewer up the privatized highway leading to this neighborhood, and even fewer past the security gates leading to this house. As neighbors gated this previously public highway, most lost access to multiple hiking trails, making this view

20 THE TWO FACES OF FEAR

increasingly difficult to access. A hiker had lamented, "It's like cutting access to the ocean."

I turned to the kids I grew up with, assembled in a circle nearby. Walking toward them, I remembered one who would not be joining us that night—another victim of the war. Our hostess lounged on a garden chair presiding over the party in a golden strapless dress. It was classmates only. No spouses. No kids. I took a spot in the circle—and a moment to figure out what they were doing. In place of open conversation, my classmates were going around the circle providing an update on their lives along four variables: education, marital status, number of children, and whether their children were attending the same private school we attended. I did not need to design a survey for them. They were surveying themselves.

"I graduated from the Tec," said one, who attended one of the most prestigious private colleges in Mexico located in southern Monterrey and modeled after the Massachusetts Institute of Technology. "I got married, we have three kids, and they're at the school." General applause. Next classmate. "I studied marketing at the UDEM." This is another prestigious private college founded by the business elite and located in San Pedro. "We got married, had two kids, and they're at the school." General applause. Next. "Well, as you all know, I got married," said one who started dating her husband while we were still in school. "Boring!" shouted another, one of our class clowns. General but kind laughter. "We had two kids, and they're at the school." General applause. Next classmate. There was some variation to this sample of college-educated, mostly married classmates with kids. A single woman carefully added that she was "happily single." A couple whose kids were not at "the school" clarified they had recently been told their kids would soon be admitted. There were digressions, but the pattern—and implicit goal—was clear. It was good to go to college, get married, have kids, and it was very good to have your kids attend the school we attended. The survey was a test and celebration of social reproduction.

Then it was my turn. "Well, I became a sociologist, and I'm studying all of you." They laughed. I had always been a bit different, very quiet, nerdy, voted *la más hippie* (the hippiest) when we graduated. I never felt that I fit in their world—the grandchild of a beer glass factory worker and a small business owner who accessed some of their institutions. Through interviews, I discovered "not belonging" was a shared experience among my former classmates. "I didn't live in San Pedro," said one, reliving the pain of a wrong address. "You can't lower your guard," said another, whose kids were enrolled in "the

FEAR AS AN EVERYDAY PROBLEM   21

school," though this was insufficient. She had to stay "on top of" new status markers, always. The upper-middle class strived for the status of the upper class (especially the heirs of the wealthy local business elite). As others have noted, they are a very close-knit group.[52] They compete and do business with each other. They have been marrying each other for generations. I recall a birthday party when we played that two of them would get married. Even as seven-year-olds, we understood the principles of social endogamy. We knew that the wealthy tend to marry the wealthy, a key mechanism of elite social reproduction.

As a child, I often wondered how some of my classmates knew so many kids from older cohorts. Of course, as elites elsewhere, they were related and meeting at multiple venues outside school, which they document and display in a local socialite magazine delivered on a weekly basis to their doors—and the doors of their second homes in Texas during the summer. This socialite magazine is often as thick as the rest of the newspaper, an indicator of the weight that displaying status has in this locality. The heirs, often featured on the cover, were among the kinder children in my experience. They had nothing to prove, at least not to other locals like me. The streets have their names. They knew they owned the city, but as this war roared on, their businesses, lives, and status were all in peril. This book tells the story of how they managed to secure themselves, their businesses, and their status in one move through further concentrating in a defended San Pedro. Their fears and defensive strategies, however, transformed the entire metropolis, far beyond what they could see from the heights of the Sierra Madre.

Previous ties were thus essential to this project. As examined in Chapter 4, "Defending San Pedro," this was a time of extreme social enclosure, when locals were more likely to speak to people they already knew. I was a college friend they had not seen in a decade, a distant acquaintance, a friend of a friend, an old schoolmate, a scholar they saw often at a public or private university. I was different people to my informants, but to all I was someone they could talk to at a time when they wanted to talk. "Studying up" beyond my social acquaintants, I interviewed a handful of businessmen who would not have given me a second of their time in another context, but this was a moment when the business elite wanted to work more closely with civic organizations and academics.[53] They too want to understand the origins of this war and what can be done to prevent such violence in the future. Beyond revamping the state police, the business elite became increasingly invested in fostering a sense of citizenship among locals to increase their demands

22 THE TWO FACES OF FEAR

on the state. Much more can be written on the role the business elite played in fostering the rise of civic organizations and increased interconnectedness between them. This book, however, focuses on the consequences of their first defensive measures for inequality in the metropolis.

Except for public figures and academics, there are no names in this book. I refer to people by profession, the municipality where they live—San Nicolás, Monterrey, Guadalupe, San Pedro—or some other detail providing relevant data for the observation in question. When places are named, the names are real. I heard all these stories in Spanish and translated them myself. English translations of media articles and local scholarship published in Spanish are also my own. At times, I incorporated expressions and key passages in Spanish when relevant. The expression "*o sea*" appears numerous times in the book and can be roughly translated as "I mean," but that is not all that it means. *O sea* is a recurrent placeholder for status, especially when pronounced with long vowels, marking belonging or aspirational belonging to the upper class. It would get lost in translation. I kept such words and expressions in Spanish for added rigor and for the pleasure of the Spanish-speaking reader who has heard them.

Outline of the Book

Why and how did violence become ubiquitous in the everyday lives of millions of Mexicans? Chapter 2 provides brief historical context for the escalation of the war on drugs in Mexico into ubiquitous criminal and state violence—impacting all, albeit unequally. It considers processes converging in the mid-2000s when President Calderón took office and launched a war on drug trafficking: intensified US-Mexico drug-prohibition policies since the 1970s; shifts in Mexican state-criminal relations as the authoritative PRI party fell in the 2000s; the restructuring of the global cocaine market in the mid-2000s; the widespread availability of military grade US-manufactured guns at the border; and more brutal groups of organized crime relying on terror to assert territory. While ubiquitous, rising criminal and state violence was unequal. As the war escalated in Monterrey, kidnapping and extortion became widespread among wealthy and poor. Marginalized youth were the worst hit, both more likely to be criminalized and forcibly recruited into organized crime. Moreover, legal cynicism, or the lack of trust in state authorities to protect people, exacerbated the experience of fear.[54] The

FEAR AS AN EVERYDAY PROBLEM   23

violence was unequal—in both the types of crimes people might fall victim to as well as the likelihood of being victimized—but all were affected by the violence, the fear of violence, and the loss of confidence that the institutions that should protect them actually would.

What do people do when they are afraid? Chapter 3, "The Logistics of Fear," provides examples of new logistical adaptations to bind fear in everyday life focusing on recalibrating and regrouping strategies. Reinforcing, relocating, and rescheduling are examined in later chapters. Crime stories circulating through social networks carried more weight than media reports, prompting locals to experience they could "be next." As kidnapping and extortion soared, wealthy and poor recommended: lower your profile. Recalibrating included downgrading cars and adopting discrete presentations of self, profession, and business. What constituted a low profile varied, but residents from all social classes sought such adjustments. People regrouped or leaned into the safety of numbers in everyday transportation for work, school, and leisure. All tried to recalibrate and regroup, though not all could. Fear deepened the preexisting criminalization of young, poor, dark-skinned men. Their attempt to recalibrate included stripping themselves from a prideful fashion "due to marginality," as one explained, for it made them more prone to police extortion. As people bound their fears using such everyday logistics, they felt safer within the parameters they created for themselves.

What do the privileged do when they are in peril? Chapter 4 traces the urban wealthy becoming increasingly concentrated within a defended San Pedro, heightening inequalities outside and within. San Pedro residents had ambivalent feelings toward the new police force protecting them, but all drew some benefits. Land values in San Pedro increased as these decreased elsewhere. The reluctance of San Pedro residents to go outside the defended city diminished opportunities for businesses and employment outside, while increasing opportunities for businesses and employment within. Although not enwalled, the municipal border enwalled social relations within classed and raced social networks. Narratives of upper-class and upper-middle-class residents revealed heightened suspicion toward the working class in their homes and in parts of the metropolis they now avoided. The wealthy who relocated across the border into Texas also regrouped. Their struggle to re-create the same privileged lives abroad prompted some to return.

How does violence and fear impact nightlife over time? Fear restructured nightlife in Monterrey in a three-stage process of destruction, small-group dispersion, and class-reconcentration, as examined in Chapter 5. The turf

24 THE TWO FACES OF FEAR

war temporarily destroyed metropolitan nightlife in the Barrio Antiguo downtown, as well as elsewhere in the metropolis where middle-class and marginalized youth gathered to drink and dance. All residents dispersed, preferring to party indoors, earlier in the day, and with those who lived nearby. Yet for the wealthy regrouping within San Pedro, fear of leaving the defended city resulted in the expansion of nightlife options. As the most privileged relocated their partying practices closer to home, they reported the new nightlife in San Pedro was "the same thing," but it was the "same" only for them. As the wealthiest spatially concentrated, the most marginal were further scattered. Violence and fear widened and solidified unequal nightlife, stretching the distance between bars catering to wealthy and poor from a few blocks to separate cities.

Fear destroys public space, but Chapter 6, "An Oasis from War," examines how fear and violence simultaneously contributed to create a massive public space in San Pedro. The chapter follows the surprising success of an open-streets program called San Pedro de Pinta. While it might be tempting to look for answers to this paradoxical public space in the physical infrastructure of this walkway—its sidewalks, lighting, shade—the most important factors lie beyond. Its sudden success is inseparable from the destruction of leisure—and particularly outdoor leisure—everywhere else. From outdoor activities to frequenting nearby towns and country homes, leisure was relocated within the metropolis and most often indoors. However, for the privileged in the defended city, a highly policed open-streets program created an oasis from war—an opportunity to "bond" and "forget about everything else." Efforts to re-create a similar open-streets program in every other municipality of the metropolis revealed deep and widening inequalities. No other municipality had the infrastructure and resources of San Pedro. While the privileged celebrated leaving their cars aside and taking the streets, poor and dark-skinned pedestrians inside and outside of San Pedro were unable to gather in streets and parks.

Some of the logistics outlined in the book are particular to contemporary urban Mexico. The far-reaching impact of fear on everyday life and multiple forms of inequality at the onset of a major societal crisis is not. Chapter 7, "Fear and Inequality at the Onset of Crises," draws parallels between social responses to fear of violence and fear of contagion at the onset of the Covid-19 pandemic. The first cases of Covid-19 in Monterrey were detected within San Pedro, yet the defended city took the strictest measures to seclude itself from the rest of the metropolis. The local government of San Pedro established police-enforced "security filters" at its borders, which media and local critics were quick to criticize as class and racial filters. As of 2023, most urban residents in Mexico do not feel safe. A national survey revealed, however, that San Pedro is now the city where residents report feeling the safest in Mexico. To illustrate this book's approach to fear at the onset of crises beyond Mexico and the "war on drugs," the chapter closes with examples of how fear relocated, rescheduled, and regrouped people and practices in New York City heightening inequality at the onset of the Covid-19 pandemic.

2

Ubiquitous Violence

May 13, 2012

"Have you noticed those shoes form a number?" a man asks a toddler holding his hand. "A two?" she asks. "Look, that is a four, and that is a nine." Using his index finger, he traces numbers in the air formed by high heels, tennis shoes, casual shoes, and children's shoes on the ground of the Explanada de los Héroes *(the Heroes Esplanade), a plaza facing the governor's office in downtown Monterrey. "Okay, let's go." They leave a small shapeless crowd of kids and adults curiously eyeing the shoes framed by handwritten signs taped to the ground. "How many in Cadereyta?" one asks near a pair of high heels. This morning, forty-nine dismembered human bodies were found on the highway between Monterrey and Cadereyta; sixty-eight was the unofficial count.*

"Their faces are unrecognizable," says Leticia Hidalgo Rea, laying down a black sign with the question "¿Dónde está?" (Where is he?) and a picture of her son Roy Rivera Hidalgo, who was forcibly abducted from their home in 2011. We met two months ago. I have seen her at several gatherings of this kind, including in this plaza just steps away from where we stand, but never as today. Her dark sunglasses cannot cover the swollenness of her red cheeks and forehead. "The police will only be able to identify the bodies using their DNA," she adds. "How will the police get the DNA samples to match them to?" I wonder out loud. "We all have them," she replies quickly ("we" as in the family members of the disappeared, including the owners of the shoes on the ground). This news, gruesome to many, has a very specific meaning for her. As she lays the picture of her abducted son on the ground between the four and the nine, she is publicly asking whether his body lies among those found on the highway to Cadereyta this morning, whether his face smiling back at her in the picture is among the unrecognizable.

It is a sunny Sunday afternoon, and most of the esplanade is covered with empty plastic water bottles. Hundreds exceptionally gathered earlier to celebrate Mother's Day and receive free hair and make-up tips from the state government. Families and couples walk around eating corn and cotton candy, making their way through lines of artisans at a crafts fair, laughing at a clown

The Two Faces of Fear. Ana Villarreal, Oxford University Press. © Oxford University Press 2024.
DOI: 10.1093/oso/9780197688007.003.0002

performing on the steps leading to the Museum of Mexican History, dancing tango on the sidewalk of an Argentinean ice cream shop, where a bandoneon player sings of love and despair. "Let's go, this gives me the creeps," says a passerby, pulling another away after realizing what the shoes were about. Few notice the shoes, and even fewer stop by. Those who do, and who are not interested in asking if they may have a pair, will listen to the organizers talk about the need for change through small actions of honesty. "Don't keep the change if you notice that the lady at the cash register made a mistake," a middle-aged woman tells the crowd. "These small changes can detonate a powerful movement." Of the bodies found on the highway she says, "We don't know who they were, cannot say they were criminals as some have implied." Most people who stop to listen leave without saying a word.

When bodies are found in Mexico, families experience that their missing loved ones might be among those found. Since President Calderón launched a "war on drug trafficking" upon taking office in 2006, thousands have been killed and thousands more have been disappeared.[1] "They are criminals killing each other" was President Calderón's official narrative for the escalating homicides, disappeared persons, as well as dismembered bodies found during his presidency. Any alternative would undermine his frail legitimacy following a contested election. Amid death threats, however, families spoke up for their murdered and missing loved ones.[2] Journalists and human rights groups put their lives on the line—and fell—reporting their stories.[3] Their courage brought victims and predators into sharper focus.

The dead and the abducted include civilians simply going about their everyday lives. In 2010, graduate students Jorge Antonio Mercado and Javier Francisco Arredondo were standing at the gates of their university when soldiers shot them and tried to frame them as *sicarios* (killers).[4] In 2011, Jorge Otilio Cantú was a newlywed driving his pick-up truck to work when soldiers shot him and similarly tried to frame him as a *sicario*. The dead include Central American migrants, miles from the border of their American dream—as in the case of seventy-two migrants executed in San Fernando, Tamaulipas, and at least some of the forty-nine found on the way to Cadereyta, although much is still unknown about such mass murders in Mexico.[5] Since 2006, almost two thousand mass graves have been found, many of the bodies still unidentified.[6] The war on drugs narrative obscures the systematic involvement of the state as a main perpetrator of violence in Mexico. The stories of the dead and disappeared, however, provide rigorous

28   THE TWO FACES OF FEAR

qualitative evidence of what the war on drugs became at this time: a blanket of impunity over ubiquitous criminal and state violence.

Roy Rivera Hidalgo, whose smiling face lay on the esplanade between the shoe-shaped 4 and the 9 that morning, was a soccer-loving eighteen-year-old college student when he was last seen. In the early hours of January 11, 2011, Roy, his mother Leticia Hidalgo Rea, and younger brother Richi woke up to the strident sounds of a commando of ten to twelve armed individuals breaking into their house in a middle-class neighborhood of the municipality of San Nicolás. Half wore local police vests of the municipality of Escobedo, located north of San Nicolás. They held the family at gunpoint and ravaged their home, taking clothes, tennis shoes, perfumes, laptops, and even meat from the refrigerator. They grabbed the keys to their two vehicles, their three mobile phones, and then they turned to the two teenagers on the ground. "*Son unos morros,*" one said. (They're kids.) "*¿Quién es el mayor?*" their leader asked. (Who is the oldest?) Four or five beat up Richi, who looked older because of his sturdier build. "*Ey, ya déjenlo. Yo soy el mayor,*" Roy replied. (Let him go. I am the oldest.) They flipped a bed over, ordered mother and brother inside the frame, took Roy, and threatened the family on their way out: if anyone reports, "they'll be back and kill them all."[7]

As soon as raucous footsteps had faded and vehicles had sped away, mother and brother went in and out of every ravaged room. They opened every closet to no avail. Barefoot, they went out on the streets looking for help. The first door they knocked on did not open. The next one did, but the neighbors kept the lights off, just in case. The military's phone number was everywhere—even on billboards—but nobody remembered it. Using a cellphone's dim light, the neighbors looked through a phone directory while the others kept their eyes on the street. Through her neighbor's window, Leticia Hidalgo Rea saw two San Nicolás police patrol cars turn a corner, stop by her house—the door still open—go in, come out, and leave. "They're protecting them, not us," she later recalled. Advised by her neighbors, she did not call the military that night. "They will return him, you'll see," they said, for others in their neighborhood had been kidnapped and returned after the ransom was paid. She delivered the ransom as requested, but they did not return Roy. The military "had no doubt" the police were responsible when she went to them, given the details of their story. "That is how the police are operating," a military officer told her. "Active police, not retired police."[8] In 2021, the United Nations condemned Roy's abduction as a case of enforced disappearance involving local, state, and federal authorities.[9]

There are no drugs in Roy's story. No drug seizures. No drug traffickers targeting each other. This is a story of a middle-class family who had dinner, went to bed, and woke up to an armed commando—including state authorities—storming into their home and forever changing their lives. Drugs came up only when Leticia Hidalgo Rea asked why they were doing this. "Because you sell drugs," they said.[10] Their words exemplify how the war on drugs provides a narrative to facilitate criminal and state violence carried out with widespread impunity. The story of Roy Rivera Hidalgo became a high-profile case following his family's efforts to bring his name and face out of anonymity locally, nationally, and internationally. Roy's story, however, is not unique. It is an all-too-familiar and heartbreaking pattern for the thousands more who have been disappeared and for those who have lost loved ones in this ongoing war. How did the war on drugs come to this? This chapter examines binational processes underlying the origins, escalation, and ramifications of the war on drugs in Mexico—from the escalation of US-Mexico prohibition policies to the breakdown of Mexican authoritative state structures, the restructuring of major illicit global drug markets, the widespread availability of guns at the US-Mexico border, and emergence of more brutal groups of organized crime. It then provides a brief overview of how the escalation of this war in Monterrey in the 2010s in particular translated into ubiquitous, though unequal, violence in the everyday lives of its residents—impacting everyone and everything.

Escalating the War on Drugs in Mexico

Prohibition, often taken for granted as an origins factor, lies at the heart of contemporary surges of violence in Mexico, including in Monterrey in the 2010s. Much has been written about the prominent role the United States played in advancing global prohibition, especially in the second half of the twentieth century.[11] Devastating consequences of the war on drugs range from mass incarceration and drug violence in the United States to mass violence and impunity in Mexico.[12] An increasing number of state officials, activists, and scholars are calling for legalization and harm-reduction policies around the globe.[13] In the Mexican case, the call is for the "relegalization" of drugs. In *Nuestra Historia Narcótica*, Enciso reveals that while proponents of the Mexican Revolution prohibited the consumption of opiates, cocaine, and marijuana in the Constitution of 1917—revolutionaries saw these

30 THE TWO FACES OF FEAR

drugs as a "threat to the race"—prohibition has been heavily questioned in medical circles in Mexico since its inception. Under the leadership of Doctor Leopoldo Salazar Viniegras, these drugs were legalized in Mexico on February 17, 1940. New policies supporting addicts with daily doses of heroin and curtailing the influence of prominent drug traffickers of the time, like Lola la Chata, were successful. The US government disapproved and suspended exports of medical drugs south of the border to pressure Mexico back into prohibition within four months.[14] In the second half of the twentieth century, four more factors contributed to escalate criminal and state violence in the late 2000s.

For much of the twentieth century, Mexico was ruled by a single party that emerged from the Mexican Revolution and sought to "institutionalize" it, at least in name—the *Partido Revolucionario Institucional* (the PRI).[15] The introduction of prohibition also instated collusion between the state and drug traffickers. Astorga finds evidence of state-criminal collusion as early as the 1920s.[16] For almost five decades, drug cultivation and trafficking, largely nonviolent, thrived among peasants disenfranchised from the Mexican Revolution in northwestern Mexico.[17] The PRI held a tight grip on Mexican politics, labor, and many aspects of the economy, including drug trafficking. As the PRI lost its hegemonic position at the turn of the twentieth century, state-criminal relations changed.[18] As Durán-Martínez argues, increased autonomy in state-criminal relations—though desirable in a democracy—hinders a state's ability to control organized crime's deployment of violence.[19] In other words, "democratization," understood as the existence of multiple parties running for and winning elections, increased violence in Mexico in part because traffickers were no longer subordinated to an authoritative and cohesive state. The fall of the hegemonic PRI party and its tightly run model of state-criminal relations is key and needs to be considered in relation to the rise and consolidation of other hegemons.

In the aftermath of the second world war, the United States became the main proponent and enforcer of global prohibition.[20] In the 1960s, US President Richard Nixon's response to US youth protesting the Vietnam War with a joint in their hands was to target suppliers abroad. Operation Intercept was the beginning. In 1969, any Mexican crossing the border into the United States became a potential drug trafficker. Two thousand custom agents were deployed to inspect all "vehicles, their component parts, personal baggage, purses, books, lunch boxes, jackets, toys, and in some cases even blouses and

UBIQUITOUS VIOLENCE   31

hairdos," forcing some border crossers to disrobe.[21] It was a costly operation that produced minimal drug seizures. Its primary purpose, Craig argues, was to pressure Mexico into cooperating in binational antidrug campaigns.[22] In this sense, Operation Intercept was a grand success. In the 1970s, operations Canador and Condor followed.[23] These included deploying the military in northwestern Mexico and spraying opium and marijuana fields with dangerous 2,4-D and Gramaxone. Peasant communities were ravaged. In the words of a US diplomat, when these military units "make ground sweeps through known or suspected drug-producing areas they are occasionally too clean," which entails abuse, as "houses are ransacked, men beaten, women violated, and belongings confiscated."[24] A child growing up in one of these ravaged peasant communities became one of Mexico's best known drug traffickers: Joaquín "El Chapo" Guzmán.[25] Rather than curtailing drug trafficking, these binational operations prompted drug traffickers to scatter and seek alliances with peasants elsewhere. As Enciso notes, "beginning with these operations, there is drug violence as such, struggles over specific sales points, instrumental violence."[26]

In 1986, US President Ronald Reagan further escalated the global war on drugs. His National Security Directive on Narcotics and National Security states, "The national security threat posed by the drug trade is particularly serious outside U.S. borders" and threatens national security "by potentially destabilizing democratic allies."[27] Drug trafficking was not a national threat in Mexico in the 1980s. As Astorga notes, the Mexican state created a self-fulfilling prophecy when it aligned with President Reagan's directive.[28] At this time, the PRI had strong domestic incentives to align. In 1988, newly elected President Carlos Salinas de Gortari faced a contested election. The PRI was falling. To win domestic and US support, President Salinas de Gortari arrested high-ranking drug traffickers and created new agencies, paving the way for the militarization of counter-narcotics affairs in Mexico in the presidencies that followed.[29] Drug violence escalated due to both the PRI's loss of hegemony and its efforts to maintain it. In 2000, the PRI conceded a presidential win to another party for the first time in seven decades—the *Partido de Acción Nacional* (PAN)—although its legitimacy was short-lived. Its second and last president to date, Felipe Calderón, faced another contested election in 2006. Like President Salinas de Gortari before him, he relied on the war on drugs for political support, declaring a "war on all drug traffickers" within weeks of taking office.[30] The results were far deadlier, with thousands killed and disappeared during his presidency. While the Mexican

32 THE TWO FACES OF FEAR

state became increasingly fragmented, major drug markets were changing as well.

Mexico borders the world's largest drug consumer and is particularly vulnerable to its shifting drug tastes and preferences. In 2006, as Mexican President Calderón took office, the US cocaine market was estimated at $58 billion; more money was spent on cocaine than on any other illicit drug. Within four years, US drug consumers temporarily dropped half of their cocaine consumption and picked up more marijuana and opioids.[31] For over a century, since its licit days as an anesthetic, the United States had been the epicenter of the global cocaine trade. Cocaine, produced using coca leaves grown in the Andean region, was primarily produced for US consumers and trafficked through the Caribbean in the 1970s and then through Mexico in the 1990s.[32] This drop, which Kilmer termed "Uncle Sam's cocaine nosedive," is indicative of a global restructuring of the cocaine market. Among other factors to consider, RAND researchers found that heavy cocaine consumers, who account for most cocaine consumption, had grown old in the United States.[33] Moreover, the US-led Plan Colombia led to temporary shortages in supply.[34] While numerous questions remain regarding these shifts in demand and supply, it became clear in the decade that followed is that the United States was no longer the epicenter of the global cocaine trade. After a temporary drop, cocaine production in Colombia ramped up and expanded into other markets across the globe.[35] The latest United Nations Office on Drugs and Crime (UNODC) Global Cocaine report clearly maps out cocaine's new major destinations in Brazil and in western and central Europe.[36]

The global restructuring of the cocaine market might also underlie, at least in part, a surge in violence in Mexico during this period. Cocaine-consuming cities are connected to cocaine-trafficking and cocaine-producing areas in long global commodity chains.[37] Shifts in supply or demand at one end of a global commodity chain can reverberate and impact cities and regions elsewhere along the chain. In the case of cocaine, Mexico is vulnerable to both shifts in supply from the south and shifts in demand from the north. Colombian researchers Castillo, Mejía, and Restrepo suggest correlations between cocaine production shortages in Colombia between 2006 and 2009—an outcome of US-led Plan Colombia previously mentioned—and increased homicide rates in Mexico.[38] These were particularly significant for municipalities closest to the US border (the main cocaine-smuggling corridor at the time). While these turf wars cannot be reduced to economic factors alone, there is a need for more transnational work that considers

Mexico's position in major and shifting global illicit commodity chains. Due to decades of escalating drug-prohibition policies, the sudden decision of more than one million people to drop a habit, temporarily or indefinitely, may have carried more weight in disrupting lives south of the border than has been previously considered. Adding gunpowder to this deadly mix, Mexico borders the world's largest gun manufacturer. There are no gun stores in Mexico, but there are two thousand located along the US-Mexico border, providing a steady stream of smuggled weapons for this ongoing war since the binational operations of the 1970s.[39]

Shifting attention to local dynamics, Monterrey made shocking world news as a site of Mexico's escalating war on drugs on August 25, 2011. On that day, young Zetas set fire to a casino in Monterrey: the Casino Royale. Fifty-two people, including two pregnant women, died in this tragic event that local artist Andrés Anza depicted in the piece *Casino Royale* shown in Figure 2.1. The *Guardian* newspaper called it "a new nadir in Mexico's drug war."[40] For *Reuters*, it was "one of the worst attacks of Mexico's drug war" and

Figure 2.1 Casino Royale

In Figure 2.1 local artist Andrés Anza Cortés depicts the violent attack on the *Casino Royale* (2011) that marked an important threshold in the escalation of violence, militarization, and human rights activism in Monterrey. Reproduced with permission from the artist.

34 THE TWO FACES OF FEAR

a particularly bitter one for President Felipe Calderón "because the victims were mainly well-to-do civilians with no link to the conflict, in an area that has traditionally been an electoral stronghold for the business-friendly PAN" party he belongs to.[41] For locals, it was a "violent event," as defined by de Lachica, one that shattered the everyday at a collective level and triggered large protests, the formation of new human rights groups, and the organization of memorials as depicted in Figure 2.2.[42] Thousands participated in the largest peace march in the recent history of the city in the days following this attack—though fewer showed up for the one-year memorial and even fewer for the second-year memorial. At a national level, the Mexican federal government sent three thousand federal police and fifteen hundred more soldiers to Monterrey following this attack, further militarizing the metropolis.[43]

President Calderón called for three days of national mourning and attempted to label the attack "terrorism" (he was heavily criticized for it). He called on the United States to take shared responsibility for fighting organized crime. President Obama called the attack "barbaric" and reiterated his government's commitment to continuing an "unprecedented cooperation in confronting these criminal organizations."[44] In brief, fifty years after US President Nixon declared a war on drugs, escalating prohibition policies helped spawn mass incarceration on one side of the border and mass violence and impunity on the other. Binational efforts are necessary when considering policies that may better serve the people living on both sides of the border.

An Unequal War

Multiple forms of violence further detailed in this section and throughout the book were not limited to major attacks like the fire at the Casino Royale or gunfights in a few neighborhoods (as is often the case with gang warfare). This turf war engulfed the entire metropolis. An eight-year analysis of the temporal and spatial evolution of homicides in the metropolis beginning in 2011 revealed the *Carretera Panamericana* (Highway 85) running through Monterrey as "a backbone of violence as many of the homicides lay directly on the highway paths."[45] Homicides increased in all municipalities in 2011 and 2012, yet "socioeconomic barriers" protected San Pedro, where homicides remained the lowest.[46] On the other end of the class spectrum, this turf war took its heaviest toll on its most marginalized sectors—especially its youth. Marginality alone, which Wacquant defines as state relegation and exclusion from the labor market, cannot explain a rise in homicide and other forms of violence in Monterrey at this time.[47] However, marginality best explains who

UBIQUITOUS VIOLENCE 35

Figure 2.2 Casino Royale One Year Memorial
Figure 2.2. shows twenty of fifty-two crosses placed in front of the Casino Royale for its victims. During the one-year memorial of the attack, human rights activists hung a row of embroidered handkerchiefs and laid shoes of the disappeared on the ground. Picture by author, August 27, 2012.

is most likely to be forcibly recruited into fighting such a war, as well as who is most likely to get targeted as criminal.

The first public signs of organized crime forcibly recruiting marginalized youth were documented in La Independencia. Located on the Loma Larga (Long Hill) dividing Monterrey and San Pedro, the residents of this hill

36 THE TWO FACES OF FEAR

have been largely invisible to city officials for centuries. The very first were Tlaxcalteca people Spanish colonizers forcibly relocated from central Mexico to build colonial Monterrey.[48] Its residents did not figure on city maps until after Mexican Independence.[49] Over the course of the nineteenth and twentieth centuries, La Independencia became the historical port of entry for migrant labor and the cradle of Monterrey's working class. Stoneworkers, shoemakers, leather craftsmen, carpenters, bakers, jewelers, candlemakers, construction workers, and other skilled workers provided vital labor in exchange for low pay, poor services, and acute vulnerability to hurricanes and floods.[50] Criminalized under many names, local authorities' first complaints of the "disorder" in this area where "messy bums gather to commit crimes" date back to 1822.[51] To fight such entrenched discrimination, the residents of this hill, like other severely marginalized populations, "turned segregation into congregation."[52] Beyond employing their skilled hands to build their own homes, they built tight-knit communities, temples, markets of secondhand and disposed objects, cinemas, and bridges to access their places of employment with dry feet and with dignity.[53]

In February 2009, the largely invisible residents of La Independencia made international headlines by blocking major avenues. The *Los Angeles Times* reported its marginalized youth, women, and children took to the streets, ostensibly to protest President Calderón's deployment of the military in the area. They covered their faces with masks, bandanas, and t-shirts, and were referred to in the media as *tapados* (the covered ones). Organized crime paid them "as little as 200 pesos, about $13," gave them a backpack filled with school supplies, and a cell phone to report police and military activity. A priest commented that they followed instructions to protest but "don't even know what it's about or why."[54] Staging public support for pay is a practice the poor know well in Mexico, long mobilized by political parties and unions. Through 2010 and 2011, marginalized youth blocked major avenues on multiple occassions.[55] The largest followed the capture of a Zetas leader and involved the closure of at least twenty avenues at rush hour for over five hours—a practice locals called a *narcobloqueo* (narco blockade). State and municipal police "took very long to respond and the city was practically in a state of siege as people were stuck for hours waiting for the roads to be unblocked and other areas of the city were the grounds for gunfights."[56]

The blockades were highly disruptive. Bus drivers were forced at gunpoint to use their buses to block traffic. One bus driver shared, "I was stopped by *los malitos* (the evil ones) once."[57] Armed men had forced her to block with her bus a private security van that was chasing them. During such blockades, drivers too were forced out of their cars used as barriers to block avenues. "That happened to a friend of mine," said a thirty-year-old woman from San Nicolás. Her friend was driving on the Miguel Alemán highway when she noticed "something strange." Traffic had stopped, and people were taken out of their cars. She did not want to lose her car, so her friend started to drive away. A guy threw himself onto the hood, holding on to the windshield wipers. "*Le dio y le dio y le dio.*" She said her friend "kept going," until the guy fell off and didn't care if she killed him. "That has never happened to me," she added, but a memory popped into her mind to prove her wrong. "Just one time, I saw a *bloqueo* close to Cervecería [Monterrey's iconic beer factory downtown], two buses blocking the avenue, I said, no, this is a *bloqueo.*" She managed to maneuver her way out, though was unsure how she did so. "*No creas que soy muy intrépida.*" (She did not consider herself audacious.)

Locals of every class were caught in the crossfire. In 2010, a woman in her forties was driving home after watching a World Cup match at her brother's house. She drove through a tunnel connecting San Pedro to Monterrey—*el túnel de la Loma Larga*—and arrived at a major intersecting avenue. Cars driving in the opposite direction jumped over the traffic island, onto and across her lane. She saw them park at a fast-food restaurant and run out of their cars. It took her a moment to realize she was in the middle of a shooting between the military on her right and an armed group on her left. Then a bus jumped over the traffic island and landed diagonally in front of her. "I was trapped. I ducked as low as I could, finding room among the pedals and called my brother," she recalled in 2012, ducking as low as she could on her couch in downtown Monterrey. Moments later, the bus began to move. "Stay still," her brother told her on the phone. She refused. The bus was her cover. Hiding among the pedals, she changed gears and drove slowly behind the bus. Both vehicles drove north to a nearby gas station where soldiers ordered them to keep driving. She drove home and did not leave her house for three days. "I felt a dagger in my stomach," she said, stabbing her gut with an imaginary blade.

To assert territory, organized crime and colluding state officials turned to blockades, shootings, and gruesome forms of public killing (including the hanging and public execution of men and women) arousing fear in the general population. The impact of this war on locals, however, does not stop there. Organized crime diversified their business and engaged in increased extortion and kidnapping across the class spectrum. Prior to this violent turf

38   THE TWO FACES OF FEAR

war, kidnapping and extortion were rare in Monterrey and mostly affected the wealthy. Both became widespread as Zetas and other groups of organized crime and colluding state officials turned to systematic kidnapping and extortion, locally referred to as *pedida de piso* (extortion) of both wealthy and poor—a pattern seen elsewhere in Mexico.[58] Most alarming was the rise of disappearances, which permanently disrupt a life and the lives around it.

In 2011, families of the disappeared gathered in public space in Monterrey for the first time. Poet Javier Sicilia provided the occasion, organizing a *Caravana por la Paz* (Caravan for Peace) from Central Mexico to Ciudad Juárez at the northern border. White paper bodies hung from ropes circling the plaza of the Colegio Civil downtown. Slowly but surely, federal police lined the street across from the plaza, with armed officers holding long guns. Organizers opened a corridor amid the crowd for the arriving caravan. "Lock your arms together in case someone tries to break the line!" cried one, instructing us on how to form a human barrier. "Who will try to break the line?" a woman standing next to me asked. "Let's hope nobody does," the organizer said nervously and continued on his way. His nervousness was contagious, especially given the increasing number of military and police surrounding us. A woman claimed, "Nah, there have been no cases of shootings at peace marches." As a precaution, many brought cameras and phones to film the arrival of more police cars and, finally, the appearance of the caravan.

The crowd cheered: "You are not alone! You are not alone!" A woman took the microphone and began to tell the story of her disappeared son. She gathered her breath to state the exact numbers of the police patrol cars responsible for his disappearance. Every time her voice broke, the crowd cheered louder, assuring her that she was not alone. "*No estás sola! No estás sola!*" She told the crowd she would not stop looking for him. "They took him alive! I want him alive!" A dozen more shared their grief, their pain, their anger, and their hope for justice as soldiers in civilian clothes strolled amid the crowd. "Where is everyone?" a father cried out. "Are they at work? Are they watching television? Are they lazy? We need to stop being afraid!" For a metropolis of five million, the gathering of a few hundred was a tangible measure of fear. "I imagine they might drop a grenade," a San Pedro resident told me later, who was aware of this and other protests but afraid to join any (particularly downtown, which she had stopped frequenting).

Protests provided occasions for rising human rights activists to meet and devise new ways of documenting violence unreported due to fear of retaliation. Amid many fleeting initiatives, one grew at a local and national scale: *Bordando por la paz* (Embroidering Peace).[59] In 2012, families of the disappeared in Monterrey, among other groups elsewhere in Mexico, began to gather in public spaces to embroider the names of their dead and disappeared loved ones on white handkerchiefs. In Monterrey, they gathered in the Macro Plaza. Embroideries included names of the dead and disappeared and a short description of the circumstances leading to their death or disappearance—in red for the dead, in green for the disappeared. "You think the world should stop but it doesn't," Leticia Hidalgo Rea explained to a group of students at the public university where her son Roy had been enrolled. "We've encountered such apathy and had to walk on our own for some time." She rearranged a pile of embroidered handkerchiefs in front of her as she spoke, including several embroidered for her son. Together with other family members of the disappeared, she founded the *Fuerzas Unidas por Nuestros Desaparecidos en Nuevo León* (FUNDENL, the United Forces for the Disappeared in Nuevo León). Embroidered handkerchiefs, including those depicted in Figure 2.3, provide evidence of the everyday circumstances in which these abductions took place (and still take place as of 2024). The following were displayed among 200 others during a peace protest in the Explanada de los Héroes on October 26, 2013:

> 23-year old. Apodaca, Nuevo León. "A woman cried out her name. She came out and gave her a kiss. Ten minutes later they took her." February 2010.
> Disappeared August 12, 2010 when he went to work, together with his brother-in-law in Villa de Juárez, Nuevo Léon. Both are still missing.
> 18-year old. La Estanzuela, Monterrey. After taking a taxi with three neighbors, none of them have returned.
> March 2011. He went out with his brother and four friends to a store in San Nicolás de los Garza, none of them returned. The six are still missing.

Stepping out of the house for a moment, going off to work, taking a taxi, going to a store—these are the incomplete stories family members repeat to themselves and to others of lives inexplicably interrupted, including in the municipalities of Apodaca, Juárez, Monterrey, and San Nicolás de los Garza embroidered in these four handkerchiefs. While locals from all social classes were abducted, disappearances in Monterrey and northeastern Mexico more broadly tend to target the most marginalized and criminalized.[60]

Figure 2.3 Embroidering Peace in Nuevo León
In Figure 2.3, a woman reads the content of one handkerchief hung as part of the *Bordando por la Paz* (Embroidering Peace) initiative in downtown Monterrey. Picture by author, October 3, 2012.

Though unequally, upper-class residents, including the business elite, were also targeted. The two most feared crimes among the wealthy at the time of my fieldwork—kidnapping and extortion—are underreported because of distrust in state institutions and fear of retaliation. In 2012, for example,

I attended a "security talk" by a military officer at a private sports club in San Pedro where a woman asked him to report on the number of kidnappings that took place in the city per day. "I can speak of reported cases because those are the ones I have knowledge of," replied the officer. "Um, last month there were only twelve reports but that would be like covering the sun with a finger if we think there were only twelve. Most people do not report. When we find out and approach them, they say, 'thank you but stay out of this, I want him back alive and if they see you they will kill him.' So, my hands are tied." A woman in the audience asked, "Is it true? If they see you come near, will they kill?" He said she would "immediately get a phone call of someone saying, I saw you told the soldiers; I'm turning him in dead." She replied, "Well in that case, it's best not to report." "Well no, it's best to report. It's best to report!"

A birthday party in 2012 also provided an occasion to sample victimization among the upper-class and upper-middle class in Monterrey, mostly residing within San Pedro. I joined a table with three women in their fifties and sixties, including a relative who invited me to the party and introduced me to the other two. "I had to close my clinic," said one. "*Me cayeron los malitos.*" (The evil ones came). They threatened her, claiming they knew where she lived and where her kids were. She closed her business and sent her children to study abroad. A second woman at the table shared a kidnapping that happened in her family. "I don't wish this on anyone," she said, recalling the pain. Another gossiped that a party guest—who was drunk and singing with a band nearby—had also been kidnapped and moved to Texas. This was the first time he was back and was only beginning to talk about it. The sample at the table was small, yet indicative of the extent of victimization among the upper and upper-middle classes. From carjacking to armed house robbery to kidnapping, the next chapters provide further examples of victimization among the most privileged residents in the metropolis. Taken together, all these examples illustrate how violence became ubiquitous in the everyday lives of wealthy, middle class, and poor. It is because violence became ubiquitous that fear became so pervasive. Such fear raised numerous logistical problems and shifts in everyday practices, examined in the chapters that follow.

Facing Ubiquitous Violence and Impunity

This chapter examined multiple factors converging to spawn increased criminal and state violence in Mexico in the mid-2000s. The term "drug violence," frequently used in the media when making reference to increased

42   THE TWO FACES OF FEAR

violence in Mexico, falls short of encompassing the scope of criminal and state violence that became ubiquitous in the lives of the general population. Victimization surveys and the stories of the disappeared make clear that drug violence coexists with the systematic targeting of civilians for labor and for profit through widespread abduction and extortion.[61] The crimes vary, but what all these crimes share is that they go unpunished. Already in 2000, scholars estimated that 97% of crime went unreported in Mexico.[62] Impunity in Mexico is not new, yet the scale of impunity post-2006 is unprecedented.

Knowledge of the deep implication of state authorities in these crimes intensified the experience of fear. In 2010, a survey revealed locals in Monterrey had very little trust in the police, as well as politicians, or judges. They placed the highest trust in the military, but within two years this trust too was dwindling—dropping from nearly half to one-third of surveyed residents.[63] Scholars call this general lack of trust in state authorities to ensure public safety "legal cynicism," and it is pervasive in Monterrey as elsewhere in Mexico.[64] The public schoolteacher cited in the introduction to the book provides a vivid example of this pattern and its impact on fear. As she hid in the corner of her office waiting for the return of the military—engaged in a shootout outside—her fears were multiple. She simultaneously worried about how to get out alive and how to avoid being framed as a criminal if she didn't. "I was so afraid. . . I was in shock, but still, my mind was coldly analyzing my choices, and I thought, 'They're going to kill me here and they're going to say that I was with the *malos*, and the military is going to say that I was among the *malas*.'" She worried that the military would frame her as a criminal and that nobody knew that she was working that Saturday afternoon in her office to prove them wrong. She continued making phone calls, leaving voice messages, praying to an image of the Virgin Mary she pulled out of her purse. "What amazed me the most was that I was doing all these things while thinking of how to get out to survive. If I stayed there, I knew what the army was going to say, '*Ella también era*' (She was a criminal). Because unfortunately, we don't fully trust that their work is clean." Her calls for help also sought to leave a trail of voice messages that could be leveraged as evidence of her innocence should clearing her name be necessary.

Extensive evidence exists of state authorities, including the military, perpetrating violence against the very citizens they swore to protect.[65] As of 2023, the five soldiers under custody for shooting two graduate students outside the Tecnológico de Monterrey in 2010 have not been sentenced.[66] In a rare case, the soldiers who shot and killed the newlywed Jorge Otilio

UBIQUITOUS VIOLENCE 43

Cantú in 2011 were sentenced a decade later.[67] This sentencing is promising in a context where crimes, including state crimes, are largely not reported, investigated, or prosecuted. As Gallagher shows through the case of organized families of the disappeared in Mexico, when citizens participate in ongoing mobilizations, their "legal consciousness," that is, the ways in which they understand the state, themselves as citizens, and their ability to challenge impunity changes.[68]

Amid impunity, new civic organizations rose. FUNDENL is an example. Their struggle for justice is one that seeks to bridge class divides. The FUNDENL members I engaged with in 2012 and 2013 were primarily middle class. The stories they embroidered, however, spanned the class spectrum. On several occasions, locals from marginalized communities approached organizers during embroideries at the Macro Plaza, requesting that they embroider the name and details of a loved one's abduction they were too afraid to report. They embroidered the names of lives lost at the Casino Royale as well, which included working-class staff and well-off residents from San Pedro. On at least one occasion, FUNDENL sought to display their handkerchiefs to San Pedro residents at San Pedro de Pinta—the new public space in San Pedro, discussed in Chapter 6. FUNDENL is a form of civic engagement calling for a joint quest for state accountability that has brought people together locally, nationally, and internationally as embroidered handkerchiefs traveled around Mexico and are sent in from abroad. Other forms of civic engagement I observed discussed in Chapter 6 focused on protecting the spaces and protesting the deaths of the privileged.

3

The Logistics of Fear

The Casino Royale marked a clear threshold in the escalation of a turf war in Monterrey, but the locals' experiences of crime, as well as the stories they heard from friends, relatives, and acquaintances, had the most impact on their everyday lives. Moreover, media reports were secondary in impact to the crime stories shared in everyday conversation. These stories could involve surviving a shooting, being extorted, hearing about a kidnapping in close social networks, or being followed home from a bus stop. The threats and experiences varied greatly, but every single Monterrey resident I spoke to had such "stories" and explicit strategies to guide their behavior and ensure their safety at this time—at least in theory.

In 2010, a journalist noted that as "fear originated by violence and insecurity," activities carried out without prior thought now required a "momentary analysis": " 'Is the neighborhood I am heading to safe?' 'Should I go out at night?' 'What street should I take to arrive safely?' "[1] Contrary to scholarship on fear of crime examining a disjuncture between levels of fear and crime, fear in this context was correlated with violent crime, especially when impacting people in close social proximity.[2] Locals distinguished between a before, when they didn't have to think twice about getting around the city, and an after, when they did. Moreover, it was locals' specific experiences with violent crime that constituted major and multiple before and after moments in their lives, raising specific logistical problems. In this chapter, I examine the logistics of fear: the ensemble of strategies people employ to bind fear on an everyday basis. As outlined in Chapter 1, these strategies encompass a wide set of practices ranging from reinforcing everyday spaces to relocating residence, work, and leisure, rescheduling activities within self-imposed curfews, recalibrating status markers, as well as regrouping in both public and private space. These strategies vary from individual to individual, as well as over time and in relation to crime. Nonetheless, these strategies are patterned, revealing how fear simultaneously isolates and regroups as people lean into the safety of numbers.

The Two Faces of Fear. Ana Villarreal, Oxford University Press. © Oxford University Press 2024.
DOI: 10.1093/oso/9780197688007.003.0003

The schoolteacher's narrative in Chapter 1 exemplifies logistical patterns of relocation and rescheduling that were quite common across social classes. I examine these patterns in greater depth in the chapters that follow, revealing how unequal resources deployed to relocate and regroup produced highly unequal outcomes—even unequal curfews—most evident in the restructuring of metropolitan nightlife and rise of a major public space within San Pedro. In this chapter, I focus on how specific experiences of crime prompt recalibrating and regrouping strategies. In high-crime contexts, recurrent crime stories do not spark "moral panics."[3] Rather, people draw morals from them, lessons on what to do and avoid doing to avoid a similar fate. As kidnapping and extortion soared, impacting wealthy, middle class, and poor, a new societal more emerged: lowering ones profile. This process of social recalibrating included downgrading status markers and adopting more discrete presentations of self, profession, and business. These practices attest to the destructive—in this case, stripping—side of fear, though fear not only destroys. To bind fear, people regrouped in their homes, on the streets, and on highways, in pairs and in larger groups. All tried to regroup and recalibrate, though these strategies were not available to all. Young, poor, dark-skinned men were discouraged from gathering in public spaces and targeted when they did. Moreover, they could not lower their profile, for they were racially profiled. Their inability to regroup and recalibrate in a high-violence context attests to fear deepening their preexisting criminalization, making the most basic strategies unavailable to those who need them the most.

Drawing Morals from Crime Stories

Crime stories carried the most weight in local narratives of escalating violence because everyone had their own. These stories emerge from and travel through social networks. They are highly specific and tend to feature stories unfolding in the everyday spaces of the storytellers shared with others of a similar socioeconomic position. Local narratives revealed that fear increased with crime, as well as with the social proximity to crime. In San Pedro, an upper-middle-class man explained:

> It all started with one or two kidnapping stories... Little by little it became clearer. Every time you would hear this happened to "the friend of a friend of a friend" and then "the friend of a friend" and then it happened

46 THE TWO FACES OF FEAR

to a friend. Then, yes, I began to feel a fear in me and in the collective as well, right?

Similarly, a middle-class man in downtown Monterrey knew "several people" who had been carjacked, robbed, and caught in crossfire. "It's no longer 'the friend of the friend of your *compadre's* (very close friend's) neighbor,'" he explained. "It's your friends who have gone through these experiences. You know that it is perhaps very likely that you'll be next, sooner or later." In contexts of high crime and impunity, sharing crime stories can prompt listeners to experience that they can "be next." The schoolteacher in Guadalupe silenced her coworkers when they attempted to share such stories with her—one way of avoiding this experience. Another is to listen to crime stories closely and draw lessons on what to do (and not) to avoid a similar fate. A mother of two in San Pedro "stopped watching the news, stopped reading the papers" to avoid going "crazy," although she paid close attention to the crime stories in her networks:

> My friend was carjacked. He had a pick-up truck, and we thought, well yeah, you're no longer driving pick-up trucks, maybe we protected ourselves with that . . . some people I know, though not friends, were out at three in the morning . . . they got them both, took them home, emptied their house . . . and the mother of a friend . . . who is 65, they kidnapped her, she was driving a Mercedes. So we looked at what was happening and thought, well, you're no longer out at three in the morning, no longer driving a Mercedes. That gave us peace of mind because we thought, we're on the right track, as low profile as possible, and that's it.

With friends and acquaintances in her immediate social network carjacked, robbed, and kidnapped, this mother of two constructed her "peace of mind" through complying with specific lessons she drew from these stories: do not drive a pick-up truck; do not go out at three in the morning; do not drive a Mercedes. Her husband had already traded his beloved pick-up truck for a smaller car because "he knew they're stealing many," and she was not out that late at night. To state that they were "on the right track" is to create symbolic security through turning a crime story into a dictum of right and wrong behavior. She thought "maybe" she and her husband "protected" themselves with that, for moralizing crime stories offers protection not from crime but from the experience that one could be next.

THE LOGISTICS OF FEAR 47

Crime stories in this context were highly specific and relied on the most to assess a threat and devise strategies in response. "You form your own criteria," explained a middle-class man in downtown Monterrey, "not with what the media tells you, but with what you've seen or what you've heard from acquaintances and friends. I think that information is more reliable." As an example, in 2012, a middle-class mother of two residing in southern Monterrey shared during a dinner with friends that the president of a sports club she frequents was kidnapped outside the club and found dead three days later. He was at a meeting with other men and had just stepped outside for a moment to fetch something from his car. "I leave the sports club by six. If I need to stay for longer, I call my husband," she resolved. A crime story unfolding in a shared everyday space prompts fear of a similar fate. To continue making use of this space, she drew a lesson—leave by six—and included a backup plan. As with the previously mentioned schoolteacher, a curfew might not protect her from a kidnapping, but it allowed her to bind fear to certain times of day and continue using an indoor space that was central to her everyday life. The backup plan involved regrouping. If leaving after her self-imposed curfew, she would call her husband to drive over and wait for her inside his car (as a means of protecting himself as well) and then escort her home. Though I did not ask, the curfew was likely contingent on her husband's work schedule. In brief, by developing new logistics this family bound fear enough to keep making use of a central space in their lives. Across the class spectrum, locals sought to bind fear through shifting their consumption practices and presentations of self as well.

Recalibrating: *Bajar el perfil*

A business owner in San Pedro described Monterrey, the metropolis, as "a city where you showed what you had." In 2010, 2011, however, "all Porsches, Carreras, and big cars like that disappeared." The owners hid them, drove them across the border to use them in Texas, or sold them. He observed his clients recalibrate their status markers, especially cars:

> They were worried about "which van or what look is good for me." They asked, "Hey, what do you think about this little ol' truck?" . . . There was an analysis of which vehicles could help you go unnoticed. . . . People who were

48 THE TWO FACES OF FEAR

driving a Ferrari a year before, you see them driving a regular little pick-up truck or a Beetle.

Among the wealthy, recalibrating status markers became a means of both downgrading and signaling status, with the wealthiest needing to lower their profile the most. As an example, an upper-middle-class woman commented on the security practices of a member of the business elite who had just left the table at a birthday party. "This man keeps a *very* low profile," she told others quietly. "Nobody in his family uses bodyguards or chauffeurs, the man bought a Beetle and drives this car around town." Widespread downgrading of cars impacted the local market. In 2010, *El Norte* reported that following a "wave of violent carjackings, *regiomontanos* (people of Monterrey) began to exchange their luxury vans at car lots . . . for more modest vehicles."[4] A local auto dealer association reported a 50% drop in luxury car sales and a simultaneous 30% increase in middle-range car sales. Its president described this recalibrating process as "reverse shopping":

> People are reverse shopping, someone who was driving a Suburban on a daily basis wants to sell it due to fear and buy a Jetta, the one who had a Jetta feels in the same situation and prefers a Monza . . . *mucha gente está bajando su perfil* [a lot of people are lowering their profile] . . . because the recommendation that we're all making right now is not having a luxury van, better to sell it or store it, get a small car, so this is why these are scarce and expensive.[5]

Sales for specific models deemed popular among organized crime dropped. "Nobody wants a Tahoe," he explained. "Actually, they have offered us several Tahoes, Suburbans, Expeditions because this is a vehicle with a high demand among organized crime."[6] A high number of used luxury cars offered at bargain prices attracted buyers from other cities. In 2013, a local businessman had just been to Guadalajara—a metropolis similar in size and economic importance to Monterrey—and learned they would come "to buy cars, because people were selling them like crazy, the BMWs, out of fear of seeming ostentatious." He too noted luxury vehicles had disappeared from the streets, "except for one or two idiots who dare." He had just seen a *súper padrote* (a pimp) driving one but thought it's neither the time nor place *para andar padroteando* (to be pimping around). This businessman had traded his beloved pick-up truck for a Civic following a close encounter with organized crime on a highway.

THE LOGISTICS OF FEAR 49

Among the middle class, Monterrey was a city where you showed what you wish you had, though violence impacted the use of aspirational status markers as well. A graduate student lived close to a major public university in the municipality of San Nicolás. He described his neighbors as "*mucha gente con aspiraciones de subir*" (people with upward-mobility dreams). To make a little extra money, most of his neighbors, like himself, rented rooms to college students. To expand their outdoor living space, they blocked their garages to host a *carne asada* (barbeque) over the weekend. Growing up in San Nicolás, he did not like the importance people gave to "status, money, the car you're driving, all of that," though trends were changing. Neighbors used to buy secondhand luxury cars, but not anymore. He knew a young man who had been kidnapped. Everyone in his family could afford the monthly payments for their luxury cars, but couldn't afford anything else. They did not have the money to pay the ransom the kidnappers demanded. The family traded the titles to two luxury cars as ransom for their family member at a parking lot. Upon his release, this man "double-checked door locks all the time." He told the graduate student, "*Ya no puedes traer nada bueno porque te secuestran.*" (You can't have nice things because you get kidnapped.) The graduate student, after hearing these real-life stories, felt worried when a friend expressed interest in buying a secondhand Audi:

> I kept telling him, don't buy it, they can kidnap you . . . how are you going to pay? But well, his desire for status was greater . . . and I'm telling you, it's a symptom, because he bought it from small business owners who . . . out of fear, were not using it.

The secondhand Audi buyer is an exception confirming that this new societal rule of keeping a low profile—as in not driving a luxury vehicle—also applied to the middle-class. Regarding his own risks, he said, "*Yo sé que no soy secuestrable.*" (I know I'm not kidnappable.) His use of the linguistic innovation *secuestrable*, however, was a clear indicator of how widespread kidnappings had become, including among the middle class.[7] "If I had an income of 100,000 pesos per month, 200,000, I would feel kidnappable, but my car is very discrete," he added. The reference to the car is key. He could define his own income as far below kidnappability levels, but he knew another middle-class man who was kidnapped outside of that income range. To claim that he "knew" he was not kidnappable is to draw symbolic security from his consumption choices, as in driving a "discrete" car. In his case,

50   THE TWO FACES OF FEAR

discretion involved avoiding aspirational status markers that would portray him as having more money than he had. This was the moral he tried to unsuccessfully impose on his friend. The public schoolteacher from Guadalupe also referenced the car of the kidnapped in her neighborhood:

> They have kidnapped a bunch of people here . . . they were keeping them . . . four blocks away because it looked like they had a lot of money, they had *un camionetón* (a large or sumptuous pick-up truck) . . . I have tried to become invisible, and I think a lot of people have experienced that as well.

A kidnapping story prompts fear of a similar fate. To distance herself from the likelihood of being kidnapped in her own neighborhood where she knows people were held hostage "four blocks away," she explains the kidnapping happened "because it looked like" her neighbors "had a lot of money." In their case, it was a *camionetón* that was to blame. She did not drive such a car. Like the graduate student in San Nicolás, she too drew symbolic security from her discrete consumption practices to become invisible.

Invisibility was sought through discrete dress codes and shifts in facial hair as well. In San Nicolás, a man in his fifties advised, "Don't carry anything in your hands, dress as austerely as possible." He no longer wore *pantalón de vestir* (formal trousers). "Now, around here, tennis shoes, jeans . . . don't carry anything of value." A middle-aged man living close to La Independencia shaved his mustache and cut his hair after two pick-up trucks followed him home from the bus stop. He was afraid he might be mistaken for someone else:

> They confuse me because some people say to me, "Aren't you Raúl? You're not the Raúl that I know." I know he lives further down, but he has been confused with me and I have been confused with him . . . ever since I realized I could be mistaken, I won't lie, I'm afraid.

In this case, the experience of being followed home is the before-and-after moment that triggers a haircut and a shave to avoid being profiled as someone else. Professionals too lowered their profiles. Following a wave of kidnappings of medical personnel, particularly of surgeons and nurses, hospitals advised doctors to refrain from wearing scrubs in public. "People should take measures to be less *secuestrable*, such as avoiding jewelry, watches and designer clothes," advised one.[8] A doctor explained, "You have

THE LOGISTICS OF FEAR   51

to be more careful, *bajar el perfil* (lower your profile), avoid wearing your coat outside or in the car. And, if they call you, verify who is calling."[9] A mother of two in San Pedro was surprised when she arrived at a hospital—her sister was going into labor—and the gynecologist and pediatrician both arrived without uniforms:

> The pediatrician was all dressed in black, that's his look, and the gynecologist was all preppy. Of course, they can't be out there dressed as doctors because they are targets . . . and I told the pediatrician, this is the first time we see you dressed up! "Yes, you can't go around dressed as a doctor anymore."

Businesses too lowered their profile. A *tortillería* down the block from the graduate student's house in San Nicolás closed after repeated extortion. The owner told the graduate student, *"No dejan trabajar."* (They don't let you work.) He moved across the border—extortion in this case prompted a relocation abroad. In a low-income Monterrey neighborhood, a man closed a beer stand set up in his house following extortion as well—just like the rest of the shops on his street. In his case, extortion led to job reconversion. He bought a small van to work as a mover but was careful to separate his home from his business. A neighbor noted, "He parks a couple of blocks away from his house. His number is listed on the van, and if he receives a call and thinks it's trustworthy, he takes the job." In San Nicolás, a small food stand managed to stay open as neighboring businesses—including a butcher and a car lot—closed due to extortion. A frequent customer attributed its exceptional survival to the owner's adoption of intentionally rundown aesthetics:

> What he sells does not match the appearance of the stand. It's horrible on the outside, but then he has kept it as a strategy . . . Don't let it seem like business is going too well and add chains . . . no, he keeps it as a stand inside a building that does not draw attention.

Discretion practices also involved the avoidance of signs. In Monterrey, a great bakery opened, but only neighbors knew about it, including the neighbor who took me there. From the outside, it looked like any other house on the block. The only sign advertising the bakery was the scent of fresh bread. In an upper-middle-class neighborhood in San Pedro, a doctor removed a sign announcing his private practice from outside the building

52 THE TWO FACES OF FEAR

and a graphic designer closed her shop and took her business online out of fear of extortion.

All these examples illustrate the deep impact of varied fears on individual and institutional consumption practices, status markers, and presentations of self and business seeking invisibility from crime. What constitutes a low profile varied greatly, but locals from all social classes adopted recalibrating practices. Fear isolates as people become increasingly suspicious and wary of others, but fear also regroups as they lean into the safety of numbers.

Regrouping: *Andar en bola*

Regrouping strategies were used at different levels and in various aspects of everyday life. These strategies were particularly visible in how people bound fear in their everyday mobility practices. At the smallest and simplest scale, regrouping could involve walking together. In San Nicolás, a father began to walk his daughter to and from the bus stop for added protection. Inside the bus, women were more likely to sit closer together and closer to the driver—another male protector, for bus drivers tend to be male.[10] Among car drivers, carpooling became more common and for new reasons. Parents already relied on carpools to optimize dropping off and picking up their kids from school, but now they carpooled to bind fear of carjacking. For example, I spoke to the principal of a private school in southern Monterrey who held security talks with parents. Given high levels of car theft, security experts specifically advised women *"que anduvieran en bola"* (to stick together). The principal said, "Right now, all moms carpool. They meet at the open house, and they organize." She heard one of them say, "If I have a van full of kids, it's less likely that something will happen to me." Fearing the solo ride to or from school, carpools included two mothers or a mother and a domestic worker riding together. "That became very common, *los grupos de viaje*" (carpools), the principal added. "Same thing with teachers, they get together and they drive in one single car."

Regrouping also involved two or more cars driving closely together, which locals called "caravans" or "convoys." These words were used interchangeably. At the end of a social gathering in a gated area outside the city, friends strategized on the logistics of getting back to Monterrey after dark. They had driven alone to the gathering by day, but one feared the return trip back at night. He suggested, *"vámonos en caravana."* (Let's drive in a caravan.) One of his friends was impatient, whispering in my ear that the man who had suggested the caravan, *"es un miedoso."* (He's a coward). Nevertheless, their friendship ensured all would wait, drive in a three-car caravan for thirty minutes on a highway, and then break the caravan once they reached Monterrey. As another example, men who previously rode their motorcycles alone through the desert in the metropolitan surroundings came to fear the paths they knew so well—even by day. "Animals travel in packs to protect themselves from lions," a local motorcyclist explained. "We work with the power of the pack." They posted videos of their expeditions to invite others to join them, which was part of their business. In one video, a motorcyclist filmed a row of pickup trucks, each with motorcycles on the back, ready to head out for a ride. "It is 7 a.m., here we are at the first toll booth, we're looking at the convoy: 1, 2, 3, 4, 5, 6, 7, 8, 9, 10." He strolled along the highway filming the line of trucks, a clear blue sky, and the sunrise. "We are approximately seventeen pick-ups . . . Here it is, the full convoy!"

Caravans ranged from highly institutionalized to spontaneous. An employee of a large steel manufacturer explained employees were "forbidden to commute to the plant" located on the outskirts of the metropolis on their own. They congregated in a hotel downtown and were driven to and from the plant in a "secure convoy." Leisure caravans, on the other hand, could be spontaneous. In 2011, *El Norte* reported daytime caravans on highways as Mexicans living in the United States traveled home for Christmas:

> Fear of violence led a great majority of *paisanos* (countrymen) who arrived for Christmas vacations to travel by day and in groups on the highways of Nuevo León, and this is how they plan to return to the United States. Many of these caravans were spontaneously formed, as individuals sought to continuously travel near others, even if they did not know them.[11]

Such spontaneous caravans reveal that while fear can certainly prompt suspicion of strangers, in specific contexts traveling close to strangers is preferred to traveling alone. Tourist buses and commercial trailers also traveled together on highways where both people and goods have gone missing. On occasions, these caravans had police or the military escorting them.[12]

54   THE TWO FACES OF FEAR

In 2011, *El Norte* reported increased demand for tourist buses between McAllen, Texas, and Monterrey during *semana santa* (Holy Week, the week leading up to Easter). Buses were scheduled during the daytime, left every five minutes, and "travelled in caravans for security reasons."[13] Among the new users was a woman from Guadalupe who felt safer in a bus rather than driving:

> I used to travel [to McAllen, Texas] on Fridays, I would go there and come back on Sunday in my car ... all women, my sisters, my daughters, my little nephews. I don't do that anymore ... I feel safer in the bus.

This resident chose a bus company she believed had some arrangement with organized crime, for it had "not suffered attacks like other companies had." Similarly, a San Nicolás resident no longer drove to the neighboring state of Tamaulipas for his routine doctor visits. He took a bus and called a taxi from the bus station. Hence, while some drivers chose to travel close to strangers, others opted to drop the car and travel with strangers inside the bus.

From walking together to a bus stop, to taking a bus rather than driving, to driving with others and in proximity of others, the common denominator of these wide-ranging mobility logistics used to bind fear is leaning into the safety of numbers. All social classes tried to regroup, but not all could. Marginalized youth could not regroup without simultaneously increasing their risk of police detention and extortion, as examined next.

The Group That Could Not Regroup

If a young and poor dark-skinned man stands alone in public, he's *un ocioso* (a bum), and up to no good. If he stands with others, he's *un pandillero* (a gang member). As violence and fear escalated, he became *un sicario* (a killer). Regrouping techniques like walking together to a bus stop or gathering in greater numbers in public worked for most sociodemographic groups, but not for young and poor dark-skinned men. As elsewhere, marginalized youth in Monterrey have long been criminalized for gathering on street corners, especially at night, as well as for dressing and walking in a stigmatized way.[14] Their criminalization predates this turf war and was greatly aggravated by it.[15] As Nateras notes, Calderón's policies contributed to further escalate the

THE LOGISTICS OF FEAR   55

criminalization of marginalized youth, the most vulnerable target for police extortion as well as for forced recruitment into organized crime.[16]

In March 2008, the secretary of public security in Nuevo León reported over eight thousand youth detentions per month in the metropolis.[17] Avilés and Berthier gathered testimonies on the circumstances for their heightened detention. In Escobedo, one youth explained that neighbors and police did not want to see them in groups—"*lo que quieren es no vernos en bolita.*" [18] In Monterrey, another did not mind getting frisked for drugs, but found it excessive that his friends were now detained for talking late at night—"*a lo mejor no te niego de que nos bolseen a ver si tenemos drogas o algo, pero de que ya se excedan porque estamos platicando ahí demasiado tarde, ese no es motivo para levantarte.*"[19] Similarly, youth in other neighborhoods explained neighbors did not like to see them in groups, even if they were only playing football, and would report them to the police—"*a muchos vecinos no les gusta vernos en bolita, que andamos jugando futbol y nos reportan.*"[20]

Young and poor men also explained that police misrepresented the reasons for detaining them, citing vandalism or harassment and demanding they pay a fine. To be freed, underaged youth "had to pay 300 pesos or 500 pesos if they were young adults."[21] In Guadalupe, one young man reported regular police raids. He was detained simply for being on the street and was also robbed if he was carrying any money. During these raids, one lost earrings to female police officers who liked them. In 2008, Avilés and Berthier alerted that marginalized youth were at high risk of forced recruitment into organized crime due to poverty, lack of education, and job opportunities. They heard from young people that "they did not want to get involved, they did not want to sell drugs or handle weapons, but they were forced to, literally, because they had no other choice."[22]

Beyond these diminished spaces and opportunities to regroup, marginalized youth were disbanded. By 2012, journalist Carrión heard it again and again in five low-income neighborhoods in Monterrey, Guadalupe, and Escobedo: there were no more *pandillas* (gangs). Ex-*pandilleros* had buried their members, dissolved, or gone into hiding.[23] In 2013, Rubio-Campos, Chávez-Elorza, and Rodríguez-Ramírez gathered testimonies from sixty-five youth living in three marginalized neighborhoods in Monterrey. In Fomerrey 45–La Estanzuela, youth reported *los malitos* came to their neighborhood "day and night" looking for young men to forcibly recruit into organized crime. These were days when they went out in the

56 THE TWO FACES OF FEAR

morning unsure if they would return, and were taken by force at any time of day—"*andaban aquí día, tarde y noche y no sabías si salías y regresabas . . . y si no quieres, te llevan a la fuerza.*"[24] A few of their friends were waiting for the bus to go to work one morning and were taken from there; regrouping at a bus stop does not protect marginalized youth from forced recruitment. They struggled with the numbers and guessed between thirty and one hundred young people had been abducted from their neighborhood. As of 2013, none had been seen again. In La Independencia, young people reported that there were few gangs left; the rest were cartels—"*ya casi no hay pandillas, solo cárteles.*"[25]

Increased criminalization of marginalized youth was also evidenced in their recalibration attempts, shifting dress codes and hairstyles to avoid attention. Since 2008, prior to this turf war, Watkins documented the original *cholombiano* or *colombiano* (Colombian) fashion of youth in La Independencia.[26] "I thought wow! This is so cool! It's quite LA-ish . . . a Mexican hip-hoppy kind of thing," she said, showing pictures of this fashion, "combining *cholo* and Colombian aesthetics." In media coverage, *Vice* singled out "its signature haircut, which draws equal parts inspiration from American hip-hop, Puerto Rican reggaeton, and ancient depictions of Aztec warriors," as shown in Figure 3.1.[27]

Watkins invited several men photographed in her book to share the stage during her book launch in 2014. None wore that haircut anymore. On stage, one man explained they had to change their style due to "marginality." When he stepped down to get a beer, I approached him and asked how they changed their style:

> I used to wear my bangs down here [he marked the spot with his hand halfway down his chest] . . . the military cut it off . . . "Hey, who are you working for?" [he recalled the military asking him]. "I work for nobody" . . . the guy on the [book] cover [also had his hair cut off] . . . neighborhood police, military and they don't cut it with scissors, they use a Rambo knife in the *granadera* [police van or truck] and then they left you in another neighborhood . . . *el morro* [a guy] had to pay 300 pesos to keep his hair.

Poor, dark-skinned men recalibrated their presentation of self, stripping a prideful fashion and haircut in an attempt to avoid police extortion and forced recruitment into organized crime, though they walked a "fine line." As Pezard-Ramírez notes, marginalized youth in Monterrey also avoided

Figure 3.1 The *Colombiano* Signature Haircut
Figure 3.1 features a young man wearing a *Colombiano* haircut with long sideburns. Picture reproduced with permission from photographer Amanda Watkins.

"looking so presentable that others may think they are *fresa*" (posh), which could get them mugged. Walking on their own made them "easy prey." Walking with others "may get them in trouble with gangs."[28] Marginalized youth thus navigated additional challenges when attempting to recalibrate and regroup, including those of being seen as a threat .

"Is It Getting Better?"

This chapter provided multiple examples of how fear impacts everyday life. In places where crime stories are frequently shared, people glean lessons from them. As kidnappings and extortion became widespread among the wealthy, middle class, and poor, locals sought to lower their profile, downgrading status markers as well as stripping themselves and businesses of personal, professional, and business identifiers. Fear impacted dress codes as well, most notably for marginalized youth. I argued fear also regroups, prompting individual practices to become collective. On streets and on highways, in cars and in buses, locals leaned into the safety of numbers to bind fear in daily routes to and from work, to and from school, as well as on occasional trips for leisure in and beyond the city. For marginalized youth, regrouping also deepened their stigma. While fear impacts practice, practices also impact the experience of fear. Through practice, the logistics of fear can bind the experience of fear and create symbolic security temporally, spatially, and in relation to consumption practices.

Examining the logistics of fear over time reveals that these practices are dynamic, shifting with a fluctuating threat. Crime stories prompt heightened vigilance and new logistics, while their absence can loosen up these strategies—reactivated as necessary. In 2012, around the same time a middle-class mother of two reported a kidnapping outside her sports club, as mentioned earlier, another middle-class mother of one living in Monterrey reassured me that "things were not as bad." As evidence, she stated she was no longer consulting her mobile phone for Twitter updates on shootings on her way out, no longer carrying her ID in a separate purse tucked in her underwear, no longer worried about carrying her computer with her to work with all her personal information (to suppress in case of a kidnapping).[29] Her husband was "calmer," too, about keeping track of where she was and which streets she was using. The general violence levels were the same for both, yet two middle-class married women with kids simultaneously reported heightened and loosened logistics because of the specific crime stories unfolding (or not) in their own networks. The main evidence the second presented to claim that "things were not as bad" was that she had loosened up her logistics and was unharmed. She was the evidence. Her narrative highlights that while tightened logistics bind fear, loosened logistics lighten fear. In both cases, a close relationship exists between the logistics and the experience of fear.

Around 2013, a new question became recurrent in everyday conversations: "Is it getting better, or have we become accustomed to it?" Becoming accustomed to a threat is not a passive process. Rather, it is the result of individually and collectively creating new customs, new logistics to learn to live with danger. The question points to the difficulty of teasing out perception from practice. "I feel safer," one businessman told another at a security talk. "Yes, but you're not going out as late anymore," said another, pointing to a self-imposed curfew the first had taken for granted. As people curtail and adjust their lives, as they develop new logistics to bind fear to the extent that they can, they feel safer within the parameters that they have created for themselves. Analyzing the logistics of fear relationally and over time ultimately reveals how fear reconfigures social practices, as well as how reorganizing everyday life reconfigures the lived experience of fear. Spatial patterns in these logistics at a metropolitan scale examined next reveal widening divides as the privileged regrouped and reconcentrated uneven resources within San Pedro.

4

Defending San Pedro

September 19, 2013

Former Mayor of San Pedro Mauricio Fernández was the main guest at a screening of The Mayor, *an award-winning documentary about himself.*[1] *Over sixty students packed a classroom in a newly inaugurated center at a private university named after his grandfather and funded by his mother. Five bodyguards stood by the entrance. Media photographers and cameramen documented Fernández as he greeted the crowd and took a seat in the front row.*

The documentary begins with shots of armed guards patrolling his home on a four-acre estate nestled up in the Sierra Madre Mountains. The nine-bedroom house featured a billiard room, two art galleries, ten storage rooms, and a library. Images of his pool, fossil collection, ivory chess set, taxidermy animals, and bear skins depicted a life lived in luxury since birth. The audience watched short family video clips of the mayor on his wedding day; holding a newborn; painting; flying a small aircraft; meeting Bill Clinton, Fidel Castro, and Gabriel García Márquez; giving talks at the Mexican Senate; and standing with former Mexican presidents Ernesto Zedillo, Vicente Fox, and Carlos Salinas de Gortari. Taken together, these images tell the story of a mayor belonging to one of the wealthiest families in northeastern Mexico with established ties to the national and international economic, political, and cultural elite, as well as a desire to further assert a place among the global elite.

While studying abroad, his daughter noticed her classmates wore "old rings" signaling their descendance from great European families. She, however, did not have one. "We solved the problem," the mayor told the camera, pointing to a ring on his finger. "I made a family ring. This thing is the very first vertebrate being on planet Earth, a trilobite, the very first bug, 550 million years old." As Monique Pinçon-Charlot and Michel Pinçon note, the wealthy assess each other through their power over space as well as their ability to project time "over a 'durée' that is not common time but extends itself across successive generations."[2] An old ring matters because it is a symbol transforming a family into a lineage. Offscreen, the mayor leaned his head on his right hand, a trilobite ring stretching his family's lineage to the origins of life on Earth.

The Two Faces of Fear. Ana Villarreal, Oxford University Press. © Oxford University Press 2024.
DOI: 10.1093/oso/9780197688007.003.0004

DEFENDING SAN PEDRO   61

The story of this family, and the local business elite more broadly, became intertwined with the urbanization of San Pedro in the mid-twentieth century. Old real estate commercials featured in the documentary advertised this former agricultural valley as "a place where corporations do business in all parts of the world . . . everyone wants to live here, buy a house in San Pedro . . . it's a lifestyle . . . most own their homes . . . it's an opportunity you cannot give up!" Students in the audience laughed. Many live in San Pedro, which surpassed these developers' dreams. It came to have "the highest GDP in the metropolis," announced the commercial, as well as one of the highest in Latin America. Until the mid-2000s, San Pedro and the broader Monterrey Metropolitan Area also boasted low crime rates, making it a desirable place to live for both local and foreign elites. The sudden and dramatic escalation of a turf war over the metropolitan area, including in its most privileged spaces, had an immediate impact on everyone, including these wealthy families.

"They tried to kidnap my daughter," the mayor said on camera. "Vamos a agarrar el toro por los cuernos" (I will grab the bull by its horns). Involved in politics from a very young age—his grandfather was a founder of the PAN party that got him elected—he ran for office following this kidnapping attempt with the slogan "We Need to Armor San Pedro." His goal: to secure the municipality of San Pedro for the business elite. Crime rates in San Pedro were lower than elsewhere in the metropolis, though the city was not free of organized crime. "The families of major drug lords live in your municipality," a filmmaker challenged him onscreen.

"Well," the mayor explained, "if you see San Pedro as the safest municipality in Mexico, then that is an invitation not only for the good but also for the bad people." He explained there were two kidnappings in San Pedro per week, pedida de piso (extortion), and that the bathrooms of clubs were drug shops. "I made the decision to make a frontal attack . . . I was convinced that we would not give San Pedro to organized crime." Now, he claimed, there were "zero shootings, zero kidnappings" in San Pedro.

"And nobody has told me this is not true," said the mayor off camera, turning to the students around him. Onscreen, he added, "Tres que anunciaron que me querían fumigar, pues salieron fumigados."(Three who claimed they would kill me are dead.) His bold statement was followed by images of his gunroom at home, of him cleaning a gun, removing and reinserting a cartridge, pulling the trigger. "I understand that this has become an island . . . Truth is, we do have a very different reality." The documentary also featured footage from his inaugural address in 2009 at the city hall. "I know we have a very difficult

62 THE TWO FACES OF FEAR

problem," he said as he took the podium. "I'll tell you, and I'm not sure this is the venue for this . . . I'm simply letting you know that I am going to take on some atribuciones *(state powers) that are not mine because we are going to grab the bull by its horns." The audience applauded onscreen and offscreen. "People are tired of politicians, liars, opportunists . . . I am not a politician. I don't give a fuck about politics. I care about my country . . . wars are not won by nuns; we haven't understood that we're at war."*

While not free of crime, including organized crime, there is clear evidence laid out in this chapter and the chapters that follow that in San Pedro locals lived in what Mayor Fernández called a "very different reality." The business elite was not unique in seeking defense of its everyday spaces, though they had far more resources than the rest to do so—including privileged access to the state. As Mayor Fernández took office in 2009, *El Norte* reported metropolitan residents had "made a decision: to lock themselves up" with gates, fences, chains, and even large flowerpots.[3] Those who had walls or gates reinforced them. In Juárez, a working-class man described his municipality as "no-man's land," where the police are "there to harass and not protect." He already had a wall, but he raised it an extra 8 feet (about 2.5 meters). In San Nicolás, a middle-class family already had a front gate, but now they closed it night and day. Middle-class and working-class residents had fewer resources to gate themselves, although the local state stepped in to provide further infrastructure. The local government of San Nicolás gated parks, soccer fields, and neighborhoods with an Armoring Neighborhoods program. In Guadalupe too, local authorities gated neighborhoods with a Safe Neighborhoods program. At a neighborhood scale, efforts to defend neighborhoods also included the formation of neighborhood watch groups.[4] Residents from all social classes pooled their resources to defend homes and neighborhoods with such measures, but only the business elite had the resources and access to the state to rely on the private use of public security.

San Pedro was not an armored city—major drug lords were captured in their homes within its borders.[5] Rather, I argue, San Pedro became a "defended city," as the local business elite leveraged far more resources to secure its business and lifestyle within than elsewhere in the metropolitan area. The most privileged residents in the metropolis had already relocated their residence from downtown Monterrey to San Pedro in the mid- to late-twentieth century. Nevertheless, they did business and frequented leisure options downtown and elsewhere in the metropolis prior to this turf war. As

San Pedro's municipal boundary was secured amid ravaging violence, corporate offices relocated to San Pedro seeking greater security. Wealthy families living in the countryside or elsewhere in the metropolis moved to San Pedro or left the metropolis.

When the residents with the most resources in a metropolis spatially regroup and pool their resources to defend themselves at a city level, their seclusion impacts the distribution of opportunities inside and outside its borders. In San Pedro, city limits bound the everyday mobility of its residents, ripping social and economic relations with outsiders. Even within privately secured and highly exclusive neighborhoods and institutions in San Pedro, fear further reinforced in-class and in-network relations as locals opted to limit their sociability to *los conocidos* (acquaintances) only. All others were suspect, especially if poor and dark-skinned. Those who moved across the border to Texas also regrouped. Most could not re-create their privileged lives abroad and, within a few years, some returned to a defended San Pedro. Fear fragments urban space, as many others have shown, through the increased gating of homes, neighborhoods, and the rise of gated communities.[6] San Pedro reveals, however, how fear can simultaneously accelerate the spatial concentration of urban wealth at a city level, regrouping the privileged and reconcentrating their resources.

Making Private Use of Public Security

The defensive tactics of the business elite included the use of private security, as well as the private use of public security. At the state level, the business elite partnered with the governor of Nuevo León to create a new state police force to patrol the metropolis. With higher salaries, better training, and tougher weapons, the first generation of *Fuerza Civil* graduated from the newly formed University of Security Sciences on September 14, 2011. The private sector provided the marketing strategy for *Fuerza Civil*, advertised in their website as "a new generation of heroes, made up of 'hero citizens,' braver, smarter men and women better trained to protect what matters the most: the security and tranquility of families." As the new state police force took to the streets in 2011, homicide rates began to decline at a metropolitan level. Ley and Guzmán note, however, that homicide rates also declined beyond the metropolis, making the impact of this new police force on public security hard to measure.[7] Moreover, as Rizzo Reyes argues, homicide rates

64   THE TWO FACES OF FEAR

need to be considered with caution because these do not encompass multiple forms of violence in the region including disappearances and mass graves.[8]

When Mayor Fernández took office, he allocated far more resources to increase the number, infrastructure, and weaponry of the local police than his predecessors. His security policies included the contested use of paramilitary groups, which he called *grupos rudos*.[9] "They can criticize me all they want, I did it to get results," he stated in *The Mayor*. While the exact impact of the revamped local and state police forces, the military patrolling the streets, as well as paramilitary groups on public security is difficult to assess, there was a clear aggregate effect in San Pedro. Through a period of heightened violence, this municipality maintained lower homicide rates than the rest of the metropolis.[10] San Pedro residents reported higher trust levels in their local police than the residents of other municipalities.[11] Like the public schoolteacher referenced in Chapter 1, a mother of two in San Pedro drew a sense of safety from living close to relatives and everyday spaces. Her children's school, her mother's house, "everyone" she relates to, her siblings and closest friends were all in "a seven-minute radius." However, and unlike the public schoolteacher, she also drew a sense of safety from heavy police presence. "We've been here [at home] and we hear shootings over there," she said, pointing to the Loma Larga hill dividing San Pedro and Monterrey:

> And we're like, are those fireworks or shootings? Damn it, it's shootings, well, I hope it's fireworks. I hear cop cars and I hear things at night, but I don't know what they've done, I don't know what Mauricio Fernández did . . . because we said to each other, how is it that things are happening in Santa Catarina, you hear of things in Monterrey, in San Nicolás, in Apodaca, at the airport, on the national highway, but in San Pedro, you don't feel like those things are happening . . . although, there was that thing.

A distant memory popped in her mind to prove her wrong. "Were you around when they killed those cops in Calzada del Valle?" I shake my head. I was abroad. She recalled learning about the shooting and having to rush to pick up her kids from the kindergarten. Then she corrected herself. "No, I already had my kids in the car." Tracing her memory, she added that she was rushing to pick up a domestic worker. "The cop thing was another day," she said, realizing she was confusing this shooting with another one that also took place on the same avenue two blocks away from her house. She tried to disentangle details of stories she had bundled together to create symbolic security and distance herself from danger. "No, more things did happen, I had blocked them," she realized. "The difference is that when there's a shooting in San Pedro, in five seconds, you've got seventeen patrol cars." Another San Pedro resident hated heightened police presence:

> I hate seeing them everywhere, they're everywhere. I hate seeing their trucks and their rifles, and they're at a traffic light and they're not paying attention and they're pointing at you with a machine gun and your son's there, a four year old, what do you do? It's the most aggressive thing I've felt in my life. And you're driving in your car, and you just want to cry from the impotence, you get me? How can I tell that guy to turn away his. . . .

Her eyes reddened with tears as she struggled to finish her sentence, unable to name the weapon she feared might inadvertently kill her or her son at a traffic light. Regardless of how they felt about heightened police presence in San Pedro, the ensemble of defensive tactics pursued by the business elite benefited its residents and drew new residents and business to San Pedro. Toward the end of his second three-year term (2009–2012), Mayor Fernández advertised the "conclusive results" of "three years of armoring San Pedro" in the *Sierra Madre,* the socialite section of the newspaper *El Norte.* He compared crime rates in San Pedro and five cities in Texas: San Antonio, Houston, Austin, Dallas, and Plano.[12] Graphs depicted significantly lower rape, theft, home burglary, and car theft in the municipality of San Pedro compared to the metropolitan areas of these Texan cities. The message: San Pedro was safer than moving to Texas. These were not the crimes San Pedro residents were most concerned about—kidnapping and extortion. Nevertheless, this comparison illustrates the two main spatial strategies the business elite pursued at this time: regroup within a defended San Pedro or cross the border and regroup in Texas. Singling out San Pedro from the Metropolitan Area of Monterrey also reveals an increasing division between this municipality and the broader metropolis.

Regrouping Urban Wealth within a Defended City

As violence increased, so did the skyline of San Pedro. Real estate dropped in the broader metropolis, but not in the defended city where the price of a square meter increased 45% in 2011 as state homicide rates peaked.[13] The

66   THE TWO FACES OF FEAR

president of the National Chamber of Housing Development for Nuevo León explained that due to "the feeling of security in San Pedro . . . we've seen a higher demand and prices increased in these districts in relation to the rest . . . where prices have dropped below market levels."[14] Upper-middle-class and upper-class families residing elsewhere relocated to San Pedro seeking security, including in its newly built and privately secured gated communities.

One family had long lived in Monterrey. Following a burglary in their home, the family moved to one of the first gated communities in San Pedro. In 2013, I joined the mother for lunch in her new apartment. We drove past a security gate and down to the parking lot. The first level was for visitors. We drove past a second security gate to access a resident-only parking lot with cars I had not seen on the streets for some time—one Ferrari, one Porsche, and several Audis. We took an elevator up to her apartment, where a domestic worker had prepared lunch. "It was hard for me to move here," she explained, as we sat down. "I thought, I'm not going to be able to fit my house here, it's not going to fit . . . [but] the feeling of insecurity was too much." She weighed advantages and disadvantages. She loved not having to worry about her house when traveling but felt spatially constrained. "Spaces are reduced," she explained. "We have one sink, and if my husband and I want to get ready at the same time, we can't do it . . . well, these are the complaints of a rich bourgeois girl, but it has been hard to adapt. It's not the same as living in a house." Another complaint stemmed from the noise of numerous gated communities under construction nearby. "When we moved here, we never imagined that there would be these many towers . . . now we want to leave. But really, I want to leave Monterrey." For this resident, moving back to their previous neighborhood for more space and quiet was not an option. Her next relocation would be to leave the metropolis.

A businessman loved living in a natural reserve with his wife, kids, and no cell phone reception. Following a kidnapping in his social networks, he met with his family and an international private security firm they hired to advise them. The firm assessed he was at greater risk due to his remote location. He moved to a house in San Pedro and sent his wife and children abroad. "That was my first reaction," he explained. "I don't want them to grow up here, but I also did not want to leave my business, my life, my city, for this shit." He too weighed advantages and disadvantages. "I thought, I won't be able to be a father to them," and brought them back to live with him in San Pedro. At the time of our interview in 2013, his brothers were still considering leaving the metropolis. "For different circumstances, we all decided to stay . . . I say, my bags are not packed, but I keep them in sight. If anything happens, we're leaving." Living in nature was no longer an option. Like the resident mentioned earlier, his next relocation would be to leave the metropolis.

A San Pedro resident who had moved to a city in the nearby state of Tamaulipas after marriage had recently returned to San Pedro with her children. "It got so rough, they were kidnapping women." She and her husband had been planning to build a house for four years but dropped the project. Her husband told her to take refuge in her mother's house in San Pedro with their kids. "I'll catch up with you, I need to leave things organized over here; *no me puedo ir como un chivo loco*." He could not leave "like a crazy goat." This strategy to relocate women and children first reveals, as in the previous case, fear reinforcing traditional male protective roles. In both cases, the male breadwinner stays in an area perceived as more dangerous to provide for a family relocated to an area perceived as safer—elsewhere in Mexico or abroad. After a few months, when her husband arrived, this family rented a house in San Pedro. They had double citizenship and were considering leaving the country, though weighed the advantages of added security with the disadvantages of living far away from their families. They eventually moved back to Tamaulipas close to the husband's family. For this family, San Pedro was a temporary refuge.

Relocating practices also took place within San Pedro. One woman lived in one of the most exclusive neighborhoods in San Pedro perched high in the Sierra Madre Mountains. She recalled a conversation with her husband in which they assessed the security strategies of a couple of friends they deemed far wealthier than them:

> We don't understand why they are still here. They are moving [changing neighborhood] because they used to live in Valle Oriente [an area within San Pedro bordering the municipality of Monterrey] and that area *ya está muy caliente para ellos* [has become too "hot" as in too dangerous for them]. These are things I'm used to hearing but now that I'm repeating it, it sounds funny. Because they thought, "We're either leaving Monterrey [the metropolis, for they live in San Pedro] or we're changing neighborhood." That was the logic.

In this example, a wealthy resident and her husband think there is no place in the metropolis that will be safe enough for their friends given how wealthy

68   THE TWO FACES OF FEAR

they are. This narrative, common among the upper class, established a direct correlation between wealth and risk, assuming that it is the wealthiest residents who are at greater risk and thus need the most protection. Their strategy was to move from a neighborhood located on the municipal border of San Pedro to another neighborhood high in the Sierra Madre Mountains—not far from the friends assessing them—secured with two private security booths. For these residents too, there were two options only: to leave or to live within a doubly secured neighborhood in San Pedro.

As wealthy residents regrouped within the defended city, and the wealthiest within even tighter doubly secured neighborhoods, businesses and corporate offices also moved to San Pedro. Since 2010, *El Norte* reported businesses "relocated to San Pedro seeking greater security."[15] In 2012, a real estate consultant explained businesses preferred San Pedro due to "the perception of increased security in this municipality" as well as its better features, given most luxury office are built there.[16] A San Pedro resident whose husband worked in construction confirmed:

> Everyone is changing their offices here . . . that is much of what he is building now . . . there is a demand for office buildings because people do not want to be in an area other than *La del Valle* . . . people do not want to leave San Pedro, so it gets more expensive; people are moving into vertical buildings.

Reluctant to travel outside city borders, businessmen opened offices within San Pedro to work remotely. One businessman used to commute to his business in downtown Monterrey every day. If leaving early enough to avoid traffic, he would make about twenty minutes driving from San Pedro to his office in downtown Monterrey. "That area got kind of dangerous, so, I changed my office over here," he explained. He transformed a property in San Pedro he rented as a home into an office. Others moved their offices into their homes. In 2012, an architect lost two projects when both of her clients were kidnapped. When released, one left the country, and the other set up a home office where he installed security cameras supervising business activities remotely. The outcome of multiple individual relocations of wealthy individuals and businesses to San Pedro was to further the concentration of urban wealth within.

The seclusion of the metropole's main employers and spenders within a defended city had consequences for business and employment. Small and large businesses located outside the defended city saw diminished opportunities, while businesses and service providers inside saw their opportunities expand. A shopping mall with luxury shops that opened in San Pedro with medium success prior to the turf war became the main and most exclusive shopping center in the metropolis. Faculty at an iconic private college in Monterrey shared that for the first time since its creation they saw a decline in student enrollment—of foreign students, as well as locals. Meanwhile, faculty at a private university located within San Pedro shared some college students transferred from the first to the second due to its location. A San Pedro resident shared a social club in downtown Monterrey that had long been a central institution for the upper class saw its activity decline—and offered a means of shuttling patrons to and from San Pedro in response.

Fear diminished and disrupted multiple employment opportunities for service providers. A graphic designer in San Pedro stopped working with a printing press downtown when the business moved to Guadalupe. "*Ahí sí dije, ni de pedo*," she said, as in there was "no way" she was going to Guadalupe. She began working with a printing press in San Pedro instead. A mother wanted to engrave a new set of cufflinks for her son. She went to La Independencia, where she knew she would find the best craftsmen. As she presented the carefully engraved gift to her son, she got scolded. "He was very upset," she said, as he thought she had endangered herself going there. He made her promise never to go to La Independencia again. Through all these individual relocations of business offices, of service providers, of hiring sites, fear and related practices rapidly deepened an already uneven geography of business and employment. The uneven impact of violence and fear on nightlife clubs and bars, discussed in Chapter 5, provides further evidence of this pattern.

Heightened Class, Racial, and In-Network Enclosure: *Sólo con los conocidos*

There is no wall enclosing the city of San Pedro, and yet its municipal border enwalled social relations and heightened distinctions between its residents and the rest. One resident never left its borders—except when taking a taxi to the airport, during which she virtually plunged into her phone looking for distractions. "The farthest I go is Costco, beyond that I'm like . . . oh, oh, I'm leaving San Pedro," she explained in 2013. Her husband, an architect,

70 THE TWO FACES OF FEAR

regularly commuted to construction sites outside San Pedro and accused her of snobbism. "*Qué fresa* (what a snob)," she recalled him telling her. She embraced the term. "*Sí . . . fresísima.*" Yes, she was "very snobbish," and demanded to stay within city borders where she felt "like there are cops" and she was "not all paranoid." City limits bound social relations as well. Another San Pedro resident stopped frequenting friends living beyond its border. "Friends of mine who live outside San Pedro . . . I don't want to visit them." One lived on the other side of a hanging bridge connecting San Pedro and Monterrey. "Something's always happening there, I wouldn't go to her house, I don't see her."

Within San Pedro, fear heightened distinctions between *los conocidos* (acquaintances) and strangers. One upper-middle-class woman lived in a privately secured neighborhood perched high in the Sierra Madre Mountains. Neighbors had recently installed a private security booth on the only road leading up to it—a public highway. Only cars were allowed in, which put pedestrian construction and domestic workers in a bind. Workers gathered outside a convenience store at the bottom of the mountain where trucks, including formal and informal taxis, shuttled them up and down. Visitors to her neighborhood had to show an ID to enter. The private security guard called residents to verify that the potential visitor was a wanted guest. "Of course, if it's a *güerita*, they won't call," she said, noting that light-skinned guests skipped one layer of security. Enclosed and guarded in her mountainous neighborhood, she was not fearful of who might come in, but rather of who lived there. Neighbors might complain about noisy dogs anywhere, but her neighbors had brutally silenced two. "The other day, they killed a pit bull with an arrow, and last year with a bullet . . . and you're like, what's their problem with dogs? . . . 'Don't let your dog bark?' They're dogs!" She walked her dog regularly but kept to herself, the neighbors she knew, and avoided neighborhood meetings. She did not want to know who she lived with.

Others did not want to know who they went to school with. A businessman learned from foreigners whose kids attended the same school as his children that there was increased distrust toward them. "When this whole mess started . . . several foreigners felt that the little opening, the community, the communion that was happening in the city disappeared, just like that." He said, "People began to be very distrustful" and limited themselves "*nada más con lo conocido y con lo suyo*" (only to the known and their own). Another reported heightened social enclosure at her children's school as well—one of the most prestigious in the city. In her case, heightened distrust among children prompted the principal to send a letter calling for a general meeting with all parents. This was the first meeting of this scale in the history of the school, but the principal told them the "social pressure was too much." He reported parents wanted their children to only "keep socializing with *los conocidos*."

For this resident, San Pedro was a city of tight-knit social networks. "Here you always know something, you know, if it's someone's cousin, you never meet a [stranger] . . . *o sea*, it doesn't take long before you find [a social connection], oh, okay, he's friends with so and so." While social networks were already central, this resident reported increased reliance on them as a means of mitigating suspicion toward strangers. "We went to this wedding, and we were seated at a table where we did not know anybody," she recalled. The other guests at the table were "on guard" until they found a common social connection. " 'Oh, you are the son of so and so,' and that was it, they lowered their guard" (*bajaron las espadas*). I asked if this was new. "I think it became accentuated with the violence . . . since *los malitos* (the evil ones) are supposed to have moved here." Even at a wedding, where guests could assume at least one mutual social connection—their hosts—strangers were potential *malitos* until a common connection was established.

A businessman in San Pedro shared a similar narrative of reduced mobility and sociability in his everyday spaces. "I became more selective in terms of where I go and with whom." He no longer frequented bars or restaurants in the Barrio Antiguo—a common choice among the upper class discussed in the next chapter. Within the privately secured spaces he frequented in San Pedro, increased spatial enclosure also involved social enclosure. "You don't necessarily talk to the person seated at a table next to you . . . because you do not know who they are . . . you became more cautious, *más selectivo*" (more selective), he added. I asked what that meant:

I mean, from the beginning I behave in the way that I usually do, *campechano* [friendly], right? But you dig a bit and then you're like, no, let's not go this way . . . [You dig a bit? I ask], You dig to find out what they do for work . . . You have this intuition, there's a certain intuition to say, *sí le pongo buena cara* [yes, I will smile], to so and so, but befriend him, well not necessarily, *o sea*, I am very diplomatic and I really do appreciate a friendship, but I have become kind of, *medio cauto* [kind of cautious].

72 THE TWO FACES OF FEAR

This businessman reported reduced interactions with strangers, as well as increased vetting practices for new acquaintances—as in the need to "dig" into their work. That he will smile but "not necessarily" befriend "so and so" means there are acquaintances he knows by name in his everyday spaces whom he finds suspect. Diplomacy, a *campechano* self, and a smile are all tools of caution to navigate distant relations in increasingly tighter spaces. Earlier in his narrative, he highlighted diminished social contact with the middle and the working class:

> When I was a college student, I was friends with everybody, foreigners and locals, and with people from every neighborhood, Contry, Anahuac, Obispado . . . I could go around Monterrey on my own, from a party in Contry to one in Anahuac, it took fifteen minutes . . . that Monterrey was delightful . . . but, nowadays, I do take care of myself, I don't do certain things anymore . . . I liked going to the *gallos* [cockfights] for example, for sociological reasons, to see the people. I loved *baños de pueblo* [to "bathe" or spend time with "the people," code here for poor people] so much . . . I went to the *gallos*, the *palenques* with my friends, no worries, no risk of anything. You would befriend people . . . we don't go anymore . . . it's unnecessary risks.

While likely tainted with nostalgia for his youth, this part of his narrative signaled further and multiple ruptured relations in the present. His college years—a time when he was "friends with everybody"—provide a contrasting template for "nowadays," when he "takes care" of himself. Specifically, heightened "care" involves avoiding interactions with the middle, and especially, the working class. He most likely did not "befriend" the poor in their leisure spaces in the same way he befriended his fellow businessmen—*hombres de bien* (good men), as he referred to them—but he did not see risks in socializing with the poor. His narrative provides another example of fear exacerbating classism, racism, and transforming the poor from people he "loved" hanging out with and wanted "to see" into an "unnecessary risk."

"I want to talk about prejudice," said a high school acquaintance I had not seen in over a decade. We met for coffee, and our conversation quickly turned into an interview. "I've noticed that I have become *muy prejuiciosa*" (very judgmental of people). She claimed she could "pretty much tell someone's status just by looking at them." She giggled. "I mean, it's true." If she sees someone shopping at a high-end store who doesn't "match" her "prejudices and they're buying a lot of things," she feels "afraid, and you're

DEFENDING SAN PEDRO 73

like, who are they and where do they get their money from?" Three months prior, she was shopping at a store where bags sell for at least 20,000 pesos (about US$2,000) each. "Two men came in with a dubious look," she recalled (*de aspecto dudoso*). They were "looking around," but she feared they were not looking at the bags. "I was afraid they would see me shopping there or as someone who could buy something there." She left, watching her back. "And it's prejudice," she added, clarifying this form of prejudice was new to her. In her youth, watching people buy similar things, she thought "good for them," with no afterthought. "Now you're more cautious. They look strange, like you don't know where they're from," she added (*"pos se ven de procedencia rara"*). She laughed a nervous laughter, noting this is "a prejudice based on other prejudices." I asked what made someone look dubious or strange. "I don't remember," she said, and then provided exact details:

> *Morenos* [brown skin], dark hair, clothes, I mean, they wore clean clothes, they looked groomed, um, I don't remember about the clothes, they were *arreglados* [well-dressed], but with a face that I'm just not used to seeing with money, *o sea*, it's prejudice . . . Two men together, they're paying attention, *o sea*, the demeanor was not one of someone who is casually shopping. I don't know, have you felt that? *O sea*, someone who goes shopping is not looking around paying attention to everything. They're more relaxed. I mean, they were on a mission, well, they did go shopping, but still.

The first dubious feature she highlighted was brown skin color. While framing concerns about prejudice in general, she was specifically concerned with racial prejudice. She was not used to seeing a brown face with money, but now felt physically endangered by it. To state "it's prejudice based on other prejudices" is to highlight how fear deepened her preexisting racial prejudice, turning brown-skinned men in her everyday spaces from men who could not afford a certain kind of bag into potential criminals she felt the need to run away from. An old college acquaintance provided a more explicit affirmation of this pattern. I ran into her at a coffee shop. As we caught up, our conversation too quickly turned into an interview:

> *Con la inseguridad me hice racista* [she became racist with "insecurity"]. I'm not ashamed to say it. Many people I know, friends of friends, my niece, a cousin, died in the Casino Royale, a friend was killed, kidnapped friends, disappeared, people very close to me . . . I closed myself to my inner

74   THE TWO FACES OF FEAR

circle only . . . and truth is, I'm not ashamed to say it, well, I am ashamed,
I wouldn't say this to anyone.

She traced a direct linkage between victimization stories of people she
knew and deepened racism. Despite the shame, to state that she simultaneously "became racist" and "closed" herself to her "inner circle only," to her
conocidos, is to highlight how race was already a core feature of her inner
circle, her closest friends, and relatives.

Institutions relied increasingly on social networks to navigate fear of
strangers as well. One priest in San Pedro lamented diminished income at a
time when he argued missionary work was most needed to keep marginalized
youth out of organized crime. "We are living in a crisis of distrust . . . You
cannot ask for people's information anymore because they will not give it
to you. You can't stop by their houses because people do not want to open
their doors." When he managed to get a foot in, he was not allowed to bring
in youth missionaries with him. Those he hoped would finance his mission
thought his missionaries looked like criminals and suspected they might
relapse. Unable to access the homes of his potential funders, he devised a
new strategy: having people be guarantors to their friends. One person took
the contact information, including credit card number, of their friends and
submitted them directly to the church. This person guaranteed good use of
their friends' information. Reliance on the *conocidos* was thus an individual
and institutional strategy.[17]

To sum up, San Pedro residents were suspicious of strangers living among
them in their neighborhoods, attending their weddings, enrolled in the same
private schools, eating and shopping at privately secured restaurants and
stores who were, presumably, from a similar socioeconomic background—
including the many moving in seeking the refuge of the defended city. They
were also increasingly weary of the working class they relied on to maintain
their lifestyle, especially inside their homes.

Intensified Suspicion Toward the Working Class

As the wealthy regrouped within San Pedro borders, on the streets and inside their homes, the working class they rely on to clean their homes, take
care of their children, cook, serve at restaurants, work as security guards
and chauffeurs, and carry out all other service work sustaining their lifestyle

became increasingly suspect. Fear of leaving city borders and heightened suspicion toward these workers reconfigured, reshuffled, and in some cases ruptured work and employment relations, exacerbating an already unequal geography of employment opportunities.

A designer in San Pedro used to employ *comunidades* (code for working-class communities) for her business. Her fear of going into a working-class neighborhood resulted in ruptured employment for these workers. "I used to go into Fomerrey [a low-income neighborhood] to look for a seam-stress . . . I would go anywhere, anytime, at night, you wouldn't believe it, *ahorita me hice muy paranoica*" (now I'm paranoid). This designer was also reluctant to go downtown. She was involved in a real estate project there and had negotiated visiting once a month at most. The distance between her neighborhood in San Pedro and the location of this development down-town could be driven in twenty to twenty-five minutes with no traffic, yet fear created long-distance work arrangements within a metropolis. "I go if they need me for some reason; otherwise, I'll send someone in my place, and I love downtown, you have no idea."

At home, she weighed the advantages of a clean house against multiple fears. For a while, her fears weighed more. "I thought I would rather clean my house than bring in someone I don't know, and I don't know where they live or who their neighbors are." As evidence, she stated her mother hired a domestic worker from a marginalized neighborhood in Monterrey. "There were killings on her block, and one of her nephews ended up with the Zetas," she added, lowering her voice. "I thought, who am I bringing into my house?" Fear thus reshuffled tasks between workers and employers. As she delegated new tasks to those going downtown for her, she temporarily took on cleaning, childcare, and driving tasks previously delegated to others.

Eventually, the need for childcare weighed more than her fears. She hired a domestic worker, though took new precautions. She used to drive domestic workers to their homes. "Not anymore," she added with a shiver. She would not leave her four-year-old son alone with her either. "I became a helicopter mom, *o sea*, I need to know where my son is all the time." This held true for other workers. "For example, other moms [told her], 'I'll send my chauf-feur over to pick up your son so he can go play with my son,' well no, I don't know your chauffeur." She drove her child to the playdate, stayed in the house for the duration of the playdate, and drove the child back. These examples highlight simultaneous spatial, economic, and social ruptures for this res-ident who no longer drove into working-class areas, no longer employed

76 THE TWO FACES OF FEAR

working-class communities, and temporarily refrained from employing a domestic worker out of fear.

Another San Pedro resident was spending more time at home and chatting more with her domestic worker. "We talk a lot; she gives me insights into the other side of the bubble." She stated these conversations heightened her awareness of class inequalities. "I have become very aware of the interaction between the upper, the middle, or rather the inexistent middle class, and the lower class," she explained in her home. Through increased time spent together, she became attuned to differences she had previously taken for granted:

> *O sea*, she always asks me, '*Señora*, where do I put the fork?' [when setting the table] And I tell her, '*Oye, qué onda*? [What's up?] Don't you use a fork, don't you use utensils when you set the table at home?' And she tells me, 'No.' *O sea*, this year, I just discovered that . . . here in Mexico, people do not use utensils, I'm like, *wey*, where the fuck are we living . . . it's two countries in one.

She argued her domestic worker's life was "the template" for the working class in Mexico. "You see everything, every major social problem, *wey*, she's got it at a micro scale, it's impressive. She's got *azúcar* [diabetes], why? Because she drinks six Pepsis a day, um, the husband is an alcoholic." While this San Pedro resident was having longer conversations with her domestic worker, another one was cutting them short. A young professional in San Pedro noted the impact of fear on her attitudes toward domestic workers:

> Before, with the *muchachas* [a classist term commonly used to refer to domestic workers as "girls"] . . . I wasn't as concerned if they overhead a conversation or saw a picture of my boyfriend, that kind of thing. Now, I'm really reserved on everything private, *o sea*, I don't like it when they're asking questions, and when they start asking too many, in my house, we would rather have them leave [fire them] . . . like she asked whether the gate was electrified, *o sea*, these types of questions might have seemed innocent, silly before, but they make us suspicious . . . it was too much.

In a context of heightened fear, a question can get a domestic worker fired. This resident assumed the question about the electric gate signaled a threat, perhaps fearing a burglary or kidnapping. On the worker's side, the worker might have been concerned about her own safety navigating increasingly secured devices. Most domestic workers in the Monterrey Metropolitan Area reside in segregated spaces within the homes of their employers. They are often young indigenous women who migrate to Monterrey from poor rural areas looking for work. As kidnappings, extortion, and burglaries escalated, so did suspicion toward them. As Durin notes, suspicion around who they befriended, dated, and the information they could reveal about their employers is not new, but rests "on a preexisting fear towards the lower classes and is exacerbated by discourses that contribute to stigmatize and present them as those responsible for actual criminal violence."[18] As a prominent example of these discourses, Mayor Fernández tried to create a database of domestic workers to improve "security" as part of his "armoring" strategy. Local human rights organizations denounced the program as a violation of human rights. Although not carried out, the program signaled escalating criminalization of domestic workers.[19]

"Leavers" Regrouping in Texas

A long history of labor migration ties Monterrey and numerous cities in Texas.[20] In the 2010s, new groups sought to migrate for new reasons.[21] On August 26, 2011, as multiple newspapers around the world reported the Casino Royale massacre, the *Houston Chronicle* advertised The Woodlands as a "Paradise for Mexican Businessmen." As early as 2010, "a great number of Mexicans from Monterrey arrived at The Woodlands to stay."[22] A financial advisor based in this Houston development of over one hundred thousand residents explained, "There was such a great need that we focused solely on helping the people from Monterrey, [who] tend to be wealthy families." Wealthy residents already owned a second home in San Antonio, Houston, Austin, South Padre Island, among other Texan cities, to facilitate weekend shopping sprees and summer vacations. This proximity, familiarity, and initial infrastructure made Texas a preferred site for temporary or indefinite relocation. To a lesser extent, I heard of families moving to Europe or other cities in Mexico, particularly Mexico City—perceived as more dangerous than Monterrey for decades, but safer in comparison to Monterrey at this time. Those who left were not the majority, but their regrouping strategies in Texas affected their lives, the lives of those they left behind, and the cities they moved into.

78   THE TWO FACES OF FEAR

The flight to Texas prompted the establishment of new classed spatial enclaves of Monterrey residents abroad. In 2010, one real estate agent who helped Mexicans open thirty businesses explained that when these Mexicans move to Houston "they bring their wealth. It's not a bad thing for Texas, it's a blessing."[23] The west side of The Woodlands became known as Little Mexico. San Antonio neighborhoods Sonterra and Stone Oak acquired new names with the influx of Monterrey residents as well: Sonterrey and Little Monterrey. By 2013, the *Los Angeles Times* reported "a wave of legal Mexican immigrants" fleeing violence "have regrouped in gated developments in several Texas cities, where their growing influence has been compared to the impact of well-heeled Cuban refugees who arrived in Miami decades ago."[24]

Wealthier families moved to San Antonio and Houston, perceived as cities of higher status than border towns like McAllen and Brownsville. Moreover, they regrouped in gated communities, though at a cost. In Houston, regrouping led to discrimination. "All I know is that in some places like The Woodlands, it came to a point where there were so many *regios afrentosos* [obnoxious Monterrey residents], that there was a movement against them," said a businessman who referred to his former San Pedro neighbors moving there as "rich immigrants." He heard this story from them. "You know how obnoxious the women can be; they go to schools and they double-park." He attributed discrimination abroad to their attempts at practicing forms of privilege they were accustomed to in Mexico. Durin notes wealthier Mexican immigrants "care about preserving the whiteness they attribute to themselves, and distance themselves from the residential areas of 'hispanic' migrants."[25] They may have the resources to move into privileged areas, but it is also in these spaces that they face new hierarchies among the privileged.

Only the most privileged were able to re-create the lives they were accustomed to abroad. Those with fewer resources found themselves trading fear of criminal and state violence in Mexico for fear of deportation and economic insecurity in the United States. For example, Durin spoke to a married couple with children who owned a hardware store in the town of Reynosa, Tamaulipas, and who moved to McAllen, Texas, following an armed attack on their business. They hid in a trailer home borrowed from local relatives, having lost their business and legal status. At first they lived in fear of being deported—keeping their lights off, keeping quiet, keeping close to the ground. "*Timbraba el teléfono y como cuando hay una balacera y vas al piso,*" the wife recalled. Hearing the phone ring was like hearing a shooting; you hit the ground for safety. After two years, they sold properties they had in

Mexico and returned to the United States on a tourist visa. They relied on their labor as a gardener and a cook to make a living and found comfort in a local church and in the hopes that their daughter, engaged to a US citizen, could eventually provide a path toward citizenship for them.[26]

Those who had enough resources to leave with a tourist or investor visa—including middle-class and upper-middle-class families—were not able to uphold the lifestyle they had in Mexico for long. Adjusting involved increased domestic labor previously borne by lower-income women. A mother of three who moved to Austin in 2010 was visiting her family in San Pedro in 2013 when we spoke. Moving across the border involved trading two full-time domestic workers for twelve hours of help a week:

> This changed everything. I had to come up with many strategies. For example, I've forced my children to become more organized . . . I now place three laundry baskets: one for whites, one for colored clothes, and one for black clothes. If they mess up, too bad! I didn't have to do any of this in Monterrey . . . I've had to learn how to do everything.

To compensate for these details disclosing a loss of status, she added, "I live in the most expensive neighborhood with other people from Monterrey." Regrouping abroad was a key spatial strategy for those seeking to reassert their status to "stayers" in Mexico as well. For some, fleeing itself was a means of signaling status. A businessman in San Pedro explained, "God forgive me, but some people left out of snobbism . . . because they felt they were so wealthy, so that people [their peers] could see that they were so wealthy that they did not want to live here."

Those fleeing violence engaged in new forms of cross-border commuting that provide more examples of fear exacerbating traditional male protective roles. In 2013, one businessman considered moving to Austin. He thought it might be a "nice experience for the children," but didn't want to feel like he was "leaving at gunpoint out of fear." He recalled the experiences of his friends:

> I have friends who have left, who have moved to the United States or elsewhere. Several acquaintances are in Austin and San Antonio, basically . . . some of them adapt and are very happy, others don't . . . some of them go through the horrific hassle of going back and forth, they have their business here [and the family in Texas], so they're here for three days, there for four days . . . every week, to move that way is really rough.

Mexican migration to the United States typically involves Mexican breadwinners moving to the United States to provide for a family staying in Mexico. In this reversed dynamic, Mexican male breadwinners stay in Mexico to keep a business running and provide for a family abroad. One upper-middle-class man drove back and forth on a weekly basis, though his wife and child took a plane when occasionally visiting Mexico. If commuting resources need to be maximized, more were destined to protect women and children. Sustaining a "double life" in Monterrey and a city in Texas, as well as commuting back and forth, was expensive. In 2012, a San Pedro resident commented, "Some of the people who left for San Antonio or Austin, many middle class, are now coming back because they can't afford that double life." Weighing status and security benefits, those wishing to maintain a certain lifestyle and status had one choice: to move back.

Defending Whom and at Whose Expense?

Locals from all social classes tried to defend their everyday spaces amid increased violence, but only the business elite could leverage state resources to make private use of public security at a city level. The consequences of defending one city with more resources than the rest were multiple. The borders of San Pedro disrupted and enwalled social relations and practices, increasingly harboring the most exclusive gated communities, clubs, schools, shopping centers, and restaurants in the metropolis. Within these highly cloistered spaces, locals guarded themselves further through diplomatically distancing themselves from all but those they already knew (*los conocidos*). Fear thus heightened spatial and social enclosure, fostering in-class and especially in-network socializing, while heightening distrust toward strangers, especially dark-skinned strangers, and the working poor newly framed as "unnecessary risks." San Pedro continues to boast the lowest crime rates in the metropolis. When assessing "successful" security policies, however, it is crucial to examine closely who is defended and at whose expense.

Business-led defense mechanisms had consequences beyond spatially and socially tightening relations among the wealthy. While San Pedro drew benefits from heightened police presence, regardless of how residents felt about them, others bore the consequences of unequal police treatment in and beyond San Pedro. For young, poor, dark-skinned men residing in marginalized neighborhoods, the new state police force was just like the old one. In La Estanzuela and La Alianza, marginalized youth reported *Fuerza Civil* beating, extorting, and threatening them. One said he was stopped "at gunpoint" with his brother and told that "next time, they'd blow off" their heads (*"te encañonan y te dicen que a la otra te revientan la cabeza"*).[27] Another said *Fuerza Civil* sometimes took them to school, "but sometimes they take your money, your clothes, and throw them on the avenue," and make them do sit-ups "because you're not supposed to be on a street corner" (*"a veces te quitan el dinero, te quitan la ropa y te la avientan a la Avenida . . . te ponen a hacer sentadillas porque . . . no debes estar en las esquinas"*).[28] Beyond unequal police treatment, heightened fear among the city's main employers had economic consequences for these youth. Their heightened criminalization translated into decreased employability, with slim job opportunities curtailed even at convenience stores. A large firm with hundreds of convenience stores in the metropolis set up a seven-month "leadership program" to "prepare" marginalized youth to take a low-wage job in one of their stores. Carrión notes, "In Monterrey, even convenience stores reject tattooed youth. Nobody wants to hire youth from marginalized neighborhoods."[29]

In La Independencia, criminalization and stigmatization go hand in hand with increased attempts to demolish homes, schools, and displace its residents in favor of new infrastructure and commercial projects.[30] Though gentrification attempts date back to the 1990s, these picked up significantly as violent crime rates declined. In 2017, the private sector and the state government launched a plan to build a large highway cutting through la Independencia to connect San Pedro and downtown Monterrey. In pursuit of "progress," this project would demolish and divide a significant part of Monterrey's first working-class district. Residents appealed to the federal government and managed to stop the project on the grounds of preserving the local flora and fauna on the hill—easier to protect than their homes. "All they say is that we don't study, that we don't have good jobs, that we get drugged, that we rob," says a local resident and activist fighting territorial stigma with graffiti, art, and cultural workshops. *"Nos han hecho muy mala fama porque nos quieren sacar de aquí,"* says another, arguing stigmatization is a strategy to displace them. They recruit children into their art collectives to ensure the survival of their tight-knit community into the future. One states, "As long as we live here, we need to defend ourselves from the government, the business people and even the church."[31] Hence, as one side of the Loma Larga was fiercely defended and its residents protected, the other became more vulnerable. Widening disparities were particularly visible at night and in public space examined next.

5

Restructuring Nightlife

May 20, 2012

A teenage girl poses for her father's camera in front of the closed doors of the Café Iguana—an icon of the Barrio Antiguo (old quarter) in downtown Monterrey. The café's bright green wall is covered with pictures of rock bands and crowds of young people singing or standing in line in front of this same wall. The teenager plays the model, shifting weight from one leg to the other. Nineteen bullet holes puncture the colorful collage of memories and mourning behind her. Graffiti on the wall reads, "No more blood. Out with the government, the narcos, and the army, R.I.P. Pablote and el enano *(the dwarf)." A black ribbon hangs from the main entrance where Pablote used to check IDs. He checked mine a few times, with his stern look and long beard. It's been almost twelve months since four people, including two staff, were shot dead on-site.*

"I won't let her go out at night now or even when she grows older, given the situation in Monterrey," her mother tells me in a low voice, looking at her from across the street. The teenager hangs out at home with her friends. They have sleepovers but no nights out. The teenager and parents continue their walk down the cobblestone streets of the Barrio Antiguo scouting different sites for their photo shoot. Lagging behind, two activists post a sign on the same bright green wall that reads: "Party in the Barrio Antiguo."

"Take a picture of me right here," a fifty-year-old activist tells another. He stands proudly next to the graffiti: "We will fight for you until you wake up." A block away, a music band is finishing a sound check, the first of a long list of bands craving a stage to perform. In the 1990s, dozens of bars in the area catered to all social classes, age groups, and varied musical tastes, including rock, metal, punk, ska, pop, and electronic music. Following numerous shootings, most bars closed or were forced to shut down. The most emblematic was the closing of the Café Iguana. Its bright green wall became a mourning site for those killed in this shooting and for metropolitan nightlife altogether. I join the activists as they walk one block to reach a small podium where musicians are gathering for a unique live music event commemorating this shooting. A crowd of nearly one hundred, many of them musicians, has gathered for the occasion.

The Two Faces of Fear. Ana Villarreal, Oxford University Press. © Oxford University Press 2024.
DOI: 10.1093/oso/9780197688007.003.0005

84   THE TWO FACES OF FEAR

One of the organizers takes the microphone on an improvised stage on the street. "The purpose of this event is to wake up the old quarter from its slumber, to promote peace, to reclaim this space that has been lost to fear," she explains to the crowd. For the next five hours, metal, rap, tango, and rock bands perform primarily for each other. As the bands play, neighbors and human rights activists provide updates on the area. "Two weeks ago, two women were shot dead two blocks away," one explains. "Their bodies were taken, and the police never showed up. The only people who knew about it were the neighbors." Crowds walk along the Macro Plaza two blocks away—the largest plaza in the metropolis—though few venture into the Barrio Antiguo aside from those craving its nightlife in broad daylight.

In 2011 and 2012, national media reported the fall of the Barrio Antiguo as a "wound to the heart of Monterrey" and "Monterrey's death by night," where "the damage to nightlife seems irreversible, at least in the short run."[1] The first and most obvious impact of numerous shootings and related fear on local nightlife was the closure of most bars in the Barrio Antiguo, which was a metropolitan nightlife center before the war. According to the local alcohol agency, out of eighty registered bars in Barrio Antiguo in 2007, only fourteen were still standing in 2012.[2] "Drug traffickers forced bars and restaurants to sell drugs; we've heard this from owners themselves," a human rights activist explained. "They had no choice. They sold or they closed."[3]

Shootings and extortion shut down dozens of bars in downtown Monterrey and elsewhere in the metropolis, but nightlife practices were not only destroyed. Rather, I argue, nightlife was restructured in three overlapping stages examined in this chapter that magnified existing socio-spatial inequalities: destruction, dispersion, and class reconcentration. As the Barrio Antiguo fell, violence and fear obliterated one of the few spaces left for residents to interact with others from across the class spectrum. Beyond the Barrio Antiguo, spaces for the large-scale gathering of marginalized youth were also impacted. Existing inequalities at an individual, neighborhood, and municipal level were magnified in subsequent stages. Bar closures and fear of traveling long distances, especially after dark, resulted in locals dispersing, trading previous clubbing practices for small indoor gatherings with friends at home to drink and to grill. The local tradition of the *carne asada* (barbeque) became a social refuge. Partying closer to home with those living in close vicinity meant residents were more likely to gather with others from a similar social position, tightening in-class and in-neighborhood

RESTRUCTURING NIGHTLIFE   85

relations. Alongside this private form of small group dispersion, violence prompted the class reconcentration of nightlife for the wealthiest residents and those seeking to party with them.

In 2012, human rights activists and musicians organized to "revive" nightlife downtown as detailed in the introductory field note to this chapter, yet in the defended city, nightlife was thriving. Crowds of San Pedro residents relocated partying practices from the Barrio Antiguo to the top floors of newly built privately secured plazas as well as the streets of a commercial district called el Centrito (little downtown), where bars accommodated the nightlife desires of the wealthy to party closer to home. This reconcentration of club nightlife within San Pedro meant that it was no longer only certain bars that were exclusive to the upper class but club nightlife altogether. Within these spaces of privilege, spatial and symbolic mechanisms further ensured exclusion of unwanted others, marking additional distinctions between the wealthy and the rest. Through this three-stage process, fear restructured metropolitan nightlife with a profound impact on the social and urban structure of the metropolis beyond the most critical years of this crisis. As violence declined and some bars reopened in the Barrio Antiguo, including the Café Iguana, the upper class did not return downtown. Fear thus widened the distance between bars catering to different social classes from a few blocks to separate cities, further solidifying unequal nightlife opportunities.

Metropolitan Nightlife Gunned Down

Numerous bars catering to the wealthy, middle class, and working class shut down because of gun violence between 2010 and 2012. Across the class spectrum, locals drew a direct connection between increased violence and decreased visits to Barrio Antiguo. In San Nicolás, a middle-class woman "stopped going when the shootings started and they were killing people in the bars, I mean my friends, nobody wanted to go." She nostalgically recalled walking one morning in front of one of her favorite bars where staff "were cleaning up the blood." This detail highlights the visual evidence sustaining residents' fear of frequenting bars. Others continued clubbing amid the shootings. A middle-class foreigner residing in San Pedro detailed her experience clubbing at Barrio Antiguo through increased violence. "When I first arrived [in 2008] . . . it was a big party place, and then there were all these different levels of society going there, and it was fine, and it was working,

86   THE TWO FACES OF FEAR

and then it just got really dangerous, and no one would go downtown." She referenced the Café Iguana shooting as a reason why "everybody stopped going to Barrio Antiguo." Later in the interview, she recalled being in a shooting at Barrio Antiguo herself.

It was a Sunday afternoon. She walked past the weekly antique market set up in a cobblestone road and past a line of young people waiting to go into a bar offering a *tardeada* (afternoon concert)—an institutional coping mechanism several bars adopted to draw in patrons fearful of going out at night. Within minutes of entering a restaurant, she heard gunshots. "The waitress grabbed me, pulled me in, turned down the shutters. We all ran upstairs. They closed the doors . . . locked everything. We're all sitting upstairs, and there's this gun battle." If she had been outside one minute before, she thought, "I would have been in the middle of the shooting." From news reports, she learned two people were killed in a drive-by shooting that day. She continued to go out in Barrio Antiguo but took extra precautions. She did not stand near bar entrances because security guards could be targeted. "If I went into the club, I wouldn't stand by the door either. I would stand in the back, to one of the front sides or wherever, in case someone came in and decided to . . . you know, that's what I mean, so stressful." She laughed nervously.

To be able to continue clubbing after a shooting, this resident bound her fear spatially inside the bar. She might have continued frequenting the same bars, but she did not stand in the same place. She did not use the toilets either, because she heard drugs were sold there. Most importantly, she checked in with locals who lived downtown. "There was one club where I was going all the time. One night, I did see a guy in there with a gun and asked [a local she trusted], 'Is it dangerous for me to go?' And then after a while he said, 'It is dangerous, don't come anymore.'" Shortly after, it closed. Her narrative reveals that the destructive stage of fear is a process in itself, as locals reassessed nightlife practices in response to experiences of violence and in conjunction with others and their experiences of violence. Although there is individual variation in how these decisions were made, thousands of people stopped frequenting the Barrio Antiguo. A middle-class couple living blocks away experienced this destruction of nightlife acoustically. When they moved into their apartment in 2007, the Barrio Antiguo was "a carnival" on weekends. "You walk by now, it's dead," said the wife in 2013:

> There were parties just across from us, right? Until dawn, Saturdays and Fridays . . . when all of this started in Monterrey, but especially with the

Casino Royale [attack] and the Sabino Gordo [a bar where twenty-one were massacred, most of them staff], everything calmed down, we noticed, and people talked about it, and it showed. People started to limit their movements, right? They went out less, and, earlier, that's what everyone said . . . *la raza le bajó, le bajó a la fiesta* (folks partied less).

These residents, too, drew a direct connection between increased violence—as in the case of two specific organized crime attacks—and declining crowds at Barrio Antiguo. They further elaborated on the auditory cues reinforcing their decision to stay home after dark.

"There were a couple of nights when we could not sleep, um, because we heard them nearby," the wife remembered. "One time it was really, really loud . . . we heard a very, very strong shooting; we went into the bathroom." Located in the center of their apartment, the bathroom was as far away as they could get from the risk of getting hit by stray bullets or broken glass. On another occasion, grenades were dropped on police cars stationed near their apartment. "There were two grenades," said the husband. "I was asleep and woke up to the shock wave . . . there was a sound . . . but because of the reverberations, it wasn't a sound." Increased militarization also registered in their experience as specific sounds. For example, they remembered the sound of the helicopters from the marina descending nearby.

Bar owners provided further evidence of the destruction of nightlife downtown as seen from the interior of the few bars that remained open during this time. One bar owner moved into his bar and explained, "People did not leave their homes. There were days when twelve people would go to the bar and we were fourteen musicians playing, I don't know how we paid them, there was no money."[4] Buildings that closed as bars reopened as research centers, foreign language institutes, or other businesses operating during the day. An upper-class resident in San Pedro who used to frequent bars in Barrio Antiguo prior to this turf war commented, "The geography, *el rostro* (the face), of the city is changing. The Barrio Antiguo is completely empty, *o sea, wey* (I mean, wow) the Barrio Antiguo!" The Barrio Antiguo was the site for the most dramatic and publicized destruction of local nightlife during the war, but it was not the only one. Drawing on a twelve-year ethnography, Saucedo Villegas observed the rapid internal transformation and temporary closure of a dance hall that was the most important place of nightlife assembly for marginalized youth at the time: La Fe Music Hall, located in the municipality of San Nicolás.[5] No place in Barrio Antiguo could host

88 THE TWO FACES OF FEAR

events of the magnitude of the *bailes colombianos* (Colombian dances) organized at La Fe Music Hall in the 2000s and early 2010s.

There is a rich history binding music from the Colombian Atlantic Coast—*cumbia* and *vallenato* especially—and marginalized youth in Monterrey dating back to the 1960s.[6] That history is anchored in La Independencia, the historic port of entry of migrant labor to Monterrey. As workers migrate, music circulates. Migrant workers returning from Texas brought the first records of *cumbia* and *vallenato*, which made their way into the collections of local *sonideros* (roughly translated as sound workers, or people who make a living and a lifestyle off sound in contexts where very few own a means of playing music). *Sonidero* Gabriel Dueñez played *cumbia* from party to party up and down the Loma Larga. Residents wanted more. The music featured instruments that were already popular in northeastern Mexico, like the accordion. The lyrics told stories of love and hardship that resonated deeply with these migrants and workers. On the Loma Larga, Colombian music was reinvented, and a new identity and culture forged around it. A technical glitch in Dueñez's sound system played a record at a slower tempo, and the young people loved it. The glitch gave rise to a *cumbia rebajada* (a slower cumbia) and new dance steps. The community on this hill birthed new *cumbia* artists, including Celso Piña, who became one of northeastern Mexico's most famous musicians. As Olvera Gudiño notes, Colombian music provided "La Independencia, marginal sectors of the Loma Larga and other parts of the Monterrey bursting at the margins, since the seventies" with a "different, beautiful, and functional way of describing, dramatizing, and sharing their world."[7] Colombian music became the soundtrack of marginality, a soundtrack that was best played live.

Colombian dances were organized in numerous sites in the urban margins. La Fe Music Hall in the 2000s, however, became the *"vallenato* temple,"* drawing thousands of marginalized young people from all edges of the metropolis.[8] Meeting young people from other neighborhoods was central to the experience. They wore their nicknames and the names of their neighborhood on their t-shirts, baseball caps, and on the soles of their shoes, often in abbreviated form—F1 for Fomerrey 1 or San Berna for San Bernabé. They also wore a 1 or a star, marking allegiance to one of two groups that formed blocks of protection all over the metropolitan margins. Each massive gathering was an opportunity to present and affirm themselves in relation to others. They wrote the name of their group on posters, hoping to catch the eye of musicians who might then give them a shout out. They formed two

RESTRUCTURING NIGHTLIFE   89

large groups on opposite sides of the dance floor in front of the stage and danced in pairs and in large rotating circles—*la rueda de la cumbia* (a cumbia circle). With their feet close together, they balanced themselves on their toes with wing-like arms stretching wide, swinging their hands and rhythmically displaying a 1 or a star at each other.[9]

As violence escalated, they leaned into the safety of numbers to travel to and from their neighborhoods and La Fe Music Hall. In the early 2000s, most of them arrived by foot, took a bus, or shared a taxi. As violence and fear increased, so did the number of cars in the parking lot, the lines of taxis, as well the number of buses waiting to take them back to their neighborhoods.[10] Such logistics, however, could not protect them from being seen and treated as criminals themselves. As violence escalated, Saucedo Villegas observed important shifts in how young people related to each other, as well as how private and public security related to them. Fights became more frequent inside, where "for aggressors, victims and spectators, violence was part of the 'show.'" Security staff lined up to form a wall dividing the 1 and the star. They started conducting full-body inspections upon entry for a growing list of prohibited items: belts, hairpins, earrings with hooks, shoelaces, lighters, matches, pens, and pencils. Inspections included checking handbags for hidden compartments, pockets, backs and fronts of bras, and closed shoes. Baseball caps were prohibited. Beer was sold in disposable cups because cans, too, were considered weapons. Younger security staff were hired (closer in age to participants) and dressed in similar baggy pants and flowered shirts to "camouflage" among them. They carried no weapons and relied on their numbers to direct patrons in, through, and out of the music hall. Inspections were more thorough for youth ages fifteen to twenty-five who featured the increasingly stigmatized *colombia* aesthetic. When young people got into a fight, security staff rounded them up, took them outside through the back door, and handed them over to the local San Nicolás police.[11]

Police extortion of young people happened often in marginalized neighborhoods, as well as in their leisure sites. Saucedo Villegas observed a young man in tears at the ticket office of La Fe Music Hall. He had traveled from a nearby state to watch *Los Diablitos de Colombia* perform. Some young people got into a fight, and when private security rounded them up, they grabbed him as well "because he was standing by looking." Private security took him out through the back door and handed him over to the San Nicolás police. They took all his money. Employees at the ticket booth were unmoved by his tears. Only a passerby acknowledged the pain. "*Sí, son bien bañados.*"

90   THE TWO FACES OF FEAR

(Yes, they're terrible).[12] Employee indifference and a passerby's reassurance both suggest police extortion of patrons at this venue likely occurred often. During the most violent years of 2010 through 2012, Saucedo Villegas observed further shifts: a decrease in the frequency of *bailes colombianos*, lower attendance, a shift in performers to primarily local musicians (as others were likely unwilling to travel to Monterrey), the relocation of police patrol cars from the back to the front entrance (most likely as a display of force), and, on one occasion, the sudden entry of armed police forces into the dance hall. La Fe Music Hall temporarily closed in 2014. For marginalized youth, fewer dances and the increased danger of violence and police extortion at La Fe Music Hall meant the loss of an important metropolitan place of assembly.

In brief, while there were abysmal differences between bars catering to the wealthy, the middle class, and poor prior to escalating violence in downtown Monterrey, these bars were nonetheless located blocks away from each other. There was, at least, some class mingling in the streets and at midnight taco stands that was obliterated. As both cross-class metropolitan nightlife downtown and marginalized metropolitan nightlife at La Fe Music Hall were destroyed, locals from across the class spectrum sought new ways to party, especially with those they lived closest to.

Partying Closer to Home

"There is nightlife, but not like there used to be years ago. Most bars, places used to be concentrated in the Barrio Antiguo, now it's dispersed," explained a 28-year-old Monterrey resident in 2013.[13] New bars and restaurants opened on the top floors of small shopping centers—especially in middle, upper-middle, and upper-class neighborhoods. In addition, this man claimed it became more common "to gather at home, to grill or to get drunk with your friends at home."[14] Similarly, a middle-class tech worker living in downtown Monterrey used to go out in "some plazas with bars that were very calm" in southern Monterrey. "Suddenly they're gone; they closed." As an alternative, his friends "no longer get together to go to a bar or a club; they get together in somebody's house, and they have their *carne asada*." The local tradition of the *carne asada*, already central to the sociability practices of wealthy and poor, became a social refuge at this time.

Where to gather? In the case of this tech worker and his friends, they met "somewhere close to everyone." Though it is common for friends to rotate homes in less-violent conditions, this example illustrates how the centrality of a home in relation to the homes of others may become a main factor determining who becomes host, allowing for the simultaneous reduction and more even distribution of risks among friends. He had heard "rumors" of other forms of nightlife continuing in San Pedro, but this was not an option for him or his friends:

> Most people now, if they go out, they'll go out for dinner early or in areas like, for the people who can do it, in San Pedro, where supposedly, it's what people have been saying, that these areas are armored or protected. San Pedro is too far, so they [his friends] think, nah, let's stay home.

The bars this man referenced in southern Monterrey were geographically farther away from his home in downtown Monterrey than bars in San Pedro. What made the bars in San Pedro "too far" at this time were the risks of being out on the streets at night. As Lindón notes, fear can symbolically stretch the distance between two geographic points.[15] "Too far" brings attention to the symbolic stretching of space that has become dangerous to travel through. Like other locals I spoke to, this tech worker and his friends sought to keep their trajectories as short as possible.

For drivers, driving home after dark, and especially arriving home, required heightened caution. In 2011, a middle-class woman in Monterrey explained, "Arriving home is a critical moment. Every time I approach my house, I become increasingly aware of who is driving behind me. If I see anything suspicious, I keep driving." She made sure nobody was inside parked cars near her house. "First, I get out and quickly go into my house, then I come out again and bring groceries or anything I might have left in the trunk. She added, "*Te agarran cuando estás en la lela.*" (They get you when you're distracted.) As an example, she shared that one of her nephews had his car stolen when he parked in his garage and got out of his car. My field note "Driving Home from a Carne Asada" illustrates one such "critical moment" in further detail.

Driving Home from a Carne Asada, April 12, 2012

A friend invites me over for a carne asada in his home in downtown Monterrey. The meat is ready around 11 p.m., and we continue our conversation indoors.

92 THE TWO FACES OF FEAR

I feel a clock ticking inside my chest. I do not want to leave, but as I hear stories of some of the things I missed while I was abroad, I begin to imagine empty streets on my way home. At midnight, the ticking gets louder. The longer I wait, the fewer cars there will be on the road, and the more nervous I will feel on my drive home. I want to leave, but we just finished dinner—leaving immediately after a meal is like saying you were there only for the food. I stay a bit longer, thinking, but this is ridiculous, if I weigh these things, I would rather be impolite than risk my life. Others are not leaving, so I can't leave either. My friends, however, live in downtown Monterrey. My drive to San Pedro is longer, and I'm driving on my own. I'm weighing all these justifications as I blurt out, "I think I might leave soon," and get a disapproving look from my friend. "But what about desert?" His girlfriend brings some chocolates. I stay for another fifteen minutes half there, half on the empty streets on my mind. A few more minutes and the balance shifts. I get up without asking, kiss everyone goodbye, and leave.

On the road, I am relieved to see dozens and dozens of cars on Gonzalitos, a major avenue, as I begin my drive home. It is now one in the morning. It will be an easy drive, I think, and turn up the radio volume as I go up and down the Loma Larga marking the limit of Monterrey and San Pedro. As I cross the city limits into San Pedro, I feel even more relieved. There are significantly more cars out in this part of the metropolis. I take Calzada del Valle west and look into a plaza with a top floor full of restaurants on my right. I exhale, there are still a lot of people out having drinks and dinner.

I make a left onto my street. A red pick-up truck makes a left onto the street behind me. As I reach my street corner, I decide to drive an extra block and make a right to go around the block and lose the truck. The pick-up truck follows. I make a right again to drive onto my block. The pick-up truck follows. Adrenaline floods my chest, legs, arms, head, and eyes as I drive by my apartment and continue an extra block again. Through my rearview mirror, I see the pick-up truck slow down and park a few houses away from mine on the opposite side of the street. Maybe that is where the pick-up truck owner lives. But what if they're just stopping realizing that I have understood I am being followed? I make a left, and there is a new car behind me. My heart and mind race as I wonder if kidnappers work in tandem to deal with people like me who might think they have lost a tail when they are actually communicating via radio or phone to pick up following a car where another has left off. I'm also thinking this is probably paranoid behavior, but I would rather trust my gut than not. I make a series of extra turns, down then up, then around the block again, and as I drive onto my block once more, I confirm there is nobody inside the truck and that lights are on in the house where it is parked. Maybe it really was just a coincidence that this neighbor was driving home at exactly one in the morning just like me. I park my car in front of my apartment, and the presence of two old men chatting a few doors away makes me feel instantly safer. I get out of my car, open the lock on my gate, go in, and lock the gate behind me. I go upstairs to my apartment, open, close and lock the door behind me as well as two extra locks on the door. I hear a truck move slowly on my street. I go out on the porch, ducking to carefully peek at the street. The neighbor's truck is still parked, and this other truck is gone. There is nobody on the streets but the old men chatting. Nobody is following me. I made it home.

Like the woman mentioned earlier, this field note illustrates a "critical moment" of arriving home with increased awareness of surroundings and strategies to mitigate the fear of being followed, like circling around a block. This field note also illustrates that a feared trajectory begins in the mind even before hitting the road, as in the anticipation of empty streets. Such fears of being out on the streets, especially at night, drove many to socialize with those living closest to them and earlier in the day.

Fear of long trajectories meant those who lived far from their friends might not be able to gather with them. An upper-middle-class woman in San Pedro resented that a friend living in Santa Catarina no longer attended their weekly social gatherings on Tuesdays (*los martecitos*). Her husband had forbidden her from driving after dark. Though she resented her friend, and her friend's husband, she was not willing to travel to Santa Catarina where her friend lived either. To continue gathering after dark, other locals relied on carpooling and sleepovers. A middle-class woman in San Nicolás explained, "I used to, when they called me, 'there's a party,' I would head out not knowing where I would end up." Now she wanted to know exactly where she was going and exactly how she would get back:

> By going out, I mean that if someone invites me to a party, then, where is it? For example, I don't like going to the southern part of the city . . . they would invite me to a party and no, because I would say, I'll show up early and stay there [sleep over]. Or I would tell a friend, hey, we go together, and then you stay at my place or I stay at your place, but I didn't want to go back home alone. I mean, the streets were so empty.

94 THE TWO FACES OF FEAR

This narrative highlights the experience of fear as a series of logistical problems and fear-binding strategies. Fear emptied streets and made it more likely for people to commute and engage in a more intimate nightlife, including sleepovers for safety. While this San Nicolás resident perceived southern Monterrey as dangerous, she revealed later in our interview that soldiers had cracked down on a *casa de seguridad* (safety house) down the block from her house where kidnapped people had been held. The belief that other places are more dangerous than where one lives is a coping strategy to distance oneself from surrounding violence, including for neighborhoods and areas of a similar class position. Middle-class residents from one area of the city referenced other middle-class areas (and not only working-class areas) as more dangerous than where they lived. A resident of downtown Monterrey thought the neighborhood of San Jerónimo was more dangerous, while a resident of San Jerónimo thought that downtown Monterrey was more dangerous. This coping strategy, together with the numerous dangers people feared being out on the streets at this time, underlies a collective preference to party closer to home.

Among the middle class, indoor parties sought to imitate club practices that were not accessible at the time. In San Nicolás, a middle-class man in his late twenties noticed friends "started renting karaokes, and you had them in every party because it's one way in which you can do everything you do in an *antro* [club]. Even if you're at home, you put on music, you sing, videos." Among marginalized youth, nightlife was dispersed as well. In 2011, Torres Escalante, like Saucedo Villegas, observed smaller crowds and fewer Colombian dances at La Fe Music Hall. Torres Escalante followed the dispersion of dancing elsewhere. He observed four smaller dance halls, two sites for bigger parties, four street concerts, and the homes of marginalized youth. While "stages have changed," he noted, "they have not disappeared, on the contrary, they have become diversified . . . scattered throughout the municipalities of Monterrey."[16]

Given that residents tend to live in close proximity with others from a similar socioeconomic position, such small-group dispersion reinforced in-class relations and neighborhood ties, further exacerbating social divisions within an already very unequal metropolis. For marginalized youth, dispersion made it harder for them to socialize with others even of their same class position who lived in different parts of the metropolis, as they were the most dispersed geographically. Moreover, this dispersion had a symbolic component as well that impacted their ability to build metropolitan social ties.

Colombian music was diffused through radio stations, which youth groups used to dedicate songs and send greetings to each other.[17] Researching this practice prior to the war, Blanco Arboleda argues that such radio stations and programming allowed youth groups to transcend neighborhood identities. Through the daily practice of sending greetings to each other over the radio, young people residing far away could "imagine" themselves as part of a "metropolitan community" and "symbolically integrate."[18] There is evidence that such greetings fostered sociability in everyday encounters. Torres Escalante observed youth who had first heard of each other over the radio bump into one another at metro stations and recognize each other. As the war escalated, however, young people stopped sending each other greetings over the radio to "lower their profile." One explained, "You used to fight for a name . . . send greetings to each other on the radio a lot. Not anymore. That kind of thing is over. The more fame you get, the more they'll look for you"— "*antes peleaba mucho el nombre . . . se mandaban saludos en la radio que se usaba mucho, ahora no . . . sí porque entre más fama tengas, más te busca.*"[19] While marginalized youth were spatially and symbolically dispersed, at the other end of the class spectrum, the wealthiest regrouped, reconcentrated their resources, and re-created forms of nightlife lost elsewhere.

San Pedro as a New Nightlife Center

As Barrio Antiguo neighbors described its formerly carnivalesque streets at "dead," a secondary nightlife center within the defended city thrived. El Centrito already had some bars and clubs prior to the turf war, but it became a primary nightlife center as many relocated their clubbing practices from downtown Monterrey into San Pedro. An upper-middle-class San Pedro resident in her early twenties explained, "You used to go out in the Barrio Antiguo. Now you go out in el Centrito. You used to go to Bar Rio [a live music bar in Barrio Antiguo that closed]. Now you go to the Pink Donkey [in el Centrito]. It's the same thing." That the shift in nightlife centers and bars appeared as the "same thing" to her meant she was able to seamlessly continue her nightlife practices amid war. A woman who lived in an apartment overlooking one of its main streets described the night scene from her balcony: "I mean, seriously, it becomes like a zoo. At the stroke of midnight, Centrito just comes alive." Elsewhere in San Pedro, bar and dining options proliferated on the top floors of newly created private plazas. A middle-class

96 THE TWO FACES OF FEAR

man who lived in Monterrey and worked in San Pedro commented on the relocation of upper- and upper-middle-class dining from Barrio Antiguo to the defended city:

> What is the safest municipality? Well of course, San Pedro. This is why you see these plazas ["plaza" here is a reference to privately secured shopping areas] are full, and [if] people say, "I'm going to the Barrio Antiguo," [others will answer] 'No!' " and suggest a private plaza instead. It's full on Saturdays and all because you can say, "I'm going home from here, it's close, we're in San Pedro."

While the preference to party closer to home was common across the class spectrum, only the wealthiest saw their nightlife options expand. In early 2012, I visited the top floor of a private plaza with a middle-class college friend who often drove about thirty minutes from Monterrey to go out in San Pedro. He didn't mind the drive, he said, for he was "used to *apocalimex*" (an apocalyptic Mexico). We parked in a privately secured parking lot and took an elevator to the top floor. The doors opened to reveal an entire floor of restaurants and bars overlooking the Sierra Madre Mountains where hundreds were out having dinner and drinks. "You see? Life as usual," he said, but it was "life as usual" only for some.

A month later, two college acquaintances, one upper-middle class and the other upper class, who lived in San Pedro invited me for drinks on the outdoor patio of a shopping mall. "We never stopped going out," said one, in response to my surprise as we took a seat amid crowds gathering in this outdoor gated area. "Even in the worst times, we were still going out." She spoke in past tense, as if the military were not stationed blocks away. Another disagreed. "I rarely go out. I usually stay at home or sleep over at a friend's house. One of my brother's friends disappeared last week, and the family doesn't know anything. Nobody has called them. No ransom has been requested. They have no idea." This second woman offered recent evidence of victimization from within her social networks to sustain the necessity of limiting her outings at night as well as her reliance on sleepovers as a safety mechanism.

Weeks later, I observed a new bar on the top floor of a smaller private shopping center in San Pedro. A private security guard indicated a spot for me to park and politely requested a tip for the service. "We're here to take care of you," he said. While tips to secure private property like a car were common before, tips were now requested in exchange for personal security.

RESTRUCTURING NIGHTLIFE 97

I counted three more security guards on my way up to a bar where youth in their twenties danced. There was a stark contrast in how private security guards approached patrons at these venues versus how they approached marginalized youth in Saucedo's study of La Fe Music Hall. In both cases, we see an increase in private security—though one seeks to "protect" upper-class patrons while the second increasingly criminalizes them. Moreover, there are racialized patterns in examining who guards whom. While the private security in La Fe Music Hall could camouflage among participants—presumably of a similar skin tone—this was not the case in the San Pedro bars I observed where private security guards had a darker skin tone than the patrons they were hired to protect.

A man who used to go out in the Barrio Antiguo tried this last bar, but "it was not the same. It was a different public. Like . . . [it] had good music. I went to several events, but it was for a different public, it was very San Pedro."[20] "Very San Pedro" meant high heels, make-up, long blonde-streaked hair, miniskirts, bottles, groups of friends singing in English. To state that this bar was for "a different public" meant that it was not for him. These new bars and clubs catered specifically to the tastes of the upper-middle class and upper class. Looking back on the transformation of nightlife in the metropolitan area, a journalist noted, "While San Pedro became the destination for those looking to party, in Monterrey, it was nearly impossible to party."[21] Hence, new bars opening in San Pedro were "the same thing" only for the most privileged residents living nearby as well those willing to run the risks of traveling a greater distance to party with them.

Inside bars and restaurants catering to the most privileged, additional symbolic mechanisms were at work to disincentivize the attendance of "undesirable" clients. One upper-middle-class woman commented on new physical and symbolic mechanisms used to discourage the presence of "new strangers" who could afford the menu of a popular restaurant among the upper-middle and upper class but did not fit the profile of desirable clients. "They started to get, a lot of men, people who were *nuevos desconocidos* (new strangers), and they were like, hmm," she said, adding a suspicious tone to her voice. As noted in Chapter 4, this was a time of heightened social enclosure when locals preferred to socialize with *los conocidos* (acquaintances). New symbolic mechanisms were deployed in response. "They started putting videos of *National Geographic*. They took football out, cars, anything *macho*. They put on cooking lessons, classical music, jazz. They introduced things in the menu that might seem strange to them." I asked for examples. "Like Vichy

98 THE TWO FACES OF FEAR

Catalan," she said, assuming I knew what that was. "It's sparkling water from Catalunya," she added commonsensically. I asked for more examples. "They added aperitifs, Campari, and all of that, digestives, grappa . . . and it worked, amazing, it worked. Now you go on a Friday night and there are tables of women . . . they destroyed that *machista* ambiance." Her acute observations of shifts in the menu and décor exemplify how the upper-class deploys symbolic tools to exclude. The restaurant might be open to the public, "but there are divisions," she clarified, pointing to new spatial mechanisms of indoor exclusion:

> There is a section that is somewhat closed, not entirely closed, but it has a half-wall. Well, that is the area where they will always seat the wealthy, the friends of the owner, *o sea*. When we go, that is where we sit. We always know those who are inside, there, in that little square, and you rarely or never know those who are outside the *cuadrito* (little square). I mean, nobody knows, it is not well-known, but I've realized how it works, because they have a client system that is *bien cabrón* (bad-ass). So every time you go, they register you, and they have hierarchies, *o sea,* and these are not necessarily based on consumption. I get the impression that the owner looks through the list, and he doesn't mix them.

This restaurant might seem like a single establishment for a common guest, including myself prior to hearing her observations. However, those who sit in the half-walled area know there are additional divisions. She knew from experience that this restaurant was, in fact, two restaurants. "It's different, because I went on my own with my friends the other day and they sat us at the bar, and it was a different place. The waiters do not treat you in the same way." I asked if these strategies were recent and what they were about. "I think it's about comfort, because you want to know who is seated next to you. It's like this column I read in the paper last Friday, where the writer said that in cafeterias in Monterrey you have to lower your voice because you do not know who is seated next to you." In this restaurant, the menu, music, and this newly added discreet half-walled *cuadrito* were all material and symbolic mechanisms of seclusion, ensuring social in-network enclosure among *los conocidos*.

A couple she knew would go to this restaurant with her but not to other restaurants that lacked mechanisms of in-network enclosure, including the dining area outside a gated shopping mall blocks from the military referenced earlier in this section. "Because you do not know who might be there," she clarified. "It's that, that language, you know the profile of what the narcos might like, *o sea*." She looked for an example and recalled a Japanese restaurant where we had previously run into each other. She thought it would be very unlikely for a narco to go there. "Don't you agree?" She laughed. "*O sea*, in that hidden place, where they cannot show off . . . and you know, that helps us . . . because we know who does not belong, and in these times of paranoia it's easier to identify." "Identify?" I asked. "Who does not belong, who is not, who is new. You immediately know this; they do not behave in the same way (*no se desenvuelven igual*)." She had been frequenting that Japanese restaurant for over a decade. "It's a very closed environment, very defined. Not that people cannot come in, but it's very defined . . . it's a very subjective language. I'm not sure how to express this." In other words, anyone who strayed from the "very defined" behavior, was suspect. These additional indoor divisions were a micro version of a broader metropolitan trend of increased seclusion of the most privileged confining themselves to tighter spaces and in-network sociability day and night.

Solidifying Nightlife Inequalities

Surveys seeking to assess the impact of fear on daily practices often ask respondents whether they have stopped going out at night. It is a key question suggesting the deep impact of fear on a wide set of practices and relations that are not easily discernible through surveys. This chapter drew on ethnographic and interview evidence to reveal how fear can impact metropolitan nightlife over time. There was deep destruction. National media picked up on the story. Dozens and dozens of bars shut down in the Barrio Antiguo amid shootings and widespread extortion. What was less visible were the forms of nightlife sociability that emerged, allowing some to continue socializing through small group dispersion favoring in-class relations.

While the most privileged further concentrated and saw their clubbing options expand within a tighter perimeter "closer to home," the most marginalized were further dispersed spatially, socially, and symbolically. Small group dispersion endured at the urban margins even after some forms of violence declined. In San Bernabé, a neighborhood commonly featured on t-shirts and caps at the dances at La Fe Music Hall, Pezard-Ramírez observed between 2013 and 2016 that "as the weekend approached, silence

100 THE TWO FACES OF FEAR

was substituted by loud music from inside the houses and from cars. There is hardly a zone in the *colonia* that is silent. However, there is no movement on the streets. The parties happen inside the houses."[22]

The long-term impact of nightlife restructuring during this period endured beyond the most critical years of the turf war. The Café Iguana, among other bars in the Barrio Antiguo, reopened, although a local journalist observed, "They can't be called survivors, rather, they reemerged after being shut down by crime and violence."[23] The upper class, however, did not return downtown. In 2013, a private college student explained, "It's not that it's unsafe, it's just not where we go." As other nightlife options emerged and were consolidated in San Pedro, nightlife in downtown Monterrey was declassed just as living or shopping in downtown Monterrey was declassed before it.[24] Violence and fear widened and solidified the distance between bars catering to different classes from a few blocks to separate cities. By 2016, the metropolitan restructuring of nightlife was obvious to travel writers. *The Rough Guide to Mexico* alerted travelers that crowds had "dropped off considerably" in Barrio Antiguo since 2011, advising partygoers to take a taxi to "San Pedro Garza García, where the latest mega clubs and bars play host to a smart, affluent set."

6

An Oasis from War

September 2, 2012

It is 10 a.m. on a Sunday morning in the Calzada del Valle, a main avenue running through San Pedro. Fear may have emptied streets and parks elsewhere in the metropolis, but not here. As of March 27, 2011, thousands transform this central 1.5-mile (2.5-kilometer) boulevard lined with luxury shops, banks, and restaurants into the largest and most vibrant public space in the metropolis. Every Sunday morning, a steady stream of cyclists, runners, parents pushing strollers, skateboarders, teenagers, and dog lovers fill up its six lanes closed to traffic between 7 a.m. and 1 p.m. Local state officials call the initiative San Pedro de Pinta, drawing on the local expression "irse de pinta" (to divert a common course to have fun). I watch the flowing scene from a Starbucks patio near one end of the boulevard. A food wrapper flies off my table, landing at the feet of a man in his mid-sixties. He hands over the wrapper and I recognize his face. "Are you Alvaro's father?" I ask. He nods with the same blue eyes, the same pointy nose as a friend, evoking distant memories of my college years in Monterrey. "Did he just have a baby?" The grandfather smiles, thrilled to be asked about the newborn. "I like to come here on Sundays," he adds, when I ask about this space. "It is calm. I walk the full Calzada del Valle, then up Humberto Lobo to a supermarket where I buy a few things and take a taxi home. It's my weekly routine."

"Calm" is not a word used to describe most streets in Monterrey these days, but it fits Calzada del Valle on a Sunday morning. A dense flow of bodies circulates in the same direction cars would: west on one side, east on the other. Tall, leafy trees shade a wide median with a snaky walkway dividing the circling flow. Amid the crowd, eleven teenage boys run in matching black shorts and yellow t-shirts. They pass an old woman walking her perfectly groomed miniature schnauzer and a middle-aged couple briskly walking side by side—each listening to their iPods. A boy, around eight, in neon running gear with an iPod strapped to his arm as well, furiously outruns the couple. Other children run or walk close to their parents, though this child appears to be running alone. "I'm going to catch up with my boyfriend!" a teenager shouts at others sipping

The Two Faces of Fear. Ana Villarreal, Oxford University Press. © Oxford University Press 2024.
DOI: 10.1093/oso/9780197688007.003.0006

102 THE TWO FACES OF FEAR

drinks by the sidewalk and bikes off. Many, including these teenagers, scan the Starbucks patio as they walk or bike by.

San Pedro de Pinta is a place to see others and be seen, to show off running gear and biceps, to exercise, to flirt, to gossip, and in the case of young ones running solo, to be left alone. I join the stream of runners, stroller-pushers, and walkers drifting west toward the roundabout at the intersection of Calzada del Valle and Calzada San Pedro where a weekly market meets. I text myself notes as I walk by numerous small and large businesses advertising their services. Capoeira, aerobics, and yoga instructors offer free lessons. A major hardware store draws kids to a large inflatable trampoline. A local state agency for families puts on a puppet show, and a staff member hands me a free notepad with the phrase "What can I do for my family today?" printed across the top of each page. A local pet shelter has brought puppies for adoption. A plant nursery offers me free plants. Dozens of others have organized activities to promote reading, attend art museums, and play chess.

This space has all the elements of a highly unlikely weekly town fair amid war. At the roundabout, a teenage boy plays the guitar and sings to a passing audience. Dozens of food stands offer grilled meat tacos, barbacoa, gourmet tamales, quesadillas, Venezuelan arepas. Dozens of sellers offer homemade seasoning mixes, salsa, cupcakes, jícama on sticks, frozen spicy fruit popsicles, jewelry, handmade clothes, and hair pieces. Among them, I spot the younger sibling of an old schoolmate I have not seen in years. "My wife makes them," he says, pointing at the small bags of spicy dried pineapple chunks laid across his stand. The kid I remembered got married, had a kid of his own, and had just renewed his permit to participate in this market. He loved San Pedro de Pinta, which he described as "a space where we're becoming more aware of the neighborhood scale." The market offered him an opportunity to connect with neighbors.

"This is about people taking public spaces, you know; it's very relevant to your study. Have you been here before?" said another at the roundabout before I had a chance to ask. The middle-aged, upper-middle-class woman had heard from relatives that I was back in town for this work. I had visited San Pedro de Pinta multiple times since my first visit during the summer of 2011. The walk had grown exponentially. Police patrol cars used to be stationed at each corner, but more discrete supervision was now in place, with cameras surveilling us from above. "Earlier this morning, I wanted to go walk in Chipinque, but there was a one-hour line of cars waiting to go in," she complained. "So, I U-turned and came to exercise here instead. There are fewer options of where to go." Chipinque, a private natural reserve in the Sierra Madre Mountains located

within San Pedro—about a twenty-minute drive from the roundabout—is a favorite exercising spot for locals. There are multiple other nature parks in the metropolis, as well as hiking paths in and out of canyons in the mountains nearby. None of these were options for her—and very likely for others waiting in unusually long lines to drive into Chipinque that morning given widespread fear of the outdoors at this time. For this San Pedro resident, San Pedro de Pinta was both the place to go for a run in the morning and the place to go out for a walk with her husband later that same day—in a new set of casual clothes, for I had seen her rush by in running gear that morning from my table at the Starbucks. Close to 1 p.m., vendors stack tables and chairs. A patrol car circles the Calzada del Valle announcing that streets will soon reopen to cars, and I make my way back to mine through the snaky shaded walkway. A girl pedals her bike ahead through a curtain of water drops, laughing at her parents and brother smiling at her from across the street. I step into the sprinkler curtain behind her—an instant relief from the intense late-summer heat. I feel at ease walking back to my car, calm like Alvaro's father, who is probably home by now.

According to most scholarship on fear and public space, San Pedro de Pinta should not exist. When people fear—the upper classes especially—they stay off the streets and replace outdoor practices with indoor gatherings in gated communities and shopping malls.[1] They do not begin to massively gather on a large boulevard with their children. In 2011, however, as state homicide rates peaked, destroying public spaces and outdoor leisure practices in and beyond the metropolis, San Pedro residents created—through weekly gatherings in this major avenue—the largest public space in its history. At its peak, over ten thousand people packed the Calzada del Valle on Sunday mornings, where locals reported feeling "calm." As an urban policy to promote the use of bicycles and exercise, San Pedro de Pinta is not new. More than two hundred cities around the world, from Bogotá to New York City, open streets for pedestrian use on Sunday mornings, particularly during the summer.[2]

The sudden success of an open-streets program in such a violent context, however, is surprising given the literature on the topic and the leisure options these residents have. Scholars of marginality reveal streets are the main sociability spaces for the poor, even in violent contexts, because they have no other choice.[3] San Pedro residents have choices. They own the largest homes in the metropolitan area and have big backyards and pools. They are members of select social and sports clubs—including the most exclusive

104 THE TWO FACES OF FEAR

golf club in northern Mexico, located within San Pedro.[4] They have privately secured shopping malls featuring luxurious global brands. What did these residents find at San Pedro de Pinta that they could not get from their backyards with pools, their private clubs, and exclusive shopping malls? At San Pedro de Pinta, the most privileged residents in the metropolis found a place of assembly to see others and be seen, to reconnect with some they had not seen in years, to protest the loss of loved ones when they feared going downtown, and to experience a "sense of freedom" amid war.

As argued throughout the book, whatever fear destroys, people will seek to re-create, relocate, and reschedule so that life can go on. A previous chapter illustrated how violence and fear prompted a process of destruction, small group dispersion, and classed reconcentration of nightlife. Using this same approach, this chapter examines the destruction and classed reconcentration of leisure—and particularly, of the simple practice of being outside walled spaces with others, which became a luxury at this time. While this boulevard was unique in the metropolis in urban design, in the abundance of tall, leafy trees to provide essential shade from scorching heat, in its high-quality running pavement, among other features, the popularity and vast range of practices that emerged in San Pedro de Pinta is inseparable from the temporary obliteration of numerous leisure options elsewhere. As violence escalated, thousands from all social classes gave up trips to nearby towns, ranches, and *quintas* (country homes), as well as outdoor practices ranging from boating to rock climbing, hiking, camping and motorcycle riding.

With unequal resources, locals from all social classes sought to relocate and re-create these leisure practices within the metropolis. A middle-class woman shared that her friends "used to celebrate their children's birthdays in a *quinta* on the highway with a pool," but "in recent years, the deal was looking for a house with a pool that they could rent here in the city and not too far, downtown or some area considered safe." All options she listed for parties and gatherings were indoors, and her extended family chose to gather in the house with the most security—in this case, a middle-class gated community. Parks and streets were not an option. In San Nicolás, a middle-aged man recalled at least thirty shootings in his neighborhood in 2012, with four to ten deaths in five of them. Despite the shootings, his elderly father did not want to stop his daily walks around the neighborhood, arguing, "*Aquí hay confianza.*" He said there was "trust" among neighbors and held on to his walks, for he hated the idea of "being locked up like an animal." When youth harassed him on the street, he changed his mind. "How our life is changed by all this, such a strong violence," his son added, for dropping a daily walk can shatter the life of a senior. The local state of San Nicolás gated the park across from his house as part of their Armoring Neighborhoods program, which resulted in decreased use. The parks were "empty even by day, on Sundays . . . they gated almost all parks in San Nicolás, they put steel fences around them . . . cameras in some of them . . . they call it armoring . . . the municipality asked the people to vote . . . they voted yes . . . but now with the armoring, they don't use it."

From middle-class to marginalized neighborhoods in Monterrey and San Nicolás, public space was ravaged. In San Bernabé, Soto Canales interviewed a young resident who drew connections between increased shootings, kidnappings, extortion, and emptied public space. When young people stopped hanging out in public plazas, their absence made her feel "more afraid," for at least young people "didn't bother people from the neighborhood. Back then, I remember, there were people going around on bicycles with a whistle to take care of the neighborhood and my mom paid a quota for this service, after that, it was patrol cars, and then, the military."[5] The occupation of the *velador* (the sentinel) patrolling a neighborhood with a bicycle and a whistle disappeared. That the military replaced the police suggests that the police in that neighborhood were likely colluding with organized crime. As mentioned in all previous chapters, both police forces and organized crime disproportionately targeted marginalized youth. One told Torres Escalante, "All preferred to stay locked up indoors than . . . be out and at risk, all the police were colluded in that time, almost nobody wanted to be out on the street"—"*todos prefieren estar en su casa encerrados que estar en la calle arriesgándose de, los policías todos estaban comprados en ese tiempo, ya casi ya, ya nadie quería andar en la calle.*"[6]

"Public space is the first thing to go, public space is the first thing we need to take back," a human rights activist told students at a public university in San Nicolás in 2013. Yet public space was thriving within the defended city, where the most privileged regrouped and relocated their leisure practices. A woman cited in the opening field note to this chapter put it simply: there were "fewer options of where to go." Thousands like her transformed a boulevard into a place of assembly for expanded sociability among the *conocidos* (acquaintances). Indeed, because the main activity at San Pedro de Pinta was to walk around in circles, it was very likely for residents to run into people they already knew, including those they had not seen in years. Violence and fear, like an inhospitable climate, reduced the spaces available

106   THE TWO FACES OF FEAR

to congregate—especially outdoors—while also increasing the density of social interactions among those residing closest to each other and able to congregate.[7]

In what follows, this chapter traces the temporary destruction of outdoor activities from local tourism to a popular dam and the nearby town of Santiago to temporarily abandoned country homes near Cadereyta and the popular mountain range La Huasteca. It then traces the surprising rise of San Pedro de Pinta, which reveals how fear can both destroy and create new forms of public space—albeit under certain conditions. Local state efforts to replicate similar open-streets programs in other municipalities did not produce the same results and revealed widening disparities.

Obliterated Outdoors

In 2010, *El Norte* reported that ten thousand people used to go to a nearby dam every weekend to enjoy a boat ride and a meal. "Today, hours can go by before the boat-owners or the waiters have anyone to serve."[8] Specific events marked a clear escalation of violence and decline of leisure in the area. A month prior, on August 16, 2010, the mayor of Santiago, a town located less than 25 miles (40 kilometers) southeast from Monterrey, was abducted from his home. Three days later, his body was found on a nearby highway leading up to a popular waterfall. The local Santiago police was disbanded, with the military and state police taking control of the town.[9] Unsurprisingly, local tourism to Santiago and nearby areas plummeted.

"You used to, for example, go to the *presa* (the dam), and then you would go for lunch in Santiago, get an ice pop in the plaza, now *wey, se fue de pueblo mágico a pueblo trágico*." An upper-class woman in San Pedro found a rhyme to capture the fall of Santiago from "magic" tourist destination to "tragic" ghost town.[10] In 2013, she nostalgically recalled her country home in the vicinity, which she had not visited in three years. "That part is really sad because that house was great . . . it's been years, but I mean, nobody goes, nobody." Her mother-in-law used to go every Saturday. "She would spend all the afternoon there . . . we don't go to *la carretera* anymore" (the highway to Santiago, a destination in itself lined with shops and restaurants). Instead, she began to travel abroad more. Noticing an uptick in international travel among her peers, she thought it might be a good time to open a travel agency.

AN OASIS FROM WAR 107

For this woman and her friends, fear relocated travel from local to international destinations.

A middle-class man in downtown Monterrey stopped going to Santiago, Montemorelos, and nearby towns, by day and by night—though things were changing in 2013 when we spoke. "This year, people have begun to go out to *la carretera* again, at least by day." He noticed "a lot of security on the highway," including "military convoys," which led him to think "the highway is, let's say, somewhat protected." He clearly distinguished these recent trips from "a few years ago when you could go out and come back anytime, that you could go to a ranch, the *presa* (dam), wherever you wanted to and there was no problem." He heard of abandoned country homes. "Nobody wants to go to a *quinta*, let alone sleep there, out of fear of what may happen at night. He had friends with ranches who had not been in years. "You feel safer in the city than on the highway." An artist living in downtown Monterrey had not been to her family's country home in over a year. We met for lunch with a mutual college friend. In 2012, I interviewed her in her two-bedroom apartment downtown, where she kept a framed picture of her country home on her desk: "a place where I could dream . . . but it wasn't paradise anymore." She held the picture of a one-floor white house with an orange tile roof against a blue sky, perfectly trimmed green grass amidst orange trees, a large pool, and wondered if she would ever return.

Six months later, she began considering the option of reclaiming that cherished place. Early in 2013, we took the highway to Cadereyta and stopped at a military checkpoint. She claimed that she no longer feared it, for she "had become accustomed to living in a state of war." We drove into town. She checked in with a local at a convenience store. "I always buy a few things," she said, though the pit stop was not to buy chips. She wanted to make sure a local knew we were going in and could update her on any recent events we should be aware of. "I have this theory that they recognize my car, that they know who I am, where I live, but they will not bother me," she explained, tacitly referencing organized crime as a "they." We drove down a narrow paved road and arrived at the front entrance of her gated property. A local gardener and his wife lived on-site. Past the gate, a narrow dirt road revealed the scene from the picture: a one-floor house on top of a hill with a pool amid orange trees. The artist took off her shoes, popped a beer open, and recalled violent events in the area. Her neighbor was murdered last year. She claimed he "most likely" was into some kind of "dirty business . . . he was from Reynosa after all." Elsewhere, I examine criminalizing the dead as a means of creating

108 THE TWO FACES OF FEAR

symbolic security amid vulnerability.[11] The alternative—that her neighbor was not into "dirty business"—might make her feel more vulnerable sipping beer in the plot next door. The son of the local butcher was kidnapped and not returned after ransom was paid. More recently, the military found a *narcofosa* (mass grave) in the direction where she heard multiple shootings years before, always at the same time of day. Taking another sip from her beer, she added:

> Never ever, in this place, which I consider paradise, where we used to walk around barefoot in our diapers, how could I ever imagine that one day I would be neighbors with someone murdered because he was in with the narcos [she paused to take another sip]. Or that the place where I learned how to drive a van, um, that two decapitated bodies would appear there. I juxtapose those images because for me, this place, I don't want it to have that meaning. I want to keep giving it that . . .

She stretched her arms forward as if she could bring paradise back. This place contained a deep part of herself that she wanted to reclaim. "I mean," she added, "the fact that all the people here are holding on and are keeping this place, and if we keep coming, in the end, this will clean it, will save it." The gardener and his wife had their own stories, including a murdered family member killed when trying to sell a car to organized crime. Unlike the artist, they had nowhere else to go (no "safer" metropolis to take refuge in). A few days later, I ran into a lecturer at a private university who greeted me with a smile and asked about my weekend. "I went to a *quinta* near Cadereyta. It was sunny, there was a pool," I answered, smiling back. She dropped the smile and advised me not to go there. Her brother-in-law owns a *quinta* in the area and stopped going because of multiple kidnappings. He recently returned and was devastated to find his *quinta* ravaged:

> They took everything, the furniture, the kitchen appliances, the water pump, everything, even the ground has begun to sink. [I asked whether he would report.] No, he's the kind who thinks that the further away you are, the better.
>
> They think filing a report is dangerous, they say they are colluded, the very police . . . they've heard many stories from the neighbors of those plots where it wasn't only about simple theft, but who have been kidnapped,

killed, who have been forced to keep, um . . . drugs in their ranch or stolen cars.

Her narrative provided further evidence of widespread kidnappings and theft in the countryside, which, given fear of reporting, are unlikely to show in officials statistics. Like the artist mentioned earlier, she and her brother-in-law hoped for a better future. "They are letting this wave of violence pass . . . so to speak, with the hopes that one day they may be able to recover their things and their land, their *quintas*, right?" While some middle-class informants were starting to go back to country homes in 2013, this was not the case for the upper-class and upper-middle-class residents I spoke to. "There is nothing left for us there," said one. "I have prohibited myself from going," said another. Like the upper-class woman traveling abroad, they had more resources and could likely afford to relocate their leisure elsewhere more comfortably than the middle class at this time.

West of the metropolis is La Huasteca, a mountain range that local and global climbers know well featured in Figure 6.1. It is striking, especially on full moon nights when its lime rock takes on a reddish lunar glaze. In 2010, a visitor from Ohio noted its beauty, and the inequality among its residents on a Tripadvisor review. The reviewer called La Huasteca "the best thing about

Figure 6.1 La Huasteca

Figure 6.1 *Nido a Huasteca II* (2018) depicts the main entry road to La Huasteca as seen from a popular climbing spot. Reproduced with permission from photographer Roberto Ortiz Giacomán.

110 THE TWO FACES OF FEAR

Monterrey . . . these mountains have ridges that are unlike any I've seen in the US. They are bizarre and random and stunning . . . we had a great time and saw interesting homes on the way there—some were shacks, others were practically mansions—all in very close proximity." The declining number and negative content of Tripadvisor reviews that followed were indicative of fewer visits to this popular leisure destination as violence escalated. In 2012, a local lamented that in La Huasteca "there is no security, and the mafia gathers inside the park." Another reviewer in 2012 advised caution: "The views at night are phenomenal, but I suggest going by day only due to insecurity and the stories people tell."[12]

A businessman who loved the outdoors had stopped going to La Huasteca when we spoke in 2013. He owned a property in the area, which he had temporarily abandoned. "What's it like now? What is your feel of things?" he asked local workers at the entrance, wondering whether he could go back. "It's all good, calm, except for that shooting range they just found," they told him. The businessman coughed a short laugh during our interview recalling this interaction. He thought it might be a rumor. However, *Excelsior* reported in 2011 that five clandestine graves were found in the road leading to the main canyon of La Huasteca. Federal police closed off a large area, for they had "found a sort of shooting range a few meters away from the graves, where they found hundreds of bullet caps of different calibers."[13] Following the beheading of two guards, the businessman said the entrance to La Huasteca was now guarded by police "with machine guns, and those bags used to take cover during shootings . . . two, four, six people, they check cars, they ask you where you're going."

I avoided La Huasteca during 2011 and 2012, but I took an opportunity to go back when rock climbers I knew invited me to join them in 2013. We gathered in one home and carpooled to La Huasteca. As expected, given the businessman's account, federal police had replaced old watchmen and guarded the entrance from behind a wall of sandbags—bunker style. As we drove into the canyon, they signaled us to stop. "Hide the [beer] can," the man driving told his wife. "You're going too fast, 10 [kilometers per hour] with caution," a federal agent told the driver, then let us continue on our way. "I'm already driving very slowly," the driver complained, once we were out of hearing range from the police. A few moments later, a black pick-up truck overtook us and sped ahead. "Why isn't he stopped?" the driver's wife protested. "Because he's a narco?" she wondered, for pick-up trucks were associated with organized crime. We parked and walked over to the spot where we would climb. As one began to prepare the ropes, another mentioned an upcoming meteor shower.

"Let's watch it!" said one of the climbers with excitement. The question was where, as the group would need to leave the city at night. Nostalgia. "Icamole," said another with a sigh, referencing a town in the middle of the desert located almost 30 miles (50 kilometers) northwest that seemed out of reach at this time. "But we would get killed. The last time I was there was with a friend who is not easily frightened . . . " The storyteller paused, waiting for someone to probe her on the details of her story but nobody did—we had all heard enough—so she kept them to herself. As we drove out of La Huasteca that afternoon, the group settled on a private option to watch the meteor shower: camping in a gated residential development. Like these climbers, other locals I spoke to were relocating their camping practices into gated areas. "Five years ago, I would gather my family, my camping tent, *mi combi* (van), and I would go camp in Bustamante, near water springs," said a middle-class nature enthusiast in 2013, citing a town about 60 miles (100 kilometers) north of Monterrey:

> The locals would show up. "Good evening, how is it going? Feel safe, we're here." . . . You can't go camping there now. Nothing might happen, but if you hear a pick-up truck, you're going to piss your pants, more if you're with the family. You don't feel safe. That has changed so much . . . Camping? Forget about it, it's not an option. We need to camp in someone's property.

A reduction in camping also meant fewer chances for urban residents to interact with locals in rural areas, typically impoverished agricultural workers and ranchers. The destruction of leisure thus entailed the temporary or indefinite destruction of these fleeting cross-class encounters. An old college friend I encountered in 2012 had also stopped camping. "Last summer, four friends and I decided to be brave and go to the desert like we used to, even if it wouldn't make much of a difference how many guys we were." His comment speaks to the cross-gender impact of fear of violence on leisure, for even men in groups felt unsafe outdoors. As they were about to drive off the highway and into the desert, they saw two black Suburbans drive out of the desert and onto the highway. "We decided to make a U-turn and go back to Monterrey. This was the last time I tried to go camping."

Like pick-up trucks, Suburbans were also associated with organized crime, particularly when driving in close proximity to each other. However, as

112 THE TWO FACES OF FEAR

mentioned in Chapter 3, caravanning was a common safety mechanism employed by residents on routes they feared. Those two Suburbans could have been residents caravanning to feel safe on their drive back to the city; thus, the very safety precautions locals adopted to bind fear could likely exacerbate fear among others. One of his friends had stopped going to La Huasteca as well: "They went inside to try their longboards on some lonely roads and two men pulled over with their truck, got out their guns, and practiced shooting cans very close to them for about an hour, then left. They also go camping," he said, tacitly referencing organized crime. "What if I'm out there and one of them likes my girl or my car? It's not worth it."

The rock climbers, motorcyclists, campers, and country-home owners in this section detailed coping strategies commonly discussed in scholarship on fear and urban life: fearful residents tend to trade outdoor practices for indoor gatherings, including in privately secured shopping malls, or in the case of campers, private properties where they could camp in secured areas.[14] It is this general backdrop of widespread violence, fear, and relocation of numerous leisure practices within gated and privately secured areas that makes the emergence of San Pedro de Pinta at the peak of this wave of violence so surprising. However, I argue that it is precisely the destruction of numerous leisure spaces and practices elsewhere that, together with classed state privileges and private resources, underlies the rise and consolidation of a new and massive public space in San Pedro.

The Surprising Success of San Pedro de Pinta

On March 27, 2011, the municipality of San Pedro launched San Pedro de Pinta, the first open-streets program in the metropolis. State officials hoped the program would be successful, but they were stunned when two thousand people showed up on the first Sunday of this program. They extended this summer program to a year, then indefinitely—though they temporarily suspended it during the Covid-19 pandemic. Interviewed in 2013, public officials exclusively appointed to run San Pedro de Pinta, given its enormous success, estimated that ten thousand people attended this program on a weekly basis. While the Calzada del Valle already existed as a public space for walkers and joggers prior to increased violence, it was nowhere as vibrant and as central to the routines of its residents as it became at the height of this turf war through the San Pedro de Pinta program.

While the initial objective of San Pedro de Pinta was to create a space for cyclists, a surprising and vast range of other activities spontaneously emerged. "Little by little, citizens began to offer activities for the walk," said one of the officials overlooking this program. "*Un espacio de convivencia* [a sociability space] began to emerge, the bikes were obviously there . . . but people accepted it because of the space it provided for sociability." Yoga and tai chi instructors were the first to offer free classes to participants. An eighty-year-old woman set up a table and began to encourage people to exchange books—over seven boxes every Sunday. A girl learned how to use the hula hoop and decided to teach a class. "She now has twenty girls. They have their hoops, and she's there to give her class every Sunday, and she cannot miss it; otherwise the girls won't have their class!" An eighty-seven-year-old man sat at a table, laid out a chessboard, and asked, "Who wants to play chess?" Three tables of chess players began to meet on a regular basis. "How should we name your project?" the officials asked. "*Reta al viejo*," he said, meaning, "challenge the senior." In strong contrast with the elderly man living in San Nicolás, who gave up his daily walk and could no longer gather with others in the park across from his house, this senior could socialize with whomever wanted to play chess with him on a weekly basis.

A group of gardeners offered to share plant seedlings. A storyteller began organizing "word picnics," laying tablecloths on the ground so mothers could take turns reading stories aloud to children. "We've looked for different activities, but the most successful ones have been those that citizens proposed themselves," the officials concluded, reporting high levels of civic engagement. "These are not charities. These are citizens who want to contribute to the program. We call these *pequeñas grandes acciones* (great small actions)." A small state-run market called the Mercado de la Fregonería was relocated to the roundabout from a nearby plaza and grew exponentially. In 2013, it had more than eighty vendors, including the man selling pineapple chunks mentioned at the beginning of this chapter. The market provided dozens with opportunities to get involved, as well as additional attractions for passersby. A photographer volunteered to document these moments on Facebook, where thousands of pictures provide further evidence of the wide range of regular activities taking place in this space over time.

While San Pedro residents spontaneously offered numerous activities to grow San Pedro de Pinta, the local state worked hard to regulate the activities and sponsors allowed in this space. Businesses approached state officials with sponsorship offers for the program, including large grocery stores,

114   THE TWO FACES OF FEAR

insurance companies, and sports brands. As sponsorship grew, the weekly program became profitable. "Sponsors were obviously interested," but not all sponsors were allowed to contribute. A luxury auto brand was rejected. "No, we're not going to exhibit cars if we're trying to get the cars off the streets to promote bicycles. Obviously, no cigarettes, no alcohol." A casino approached them to offer free breakfasts. "We said no. This is a family space. These are very delicate points: nothing religious, nothing partisan." Similarly, not all professionals who offered free services were allowed to participate. "A massage therapist contacted us. We said no, that's too much physical contact." No reiki or other healing practices of the kind. "We want to preserve a family image, to promote sociability and sport." A pit bull association approached them. "We didn't like them. We said no, that's aggressive. Boxers too, we said no. 'It's a sport' [boxers argued]. No, not now, no punches, no," she said, laughing. "No Krav Maga. These are all martial arts, but to preserve the image and the environment. 'It's to teach kids self-defense at this time of insecurity' [she recalled the Krav Maga practitioners saying], but no, why don't you focus on the positive side?" said the official. Once, a Krav Maga association did a demonstration with plastic toy weapons. "People didn't like it; they didn't want to see that, no aggression."

When asked about security, both officials stressed the centrality of keeping cars off the road. "Our main security concern is not necessarily to catch thieves because we haven't had any, but to make sure that streets are closed. These are not steel walls; we're using plastic cones [to block traffic in eighteen street corners]." The state officials made an interesting point. There are no "steel walls" enclosing the wealthiest metropolitan residents as they go out for a walk with their children amid war. Steel walls were unnecessary because other defense mechanisms were in place at the city level. While these state officials had an agenda for the kind of environment they wanted to create, participants too called on the state to ensure that this space was free of references to violence and aggression. Two weeks prior, a man in his fifties or sixties approached them to complain that someone had painted machine guns on the sidewalk on one end of the avenue.

"He was very upset, very disturbed, he said, 'my son-in-law was killed, and I don't want to come here to see this,' I mean, people come here to feel something different from everywhere else, the media, the newspapers, everywhere people are talking about, well, now..." The verb tense changed. "Not as much," added the other one. "Not as much, but there was a time when there was no way of avoiding the subject. Who was kidnapped? Who was killed? So, for him, it was too much, I went to see them [the machine gun drawings], they were barely visible, I took a picture, I mean, I didn't feel as affected, but we removed them . . . the cops said it was just mischief." This story led the other official to recall the time when a crime-prevention unit wanted to demonstrate how their dogs act in case of an attack. "I said no; why don't you just throw a ball at them and have them fetch it?" Her supervisor scolded her for giving them this much entry—her comment revealed that regulating tranquility was also an instruction from above. "I told them that it was okay for them to show their obedience training, but not the attack, because that is not the message and it's unsettling, I mean, we want to keep violence out of San Pedro de Pinta . . . even if these actions are not violent in themselves, to give the community a tranquil space."

In 2013, I volunteered to design a survey for Consejo Cívico, a business-backed civic organization, to help evaluate San Pedro de Pinta and eight other open-streets programs launched that year, further discussed in the the next section. Each municipality had their own survey, making comparisons across municipalities challenging. On June 16, 2013, and with the help of twelve other Consejo Cívico volunteers, we applied the survey to 270 attendees at San Pedro de Pinta.[15] The grand majority resided in San Pedro or Monterrey, though a few also visited from other municipalities, including San Nicolás, Guadalupe, Apodaca, Santa Catarina, and the nearby town of Santiago—mentioned in the previous section and suggesting a reversal of leisure flows with people from Santiago coming to San Pedro for a Sunday stroll.[16] Most San Pedro residents surveyed that day reported regular attendance.[17]

The survey asked whether respondents felt safe and why. Out of 101 San Pedro residents, only two said no. One man said, "A group of cyclists were biking too fast," and one woman recalled a shooting that took place on the Calzada del Valle two years before. That is, only one San Pedro resident referenced violence as a source of insecurity while at the open-streets program. All others responded yes. When asked to expand on why, a thirty-one-year-old woman said, "Because of the security in San Pedro, we never leave San Pedro, unless it's urgent." A fifty-four-year-old man said, "Yes, this is a violence-free zone; we are armored." Similarly, two women, one fifty-four and the other twenty-five claimed, "San Pedro is safe," and "because I'm in San Pedro." All these respondents highlighted security as a feature of the municipality. All respondents from other municipalities present at San Pedro de Pinta responded yes. When asked why, they referenced the "family environment," said there were "a lot of people," and, again, pointed to the security

116   THE TWO FACES OF FEAR

of the municipality. A fifty-eight-year-old man from Monterrey said, "My criteria is that this is a municipality that has security, it is a safe municipality." A sixty-two-year-old resident from San Nicolás said, "This is San Pedro." A thirty-one-year-old woman from Monterrey said, "It's the safest municipality in Nuevo León." Two women from Monterrey, one forty-six and the other fifty-two, said, "You're in San Pedro" and "I trust the municipality." These examples provide evidence that residents from other municipalities were willing to travel to San Pedro and participate in activities on the streets there because they felt safe doing so in San Pedro, although San Pedro residents were less willing to go outside their municipality. We surveyed a handful in Monterrey and none at the open-streets programs elsewhere in the metropolis.

One of the state officials responsible for San Pedro de Pinta loved the attendance but also found it puzzling. "I love seeing families together, a lot of fathers. I recall a woman saying, 'My husband exchanged golf for coming to San Pedro de Pinta.' I've asked myself this [question]. This is one of the wealthiest cities, where many belong to some of the most expensive social clubs in the world, right?" She looked for answers. "Everyone can come, members and nonmembers . . . people at the social club dress up, bring their [designer] purse, nobody can flash their car around here. You don't know who is rich and who is poor. I mean, I like this." Upon further reflection, the state official revised her own narrative: "You notice *la sociedad* (society, code for class) in the dogs, right? The exotic ones, I mean, they're not wearing a bag to show off, but they bring their dog." San Pedro de Pinta was a site where dogs, among other means, signalled status when other status markers, like luxury cars, were downgraded as discussed in Chapter 2. For the residents of San Pedro, the primary draw at San Pedro de Pinta, however, were not the numerous food stands or sponsored activities, the hula hoops or the book exchanges, although all provided people with things to do. What mainly attracted San Pedro residents were the other San Pedro residents. As mentioned earlier in this chapter, because there was "nowhere to go" and because the main activity at San Pedro de Pinta was to walk around in circles, it was very likely that San Pedro residents would run into people they knew, including people they had not been in touch with for years.

Nearly eight of ten surveyed San Pedro respondents reencountered old friendships or acquaintances at San Pedro de Pinta. They ran into schoolmates, college friends, former bosses, former clients, childhood friends, workmates, parents of their kids' friends, people they had not seen in decades, like a sixty-year old man who ran into a friend he had not seen "since the 1980s when we were both motorcyclists." On some occasions, these encounters led residents to pursue these relations outside this space. A fifty-three-year-old man ran into the parents of his children's friends and "continue[d] to see them." A forty-six-year-old man ran into an old friend and "it turned out we both play soccer, and we started a soccer team." A thirty-seven-year-old man ran into an old acquaintance and "followed up, went out for lunch, exchanged emails and Facebook [contacts]." A forty-one-year-old woman ran into friends, talked, and then got together to catch up ("*para ver qué onda con nuestras vidas*"). On other occasions, respondents said they did not meet outside the family walk but continued to see these relations at San Pedro de Pinta. "Friends from school, I continue to see them here," said a fifty-four-year-old woman. A fifty-one-year-old man said, "My son-in-law, I see him here every Sunday, more often than in my house." This was a site to leisure among *los conocidos*.

Over the course of observing San Pedro de Pinta, I too ran into college friends and distant acquaintances I had not seen in years. On March 25, 2012, as I strolled through the Mercado de la Fregonería, I spotted a woman behind a jewelry stand who looked familiar. I looked familiar to her too. We probed each other and discovered we were the same age, had attended the same college and the same high school—though we hung out in different parts of the building. After navigating the same institutions for seven years without engaging each other in conversation, it is paradoxical that we should finally meet in the midst of war. "I used to go to *las termas*," she said nostalgically, referencing hot springs about an hour's drive northwest, where she might have been that morning in other times. However, something "positive" had emerged for her. "Everyone here has a garden and no need to go out. There is little use of public spaces . . . [but] with all of these things that are happening [a tacit reference to violence], people are bonding, they come out with their families to enjoy this space, to exercise, to eat food, and I like that." She compared San Pedro to Madrid, where she had just been and seen people using public spaces much more frequently.

San Pedro de Pinta provided these residents with "bonding" opportunities and a unique diversion from war. A yoga instructor who lived blocks away from the Calzada del Valle was a regular attendee. "We were there from the very first one. It was key for us, for life here; it gives us a sense of freedom, to see everyone behave. Nobody is throwing garbage around. Everything is in order. They start setting up around 5 a.m. or 6 a.m., but when they leave, it's

118 THE TWO FACES OF FEAR

like nothing happened." Given the context, her reference to "order" is not only about the absence of garbage but also of violence and references to violence. San Pedro de Pinta provided a state-sponsored and regulated oasis of tranquility where residents could forget about "life here" for a while. The yoga instructor, and mother of three, felt safer taking her children to San Pedro de Pinta than the Parque Fundidora downtown where she used to go before—an example of relocated leisure from downtown to blocks from her house in San Pedro. She provided further details on her fears.

"Imagine losing sight of your kids anywhere else, but in San Pedro de Pinta, you don't freak out. You know they are safe. It's not as if you were downtown and you suddenly turn around and nothing." She mimicked panic at the thought. "Here you give them more freedom, like that freedom we had growing up." I had attended her yoga class for a year prior to this interview and probed her on this point, recalling a previous conversation before class. "There was that time when you lost sight of your daughter in San Pedro de Pinta and said you began to scream." She immediately recalled the story:

> Oh yes, for forty minutes, I screamed, what horror . . . I was walking on the walkway . . . [but] if this were downtown, in ten minutes I would have gone to the police or would have gone mad . . . this is a space where people are trying to be a better person, to enjoy themselves, like all of us who are here like to socialize, exercise, to enjoy a walk, to support local initiatives, the one who sells food, the guy that makes salsa. For me it's essential, before, we felt there were not many spaces [to go to].

This woman revised her narrative of not "freaking out" at San Pedro de Pinta if losing sight of her child, for she had screamed with "horror" for forty minutes when the first fear that came to her mind was a temporary reality. Still, downtown her tolerance for madness had a shorter imaginary time limit. Nowhere else did I hear respondents reference their municipality as a source of security. San Pedro de Pinta was a weekly, temporary escape from entrapment. Another upper-middle-class mother of two put it this way, "They give us San Pedro de Pinta, and that's it. We're happy and we forget about everything else . . . everything was solved, we were all there in the roundabout, as if it were our mini *Arc de Triomphe*."

A turf war obliterated leisure options and public spaces across the metropolis and created the conditions for the emergence of a new classed place of assembly where privileged ties could be renewed. In 2014, urbanists

AN OASIS FROM WAR   119

Hinojosa and Aparicio described San Pedro de Pinta as "a real community fair. What started as a simple cyclist activity became, in the midst of a wave of violence and suspicion, a model to reclaim a sense of community, security and peace."[18] The model, however, was challenging to reproduce elsewhere in the metropolis.

Urban Privilege Cannot Be Replicated

Following the success of San Pedro de Pinta, Consejo Cívico pressured all incoming municipal state governments in 2013 to create a similar open-streets program in their municipalities.[19] The names of all open-streets programs evoked themes of sociability and enjoying urban life, including Convive, Monterrey (Monterrey, Socialize) and Vive tu Ciudad Guadalupe (Guadalupe, Live your City). Attempts to replicate San Pedro de Pinta elsewhere, however, revealed widening disparities. In San Pedro, police patrol cars stood at each street corner on both sides of the Calzada del Valle when I first observed the program during the summer of 2011. Over time, patrol cars were replaced with cameras surveilling the space from above and police using two-wheeled, motorized stand-on devices to patrol the avenue. Meanwhile, a public official responsible for a temporary open-streets program in Santa Catarina I spoke to in 2013 said there were only two patrol cars in the entire municipality, for most of the police was disbanded following failed "trust" exams.

No other municipality had an equivalent 1.5-mile (2.5-kilometer) boulevard with trees and a broad natural shaded walkway to work with either. The Calzada del Valle had been envisioned as a public space since the 1940s when the Colonia del Valle was developed. It was already an established public space before the war, with tall trees shading its walkway that require decades of planning and care. Maricarmen Elosúa, director of the Municipal Institute for Urban Development in San Pedro at the time, argued, "Given Monterrey's climate, this would not have worked without Calzada's trees."[20] At the other end of the class spectrum, the open-streets program in Juárez was organized on a blocked section of a highway. A couple of tents were set up to provide some shade from the scorching heat for the few families that ventured to go. Even in downtown Monterrey, shade was scarce.

On March 17, 2013, the city of Monterrey closed more than a mile (specifically 2.2 kilometers) of streets to vehicular traffic along the historic Macro

120 THE TWO FACES OF FEAR

Plaza, the largest plaza in the metropolis, stretching from the Monterrey mayor's office to the governor's office. I had seen families gather, couples make out on the grass, and street vendors sell corn, tostadas, and toys over the weekend at the Macro Plaza over the years. But the site was empty on the inauguration day for its open-streets program Convive Monterrey. Mayor Margarita Arellanes toured avenues blocked to traffic on a pink bicycle dressed in sports clothes, her long hair tied up in a high ponytail. A policeman on a motorcycle rode in front of her and a second policeman and bodyguard rode behind her, followed by a municipal police pick-up truck not far away—indicators of how the generalized fear of being out on the streets extended to public officials. Cameras filmed her touring the open-streets program, from a rock-climbing wall to a capoeira station to a karate performance—her staff bustling ahead to create a crowd. At the end of the walk, she addressed the media:

> Each one of these kilometers, each part has signs where we can see tae kwon do, we can see sports, we can see painting for our youth, we can see that there is a family environment, with sack races, we see youth, children and parents *conviviendo* [socializing], and the purpose, well, is to have a place to socialize and enjoy on Sundays ... to participate with your family stretching social ties not only within the family but also with the rest of *regiomontanos* [people from Monterrey].

Monterrey had a space—the Macro Plaza—but no shade. "There are no trees. The most comfortable spot is under the bridge," said an architect who worked with the local urban planning agency in Monterrey as we walked along the open-streets program on its inauguration day. He thought the local state should widen the sidewalks "so that they are inclusive, and include trees to begin to change the perception of public space, because they are dead right now; *no sirven para convivir*" (they're not good for socializing). The features of the space were important, but so were the much higher reported violence rates for Monterrey at this time. No other open-streets program gathered ten thousand residents on a weekly basis, even though other municipalities have larger populations. In Santa Catarina, Apodaca, San Nicolás, Escobedo, and Juárez, I observed fewer than one hundred participants during my visit. The second-largest open-streets program was in Guadalupe, where Mayor César Garza stated his objective as follows:

> What we are aiming for is clear, to establish an attractive and safe urban space so that our families can go out on the streets again and mingle with each other and the rest of Guadalupe residents, through leisure, physical activities, culture and sports . . . the idea is for citizens to find in this *vía recreativa* [leisure avenue] all that is needed to really feel that we are beginning to reclaim public space.[21]

These mayors called on residents to "go out" and "socialize" in Monterrey and Guadalupe at a time when residents were staying off the streets. There was also an abysmal gap in the variety of activities available in these programs. While San Pedro residents brought private activities out onto public space, I only observed state-sponsored activities at other open-streets programs. In Santa Catarina, one of the activities residents engaged in was painting the borders of sidewalks. Activities banned at San Pedro de Pinta were main attractions elsewhere. For example, while San Pedro state officials considered martial arts "too aggressive" for its residents, karate groups performed in Monterrey and San Nicolás. A pit bull association turned down at San Pedro drew crowds in Guadalupe—as well as many pit bulls. In Juárez, a security talk was the main attraction that brought a family I spoke to during my visit out of their homes and onto the highway.

Despite these abysmal differences, there were some similarities. Initiating conversation with multiple passersby, I learned locals who attended these programs regularly would be at home otherwise because there was "nowhere else to go." Open-streets programs provided a space for some, even if few in number, to establish or renew social ties with their neighbors. In Escobedo, a woman began to practice yoga on a weekly basis. "It's a healthy environment," she said. "I think this is what the city needs, given the things we've been through and that seem to be calming down. It's good for the children. We were very scared. We didn't want to socialize with neighbors or friends, and this does motivate me to come out, and I've made new friends here." Others reported running into old friends or work colleagues they had not seen in years. A thirty-eight-year-old woman in Guadalupe said she ran into one of her mother's friends: "I hadn't seen her in ten years. Ironically, we live two, three blocks away from each other." These initiatives created an opportunity for residents to go back to streets they evaded. One resident in San Nicolás avoided the avenue where the open-streets program was set up for some time, for "it smelled like death." Dressed in a karate uniform after a martial arts display, he explained:

122   THE TWO FACES OF FEAR

> The problem was severe because different commandos were constantly driving through this avenue displaying their AK-47 . . . asking for, well, *derecho de piso* [extortion] . . . the one who sold *barbacoa* [shredded beef], the one who sold electric parts, the one who rented music, the one with the taco stand, the little store owner, the *tamales* guy, so it was a very serious problem . . . because behind these different flashing trucks with armed men you saw the local police, so it was all organized, until this whole [military] confrontation against them took place freeing things up.

Considering the recent history of these streets—as narrated by this resident—the initiative to "open" streets in the Monterrey Metropolitan Area was about much more than promoting cycling and pedestrian sociability as is commonly done elsewhere. Pressured by the business elite via the Consejo Cívico, local state governments attempted to re-create forms of sociability that police in collusion with organized crime had played a role in destroying. Consejo Cívico evaluated and ranked open-street programs in an effort to foster competition among public officials who would seek to improve their *vía recreativa* to obtain the highest score. San Pedro de Pinta was routinely ranked the highest during my fieldwork. Frustrated with low evaluations, state officials in charge of open-streets programs elsewhere requested that the Consejo Cívico leave San Pedro out of the competition. "The conditions of each municipality are very different," one argued at a meeting with Consejo Cívico staff I observed in 2013. "San Pedro already has the space . . . leave San Pedro out," another requested. The stark differences between San Pedro de Pinta and other open-streets initiatives discussed in this section offered yet another indicator of the growing abyss between the defended city and the rest of the metropolitan area. Most municipal open-streets programs stopped at the end of these mayors' terms.

The Relative Privilege of Being Unwalled

This chapter examined the impact of increased violence and fear on leisure as a process of destruction and classed reconcentration that destroyed and produced new forms of public space. As leisure options declined for all, San Pedro de Pinta emerged as an option for some to bond and experience a sense of freedom amid war. Such an oasis thrived with San Pedro residents' fear of leaving the defended city. It declined in size as its residents began to reengage in forms of leisure they had abandoned. Nonetheless, it endured. San Pedro de Pinta continues to be hailed as a local tradition, even after a temporary shutdown during the Covid-19 pandemic.

While the municipality with the highest rate of car users hosted the largest space for the privileged to leave their cars aside for a few hours and divert attention from the war, pedestrians elsewhere relying on their feet to get anywhere had a harder time transiting and gathering. Construction workers and domestic workers who were on foot were not allowed into privately secured neighborhoods. Moreover, San Pedro residents lobbied against the expansion of bus lines and bus stops that might bring "insecurity" to their neighborhoods. Beyond San Pedro, defensive mechanisms at a neighborhood level further excluded dark-skinned, low-income residents from public space. Pezard-Ramírez observed this pattern in northwestern Monterrey, where middle-class residents "dislike the use of *their* parks and streets by those who do not live in their *colonia*."[22] These neighbors saw pedestrians walking by as "suspicious" criminals and most often approached young dark-skinned men walking alone or sitting on a bench to demand that they leave. On one occasion, she observed a resident threaten a *pepenador* (informal garbage collector) with his pick-up truck driving very closely to him.[23] In low-income neighborhoods, marginalized youth were unable to gather, as discussed in Chapter 3.

To walk and to gather, as thousands did in San Pedro de Pinta, became a rare privilege, but the privileged also fell in this war. Within a week of writing the opening field note to this chapter, four men were abducted in San Pedro, including close family members of top state officials. Two, including a former public official and a former congressman, were found dead—one by a dry river and the other in the nearby canyon of La Huasteca. The following week, San Pedro residents called for a march for peace. Such protests typically take place downtown, yet San Pedro residents had become reluctant to leave this municipality. To mourn and protest the loss of their own, this march was organized within San Pedro de Pinta. On September 23, 2012, I observed a crowd of dozens dressed in white gather at one end of the boulevard and carry a banner inviting others to "Join the March for Peace." Photographers and cameramen followed as the crowd reached the roundabout, marched in circles, and then dissolved into a mass of market vendors, food stands, and cyclists. Four days later, socialite magazine *Chic* published four pages of pictures featuring San Pedro residents "raising their voices" among its coverage of bachelorette luncheons, birthday parties, and a ballet gala (even

124   THE TWO FACES OF FEAR

during a protest, San Pedro de Pinta was a place to be seen).[24] An open-streets program thus became a place to forget the war and a site where lost lives of particular interest to the upper class could be remembered.

Meanwhile, downtown, peace protests continued, calling for broader cross-class civic engagement to demand state accountability. Of particular interest is the takeover of a plaza in downtown Monterrey on one side of the governor's office that was re-signified as the Plaza of the Disappeared on January 11, 2014. This was the third anniversary of Roy Rivera Hidalgo's disappearance. His mother Leticia Hidalgo Rea and other FUNDENL members made green decals with the names of thirteen disappeared loved ones and placed them on a crystal monolith at the center of this plaza. "This is not a memorial," Leticia Hidalgo Rea explained. Rather, taking this plaza, a nearby plaque read, is "*un dispositivo de esperanza* (a tool for hope)." FUNDENL publicly reiterated their commitment to look for the disappeared until every single person with a name on that monolith can stand before it to remove their name themselves. Only then will the monolith become transparent as a state's actions should be. Far from calling on the state to avoid references to violence, as some San Pedro de Pinta users did, those who gather here call on the state to end the violence. As of 2024, gatherings and peaceful protests continue at the Plaza of the Disappeared. The much longer list of decals on the crystal monolith reminds all that civic engagement, including the many actions that can bring streets to life, will fall short of redressing the violence that emptied streets in the first place if these actions do not call for state accountability.

7

Fear and Inequality at the Onset of Crises

"I was in Munich for a two-day conference with approximately 300 people from the US, Canada, Brazil, Argentina, and Mexico. In Madrid, I went to the Real Madrid vs Barcelona match. I have no idea of where or how I got infected. I didn't suspect a thing."[1] A businessman in San Pedro shared his story with the *Sierra Madre*, the main socialite supplement of *El Norte*, published on March 19, 2020. His testimony featured a picture of himself wearing a face mask and standing in front of a laptop, a pair of reading glasses resting over a pile of papers, signaling he was fine and working. He was the first confirmed case of Covid-19 in the state of Nuevo León and one of the first in Mexico, where a health secretary later explained the virus "was imported by . . . the wealthiest social groups in the country."[2] To "diminish panic, discrimination and negativity," the businessman's three daughters created an Instagram account posting videos and pictures of their lives "living in quarantine."[3] They dismissed rumors that their father had been traveling on a private jet. They recommended hand washing, meditation, and light exercise, and featured pictures of workers disinfecting their everyday spaces. Parodies circulated, for these images were rare windows into their gated-community lives overlooking the most exclusive golf club in northern Mexico. Within days, a dozen more cases were confirmed in San Pedro.

Despite the difference in these threats, there were parallels in how individuals and institutions—including the local government of San Pedro—responded to fear of violence in a turf war and fear of contagion during the Covid-19 pandemic. Even though the first cases were detected in San Pedro, this municipality took the strictest anti-Covid measures to seclude itself from the rest of the metropolis. As cases rose in other municipalities, surpassing the number of cases in San Pedro, local state authorities argued that a higher influx of vehicles required the adoption of measures to discourage access. While Mexico's national response to the pandemic was in phase three—the highest alert, indicating rapid spread—San Pedro abruptly declared a localized phase four. Under phase four, the San Pedro local government deployed three hundred police at its city limits tasked, twenty-four

The Two Faces of Fear. Ana Villarreal, Oxford University Press. © Oxford University Press 2024.
DOI: 10.1093/oso/9780197688007.003.0007

126   THE TWO FACES OF FEAR

hours a day, with taking people's temperature, verifying mask usage, and asking nonresidents why they want to enter. These *filtros de seguridad* (security filters) sought to discourage entrance to all except those with "essential business" within.

To defend is to exclude. As examined in Chapter 4, such mechanisms of municipal seclusion can aggravate an already uneven geography of employment. In a turf war, the dark-skinned poor were increasingly scrutinized in the streets and inside the homes of the wealthy. This was also true at the onset of the Covid-19 pandemic. State brochures clearly stated such filters could not refuse entry to the municipality, but instead only "invite" those with nonessential business to go home.[4] *El Norte*, however, filmed interactions between police officers and the people filtered out that suggested uneven entry restrictions. One police officer explained the new measures to a woman riding a bus by saying that they were returning taxi drivers, construction workers, gardeners and that she should tell her employer she would not be able to enter the next day either ("*taxistas . . . albañiles, jardineros, todos ya los estamos regresando, para que le diga a su patrón que mañana ya no va a pasar*.") Moreover, older vehicles were more likely to be inspected and discouraged from entering San Pedro.[5]

Local police stopped two carpenters driving a small pick-up truck with a ladder attached to its roof. The carpenters wore masks and were heading to work. A police officer told them that although he understood they wanted to go to work, these were the instructions he received for everyone's protection ("*lo entiendo, sé que va a laborar, pero es la instrucción que tenemos, digo es para protección de todos, tanto de usted como de nosotros*"). A construction worker also lamented not being able to access this municipality where he was called to fix a leaky roof.[6] San Pedro is the municipality with the highest purchasing power in the metropolis. It is a primary site of employment for domestic and construction workers, for gardeners, and for service workers, all of whom would find it more difficult to access their places of employment during this period. As taxis were filtered out, workers relying on shared taxis to access their places of employment perched high in the Sierra Madre Mountains, inaccessible by bus and inaccessible to pedestrians, would also have a harder time getting to work.

For the privileged in San Pedro—who moved into newly constructed office buildings closer to their homes at the onset of the turf war—such filters were less cumbersome. A man in his thirties who lived and worked in San Pedro took a shortcut in his commute to work that involved crossing city limits into Monterrey to take advantage of a high-speed avenue. In total, his route involved crossing three checkpoints, but they were not as disruptive for him. "They're supposed to take your temperature and ask you things, but you know how it is when you've got blue eyes," he told Hassaine-Bau in 2020.[7] Like the *güeritas* (light-skinned women) skipping private security clearance when accessing gated neighborhoods, mentioned in Chapter 4, such measures evidence and deepen class and racial inequalities, making places of employment harder to access for the residents who need them the most.

Social media users criticized the "security filters," likening the San Pedro municipal border to the US-Mexico border in numerous memes. One meme mockingly asked if someone knew a *coyote* (migrant smuggler) to cross him over to San Pedro ("*Algún coyote o pollero que me cruce a San Pedro?*")[8] Others called out the racial dimensions of these filters, depicting lighter skin tones as essential and darker as nonessential. These were new iterations of old memes. A decade before, when the first checkpoints were established, the San Pedro border had already been likened to the US-Mexico border. Back then, memes depicted dark-skinned men crossing an empty desert-like Santa Catarina River toward San Pedro. In a pandemic, as in a turf war, both the movements and bodies of the dark-skinned poor are more closely surveilled when they are seeking to access privileged spaces.

For nations and individuals, crises are periods that expose and heighten the hoarding mechanisms of the privileged, which have consequences for all. On March 31, 2021, the *Los Angeles Times* reported the rise of vaccine tourism among wealthy Mexicans flying to the United States ahead of Mexico's vaccine program rollout. Reporting from San Pedro, "The wealthiest city in Latin America" where "there is almost nothing money can't buy," a reporter noted residents might be able to purchase top luxury brands from around the globe, "but there is one sought-after item that isn't readily available in San Pedro Garza García: COVID-19 vaccine." Interviewed for this piece, former Mayor of San Pedro Mauricio Fernández stated, "A lot of people have access to the United States, and they are going to protect themselves." The US border might have been closed to foreign pedestrians and cars, but it was open to those who held dual citizenship, as well as to those who could charter private jets to second homes on the other side of the border. Fernández himself chartered a private jet, flew to Brownsville, Texas, and drove to the small farming community of Los Fresnos, where he received his first Covid-19 vaccine shot in January 2021. He guessed "a few thousand" more San Pedro residents had

128   THE TWO FACES OF FEAR

done the same. Moreover, he argued their vaccine tourism brought economic benefits to Texas, because people spent "a lot of money on food and hotels."[9]

In late May 2021, bars that had been shut down due to the pandemic reopened. Long lines of people waited to enter the Café Iguana in the Barrio Antiguo—previously shut down after a shooting, as discussed in Chapter 5. Patrons were seated at a distance from each other and asked not to interact much with others. *El Norte* noted that this bar followed safety protocols more closely than others observed in el Centrito in San Pedro. "We were locked up for so long, it's really hard to stay home," said one leaving a bar in el Centrito, which became the main partying center for the privileged amid the turf war. "Everything's open now. Why can't we have fun?"[10] San Pedro de Pinta, suspended temporarily for fifteen months due to the pandemic, reopened shortly after on June 27, 2021. Around five thousand people took to the streets, which state authorities estimated was around the same number as prior to the pandemic—though half the number regularly going out during the height of the turf war. "It was necessary, because this is a space that had become a tradition prior to Covid," said one, a "tradition" that emerged as numerous outdoor leisure options were temporarily destroyed, as discussed in Chapter 6. "We're happy here, walking at a safe distance and seeing that there are health measures."[11] This resident's words echoed those of others who, a decade before, reported feeling safe and "like there was security" in San Pedro de Pinta, an unwalled yet protected oasis for the most privileged in the metropolis.

In a turf war, as in a pandemic, income is a strong predictor of mortality. In 2020, before vaccines were available, San Pedro had the lowest mortality rate in the metropolis.[12] Its residents had more space to distance themselves. Their professions made them more likely to work from home. They were also more likely to delegate risks to others working for them; as discussed in Chapter 4, fear reshuffles who does what inside and outside the home. They had access to the best private healthcare in case of infection as well as earlier access to vaccines in the United States. By 2022, San Pedro had one of the lowest mortality rates in Latin America. Journalists from Red Palta analyzed the pandemic responses of sixty municipalities in the region. The two with the highest income per capita rates had the lowest death rates: San Pedro in Mexico and Vitacura in Chile. The most affected areas were among the poorest in Mexico, Chile, and Peru.[13]

All these advantages add up as Mexico continues to face a crisis of criminal and state violence. In 2023, a national public security survey revealed that over 60% of Mexicans feel unsafe in their cities. The municipality of Monterrey ranks above average, with almost 70% of its residents feeling unsafe. In San Pedro, however, only 8% of residents reported feeling unsafe. San Pedro stands out locally and nationally. The wealthiest in Guadalajara—a large metropolis of similar population and economic importance—live in Zapopan, where over 60% of residents reported feeling unsafe (with even higher rates for surrounding areas). The wealthiest in Mexico City are not spatially concentrated in one delegation—Mexico City has delegations, not municipalities—but some live in Benito Juárez, where 20% reported feeling unsafe.[14]

Given the extreme levels of violence and fear analyzed in every previous chapter, it is striking that San Pedro should become the municipality where urban residents report feeling the safest in Mexico. These numbers position San Pedro as a national "success" story deserving further attention. What did San Pedro do? As argued throughout the book, what sets San Pedro apart is having a well-organized and very wealthy business elite able to leverage the local state to defend its residents and the business carried out in its territory. Since 2011, net international trade in San Pedro has boomed, suggesting fear can further the spatial concentration of capital. Prior to the turf war, net international trade was under $200 million. Both imports and exports doubled within two years—a period that was marked by the increased concentration of wealthy residents and businesses relocating from elsewhere into a defended San Pedro, as discussed in Chapter 4. By 2022, imports and exports were estimated at almost $600 million.[15] Taken together, these numbers tell a success story of security and economic growth in the face of severe security adversity. However, ranking the average reported feelings of urban residents in isolation of nearby municipalities overlooks the processes widening and sustaining these emotional disparities.

How does the safety of some heighten the vulnerability of others? Most Mexicans, including most residents of the Metropolitan Area of Monterrey today, do not feel safe and do not trust that state authorities are there to protect them. A high-profile recent example explains why. In 2022, eighteen-year-old law student Debanhi Escobar made world headlines when she did not make it home after a party. The taxi driver who picked her up harassed her, prompting her to get out of the car on a highway. The driver took a picture as evidence that he had dropped her off alive. She was found dead inside a motel water cistern two weeks later. "They searched this place four times and only on the fifth time they found the body of my daughter," her father said

130 THE TWO FACES OF FEAR

during a press conference. "How is that even possible?" An activist protesting her abduction and murder knew Debanhi because she had attended similar protests over the abduction of other women herself.[16]

Debanhi's case is not unique. More than eighteen hundred women have gone missing in the state of Nuevo León since 2021.[17] These numbers, as other crime rates in Mexico, likely lag behind the horror. As some people report feeling safe, others are terrified to report multiple crimes, including the disappearance of their loved ones. Roy, too, was an eighteen-year-old college student when he was abducted from his home in 2011, as discussed in Chapter 2. "I couldn't even say his name without crying at first," his mother, Leticia Hidalgo Rea, told the press in 2021. "Tears don't come as easily now." After more than a decade of facing unresponsive authorities, she states with clarity: "civic organizations are all that is left."[18] Together with other families of the disappeared, Leticia Hidalgo Rea and so many more continue to search for their loved ones, to demand state accountability.[19]

Civic engagement is key in Mexico and elsewhere in Latin America where so many "citizens of fear," as Rotker put it, face criminal and state violence as well as widespread impunity in their everyday lives. As Arias notes, there is scarce information on "successful cases" of social responses to pervasive violence in the region.[20] This book brings attention to the largely understudied social responses of the privileged to violence and fear. While fear may impact other social responses—such as elections or protests—fear is a social response in and of itself.[21] In high-violence contexts, fear matters on election day and every day after. It matters on the day when a victimization story sparks outrage and brings people onto the streets—or not—as well as every day that crime stories, unfolding in the spaces of urban residents, prompt people to adjust their routines, their routes, and their social relations. Fear is a daily response to violence and a particularly powerful one when we consider the fears of the powerful. Taking fear as a vantage point rather than victimization alone—as is often done in the literature—allows for the consideration of a broader set of actors, strategies, and consequences than have been previously considered. Moreover, as civic organizations play an ever-more-prominent role in defining the possibilities of everyday life in Mexico, as elsewhere in Latin America, and as more scholarly attention is devoted to understanding them, San Pedro illustrates the importance of centering inequality in any discussion about security.

The Logistics of Fear in a Global Pandemic

This book is an invitation to approach fear as an everyday problem at the onset of crises, which is to center how people experience the breakdown of their everyday routines, the uneven resources they can leverage to bind their fears, and the consequences of their strategies for themselves and for others. As Covid-19 cases rose, fear of contagion permeated every aspect of everyday life in Monterrey and around the world. Where to live? Where to work? How to move around the city? How to organize a social gathering as safely as possible? While all faced similar problems, people leveraged vastly unequal resources to deal with them, deepening inequalities in the process. What made the Metropolitan Area of Monterrey an unfortunately excellent case to theorize the logistics of fear is the collision of extreme inequality and extreme danger. Following this same logic, the impact of the logistics of fear on inequality should be most visible in sites with a high concentration of wealth and high vulnerability to a new threat.

New York City, a global city, highly connected and dense, was one of the first global epicenters of the Covid-19 pandemic.[22] It is a "monied metropolis," home to some of the most privileged families in the world.[23] Through the lens of emotion, scholars examine, as Sherman does in Manhattan, how the wealthy understand their privilege and place in society.[24] In times of crises, emotion provides a powerful entry to scrutinize uneven resources laid bare and leveraged to further concentrate advantages among the few at the top. The logistics of fear—what people do when they are afraid—and the many ways in which such practical responses to fear are both unequal and aggravating of inequality should be particularly visible in a place like New York City and at a time such as the onset of the Covid-19 pandemic.

Fear relocates. As cases of Covid-19 rose, health authorities around the world called for social distancing and measures to shelter in place. All faced the problem of increasing physical distance from others, but the resources available to do so were vastly unequal. As cases rose in New York, the media ran hundreds of headlines about wealthy, primarily white, New Yorkers fleeing their primary residences. *The New York Times* relied on mail-forwarding requests to track the rapid relocation of thousands—particularly from the wealthy Upper West and Upper East Sides of Manhattan—to second homes, vacation rentals, or newly purchased homes in the Hamptons, Connecticut, and Florida, among other destinations within the United States. "Right after Covid hit, everyone just blasted out of here," said a councilwoman on the

132 THE TWO FACES OF FEAR

Upper West Side who was surprised she could walk on an empty Columbus Avenue.[25] Cell phone data revealed some 420,000 people—about 5% of the local population—left between March 1 and May 1, particularly after school closures were announced. The spatial pattern was clear: "The higher-earning a neighborhood is, the more likely it is to have emptied out."[26]

While the wealthy and white left, the grand majority of New Yorkers, who are primarily people of color, migrant, and poor, could not leave or even isolate within their homes or homeless shelters. Even with state measures seeking to expand temporary housing options, including into emptied hotels, the mortality rate among the homeless was higher than the city-wide average.[27] Constraints on social distancing also applied to work, with more privileged workers going virtual while others—considered "essential"—could not. On March 22, 2020, New York State launched PAUSE to halt all but essential business, which lasted eleven weeks. During this time, 1.1 million workers deemed essential worked outside their homes. They were more likely to be low-income people of color and more likely to contract and spread the virus within their communities. Data from the 2021 New York City Housing and Vacancy Survey recorded devastating and unequal losses for essential workers.

About one in four New Yorkers lost someone they were close to in the early stages of the pandemic—a family member, a close friend, a neighbor, a colleague. Among essential workers, the rate of loss was one in three. Moreover, one in six essential workers lost at least three people they were close to. "The households where NYC's 1.1 million essential workers live are one-and-a-half times as likely to be crowded compared to NYC overall," particularly for people of color residing in southeast Brooklyn, the Bronx, Upper Manhattan, and southeast Queens, which were worst-hit. "Essential work reflects and reinforces existing disparities, but the pandemic widened the gap for thousands of New Yorkers," in loss of life, in loss of loved ones, and in many ways that are still unknown.[28] State definitions of who and what is deemed essential frame the options within which people can reorganize their lives. As also seen in San Pedro, these categories can aggravate preexisting uneven geographies of employment, and in a pandemic context, result in uneven infections and loss of life.

Fear reschedules. In high-violence environments, residents meet earlier in the day to lean into the safety of numbers. In a pandemic, crowds heighten

FEAR AND INEQUALITY AT THE ONSET OF CRISES   133

the threat. Daytime activities, from exercising to grocery shopping, were rescheduled to early morning or night to avoid crowds. Fear impacts perceptions of time, tethering people to the present. A family in San Pedro dropped their plans to build a permanent home and adjusted their planning to the short-term: "We can't plan anymore, six months at a time." Similarly, Covid-19 canceled and severely impeded the ability to plan basic activities beyond the short term.

Fear isolates and regroups. In the face of criminal and state violence, people size up their social activities and gatherings, turning individual practices into collective practices. In a pandemic, people size down, but they nonetheless regroup. The pandemic involved deep isolation—walking apart on sidewalks, shutting down in-person activities—as well as numerous forms of indoor and neighborhood regroupings. From the rise of pandemic pods to increased socializing among neighbors, New Yorkers regrouped. Drawing on a series of neighborhood walks, an architecture critic wrote of the more "intimate" city New York had become, in which "New Yorkers found strength in their shared neighborhoods and one another."[29] The benefits of increased intimacy varied, however, for regroupings in the face of fear of contagion also laid bare and exacerbated inequality. In the face of school closures, for example, families with the means to do so relocated teachers into their households to provide a small-group learning environment lost to others, widening educational gaps in ways that are still unknown.[30]

Emptied-out neighborhoods in the Upper West Side delineated an understudied city-within-a-city in New York. Urban sociologists dating back to Du Bois have been interested in examining cities-within-cities, most often in terms of accumulated disadvantage.[31] Following calls to rethink urban categories in light of undertheorized metropolises in the Global South and to challenge "metrocentrism in sociology," San Pedro provides the basis to rethink the city-within-a-city as a site of concentrated advantage.[32] San Pedro is a city of 130,000 within a metropolis of over five million. It is a city-within-a-city, but it is a city of privilege. As Pinçon and Pinçon also observed in Paris, it is the wealthy who are spatially clustering in ever-tighter spaces seeking to be among themselves.[33] San Pedro adds fear at the onset of crises to the factors that can aggravate such spatial classed clustering and seclusion. As global inequality continues to rise and as new and old threats loom ahead— pandemics, climate change, as well as criminal and state violence—fear will

134 THE TWO FACES OF FEAR

continue to refashion people and places. Paying attention to what people do when they fear, the resources they leverage, and the consequences of their actions for others might help alleviate some of its impact. At the very least, it should help clarify that successful measures to contend with these issues are often based on depriving others of the resources that are needed to follow the model.

Acknowledgments

I thank all who entrusted me with their fears. I am especially thankful to those who, despite the fear, are forging hope across civic fronts. They may be a minority—engaged citizens often are—but they are tenacious. I could not have written this book without this silver lining. I am especially thankful to the families and activists of the *Fuerzas Unidas por Nuestros Desaparecidos en Nuevo León* (the United Forces for the Disappeared in Nuevo León). Their daily work pursuing state accountability is work they do for all. Much more can be done to support these efforts from a civic front. It is my hope that this book can, in a small way, contribute to understand the depth of the damage fear can do to social ties and everyday spaces in sites of conflict, in times of crisis, as well as the importance of centering inequality in any discussion or evaluation of security policies.

Many people and institutions shaped and supported the ideas in this book. At the University of California, Berkeley, I worked with Loïc Wacquant who inspired me to read widely, think deeply and historically, and to hone in on the complexity, tensions, and two-facedness of social phenomena. Thank you, Loïc, your approach to sociology as a craft is one I seek to emulate with my students. My dissertation committee members Laura Enriquez, Mara Loveman, Teresa Caldeira, and Javier Auyero provided rounds of feedback and encouragement. I am especially grateful to Javier who provided strict book deadlines as well. Javier, this book would not be done without you. I thank Michael Burawoy who mentored me through my bus driver ethnography and welcomed me to Berkeley. How I loved teaching theory with you, Michael. As you retire, I thank you for training dozens and dozens of us to make theory approachable, relevant, even fun. Prior to joining Berkeley as a graduate student, Delphine Mercier inspired me to become a sociologist. She mentored me as a college student at the Universidad de Monterrey and took me under her wing to the Université de Provence in France and the industrial zones of Tangier, Morocco. She has been a mentor, colleague, and dear friend all these years. With Maria Eugenia Longo, Mariana Busso, and Manuela Bardet, we created a community that endured long after we graduated.

136 ACKNOWLEDGMENTS

Colleagues at Boston University believed in this project from job talk to final book manuscript. Some have taken jobs elsewhere or retired, and I want to thank all for providing tools, support, encouragement, and valuable critiques over the years. A heartfelt thank you to Michel Anteby, Emily Barman, Japonica Brown-Saracino, Debby Carr, Cati Connell, Celeste Curington, Susan Eckstein, Neha Gondal, Julian Go, Heba Gowayed, Liah Greenfield, Saida Grundy, Alya Guseva, Joseph Harris, Stephen Kalberg, Nazli Kibria, Daniel Kleinman, Loretta Lees, Ashley Mears, Jonathan Mijs, Heather Schoenfeld, Jessica Simes, and John Stone. Julian Go generously organized a book workshop for me with Japonica Brown-Saracino, Fatma Müge Goçek, Forrest Stuart and Jocelyn Viterna that was invaluable in steering the manuscript into its final form. The BU Center for Latin American Studies has been a second home with Adela Pineda, Jeff Rubin, Rady Roldán-Figueroa, Elizabeth Amrien, and many more.

From fieldwork to dissertation to book, many institutions supported this project. I thank the Harry Frank Guggenheim Foundation and especially Joel Wallman, who organized a seminar at UC San Diego that was very influential in the early stages of this project. The University of California Institute for Mexico and the United States, the Mexican National Foundation for Science and Technology, the BU Pardee School of Global Studies, the BU Initiative on Cities, and the BU Center for the Humanities all provided funding and time off teaching at different stages. This research was also assisted by a grant from the Drugs, Security, and Democracy Fellowship Program administered by the Social Science Research Council and the Universidad de los Andes in cooperation with funds provided by the Open Society Foundation and the International Development Research Centre, Ottawa, Canada. This last fellowship introduced me to my intellectual soulmates, scholars of drugs, violence, and Latin America who have greatly shaped my mind and without whom I would not do this work: Froylán Enciso, Yanilda González, Angélica Durán-Martínez, Lina Britto, Ana Arjona, Eduardo Moncada, Annette Idler, Anthony Fontes, Robert Samet, Winifred Tate, and many more. Conversations with them and dear friends underlie every page, including Maria Fernanda Barrero, Norma Caballero, Ieva Jusionyte, Nazanin Shahrokni, Kara Young, Silvia Pasquetti, Katherine Maich, Gowri Vijayakumar, Julia Chuang, and Zozu. Ale Délano and Fabiola de Lachica read every word, multiple times, and offered a bonfire to let it all go.

For their developmental editing brilliance, I thank Malgorzata Kurjanska and Rachel Kravetz who provided key suggestions for the entire

ACKNOWLEDGMENTS 137

manuscript and encouragement to wrap it up. At Oxford University Press, I am indebted to James Cook for his excitement and encouragement from the beginning and to Emily Benitez and Bala Subramanian at Newgen for their generous assistance in the production process. I thank my three reviewers whose insightful suggestions allowed me to expand and deepen key points of the argument into its final form. I am particularly indebted to Angélica Durán-Martínez and Hugo Cerón-Anaya, who revealed themselves as reviewers and provided in-depth feedback and generous blurbs for the book.

A first draft of Chapter 3, "The Logistics of Fear," was published as the chapter "Fear and Spectacular Drug Violence in Monterrey," in the edited volume *Violence at the Urban Margins* edited by Javier Auyero, Philippe Bourgois, and Nancy Scheper-Hughes and published by Oxford University Press, though has changed significantly. Parts of Chapter 5, "Restructuring Nightlife," were published in "The Logistics of Fear: Violence and the Stratifying Power of Emotion" in *Emotions and Society*. Sections of the theoretical framing and data interspersed throughout the chapters were previously published in "Reconceptualizing Urban Violence from the Global South" in *City & Community*. Two observations—one in Chapter 2 and one in Chapter 3—were first included in the piece "Domesticating Danger: Copings Codes and Symbolic Security amid Violent Organized Crime in Mexico" in *Sociological Theory*.

I thank Roberto Ortiz Giacomán for allowing me to include his stunning photographs on the cover and inside the book. Monterrey is best known for its mountains, and Roberto has climbed and photographed them from every angle and in every light. Amanda Watkins captured the *colombiano* aesthetic like nobody else and allowed me to include one of her great pictures in Chapter 3. I thank Andrés Anza Cortés for the use of the Casino Royale print in Chapter 2, which captures a critical moment in the history of the city. During my fieldwork in Monterrey, I had many influential conversations with journalists, urbanists, human rights activists, and multiple colleagues at the Instituto Tecnológico y de Estudios Superiores de Monterrey, the Universidad de Monterrey, where I was generously offered office space, and the Universidad Autónoma de Nuevo León. I thank José Manuel Prieto González, Ricardo Lazcano, Leticia Saucedo Villegas, Socorro Arzaluz, Diego Enrique Osorno, Anne Fouquet, Ignacio Irazuzta, Víctor Zúñiga, Leticia Hidalgo Rea, Cordelia Rizzo Reyes, Jesús Ramírez, Sandrine Molinard, Luis Ávila, Helke Enkerlin, and Eva Nájera.

138 ACKNOWLEDGMENTS

For comments on previous chapter drafts, I am indebted to colleagues at the Latin America Working Group at the University of California, Berkeley, the Latin America and Caribbean Workshop at the University of Chicago, and the Contemporary Latin American Anthropology Workshop at Harvard University. Talks at the Watson Center for International Affairs at Brown University and Boston College provided further opportunities to clarify the book's main contributions. For comments on chapters, sections, and early drafts of my book proposal, I thank Paul Gootenberg, Kirsten Weld, Sergio Delgado, María Cervantes, Dairee Ramírez, and developmental editor David Lobenstine. Landon Lauder, Cristian Morales, Cristian Maldonado, Andrea Beltrán-Lizarazo, and Ramona Leung provided research assistance at different stages. I thank my undergraduate students who read drafts of the introduction and some chapters. I wrote for more than I can name, but especially for my Sociological Theory and Urban Inequality classrooms of Spring 2023. My parents and siblings have been an unfaltering support over the years, as well as my extended family. I thank my mother Cecilia especially, who I admire beyond words. For the love, joy, and brightest light in my life, I thank Daniel and Luna.

APPENDIX

Gaining Distance

I had the advantage of access to the people and places in this book at a time of severe spatial and social enclosure. As examined in Chapter 4, locals were more likely to socialize with people whom they knew, and I was local. I drew on trust networks to build a sample of 154 residents spanning the class spectrum featured in my field notes and interview transcripts. Insider access came with its own challenges. This methodological appendix briefly examines insider advantages, challenges, and tools that were most helpful to circumvent them.

Looking back on my data, I realize some of the very best resulted from fleeting reencounters with locals I had not seen in years and met again only briefly. Take, for instance, the conversations with a high school and college acquaintance cited in Chapter 4. Both were upper-middle-class women residing and working in San Pedro. I had not seen either in over a decade, but we had once shared car rides and gone on college trips abroad. We had the kind of trust that takes years to build because we had built it over the years. We were not close, however, and this too was important. I ran into one at a coffee shop and the other at a baby shower. Both reencounters gave way to warm greetings, an update request—"what are you up to these days?"—and great data. I was purposefully vague in replying, "I came back to study how Monterrey has changed in recent years," in this and similar instances, curious about when and how violence and fear might emerge. In both these cases, a fleeting reencounter gave way to open declarations of deepened racism— some of the toughest data to gather in this book. "I want to talk about prejudice," said one, who later made clear she meant racial prejudice. "I became racist," said the other, adding, "I'm not ashamed to say it, well, I am ashamed, I wouldn't say this to anyone." I was someone they could say this to. We had similarly light skin tones, trust, and we were not going to hang out after this conversation.

Occupying a liminal position in the lives of acquaintances allowed me to hear things from them I did not hear from people I was closer to and interacting with every day. As my college acquaintance noted, there is "shame" in admitting deepened racism and likely more shame in admitting it to someone one is closer to. The public schoolteacher living in a working-class neighborhood cited at the beginning of Chapter 1 also confided details of her life with me—a face she remembered—that she would not share with the people she was closest to. "I have never let my daughters see this side I have just shown you. I don't want to worry them," she said, for she did not have to think about me "worrying" about her safety as a daughter would. For an outsider ethnographer, the rich outpour of data that comes from reencountering those who trust us and seek to quickly update us on their lives takes years of fieldwork, plus a revisit. For an insider, fleeting reencounters are built into the structures of everyday life and are almost inevitable. This was an advantage I exploited, focusing data collection among acquaintances, including friends of friends and relatives of friends.

Except when referring to public figures and officials, I use no names or pseudonyms. In the case of prominent human rights activist Leticia Hidalgo Rea named in Chapter 2, I confirmed with her directly that naming her in the book was her preference. Anonymizing a

140   APPENDIX

human rights activist in Mexico undoes in a text the important work the families of the disappeared are doing every day to bring their loved ones out of anonymity. Moreover, both human rights activists and journalists told me prominence provides more protection than anonymity, though neither is a guarantee. For everyone else, I use no names. I drew inspiration from José Saramago, who refers to the handful of characters in his novel *Blindness* by profession or some specific trait, like wearing dark glasses. I refer to people by profession, as in the case of a public schoolteacher, a tech worker, a graphic designer, a bus driver, an artist, or a businessman to diminish any risk of identification. On other occasions, I reference a detail of a person's family structure—as in the case of a mother of two, a mother of one, or a father walking a daughter to highlight a relationship when useful. I also refer to people noting the origin of our relationship, as in the case of a college acquaintance or high school acquaintance, to signal how I came to know them when trust is particularly important. I tried pseudonyms in an earlier draft but found them distracting for a sample of this size as some people are referenced only once.

More importantly, I was concerned that using pseudonyms for those referenced more than once might allow local readers to piece different observations together and potentially identify someone. Because I drew from my social networks to compose this sample, I know some participants know each other. Sherman, too, faced this difficulty in her study of wealthy New Yorkers. Like Sherman, I was "extremely concerned about preserving the anonymity" of these respondents not to the general reader, but to other locals who might identify them.[1] To further anonymize my data, I disaggregated observations throughout the book. The public schoolteacher in Chapter 1 is an exception. I felt comfortable presenting her story in more detail since she was, to the best of my knowledge, far removed from other participants. Moreover, she has physically left the country since our interview, joining one of her daughters who had been begging her to leave the municipality of Guadalupe.

There was also the question of what places to name. I name bars and other sites that have been in the news due to violent attacks—the Café Iguana, the Sabino Gordo, the Casino Royale—and that became important landmarks in the history of violence in the city. I name bars that closed permanently or are referenced in secondary sources— Bar Rio, La Fe Music Hall—though I do not disclose the names of specific restaurants or bars that I observed. I name broad areas of the city and countryside that are relevant to the analysis and have also been covered in the news, such as the Barrio Antiguo, el Centrito, the Huasteca, the Macro Plaza, San Pedro de Pinta. I name major avenues like Gonzalitos and Calzada del Valle as well as neighborhoods when relevant—Colonia del Valle, Independencia, San Bernabé—though not when this might assist in identifying an informant. Unless naming a place was essential to the observation in question, I stuck to broad spatial identifiers such as a university, a shopping mall, and so forth. My field notes feature observations of forty-seven everyday spaces as well as fifty events, including peace protests, civic organization meetings, and political rallies. I volunteered for three civic organizations—one major business-led civic organization, one smaller organization seeking to advance sustainable mobility, and another that sought to work with a disadvantaged community in Monterrey—and met with other local scholars to discuss escalating violence in a year-long seminar at a public university.

Drawing on previous social networks, I had best access to the upper-middle class and middle class and sought to stretch my sample further in both directions leveraging old and new contacts made through the volunteering opportunities listed above and everyday routines. My field notes feature fourteen working-class, sixty-six middle-class, thirty-six

APPENDIX 141

upper-middle-class, and twelve upper-class residents. I did not collect enough information on the education and profession of twenty-six more informants to assess their class position. All upper-middle and upper-class residents I spoke to, including members of the business elite, resided in San Pedro. Middle-class residents I spoke to resided primarily in Monterrey and San Nicolás. Working-class residents I spoke to resided in Monterrey, Guadalupe, San Nicolás, and Juárez. Most of the people I spoke to were in their thirties and forties. To a lesser extent, I spoke to people in their twenties, fifties, and a few people in their sixties, seventies, and eighties. I spoke to six individuals without collecting data on their age. From within this sample, I conducted sixty-nine interviews—two-thirds were conversational interviews embedded in ethnographic observations, while one-third were scheduled and semi-structured interviews conducted in homes, cafés, and restaurants. I drew on secondary sources, including local scholarship, news articles, and one documentary to triangulate my data and deepen my analysis at both ends of the class spectrum.

Timing was key for this study. "Everything changed," is how a bus line secretary, a taxi driver, and a businessman, among others, put it in 2012. They referenced a time "before," providing detail of the practices they had to abandon to violence and fear. They "used to" go here or there, but "now" they had to think about it. Halfway through my fieldwork, in 2013, discourses and practices shifted rapidly. There were still individual before and after moments with strong consequences as detailed in Chapter 3, but there was a new and broader "before" referencing a period of heightened violence that was now referred to in past tense. In 2013, locals talked about "going back" to places they had abandoned, providing their own ethnographic observations of improvement such as seeing women on rocking chairs outside their homes again: *"ya se puede ir al rancho"* and *"ya están las señoras con sus mecedoras afuera en las tardes otra vez."*

Conversational interviews were well suited for an ethnographic revisit, especially in the beginning. These were mostly spontaneous and flexible in content, and allowed me to gather information on a wide range of subjects related to this study as they emerged in casual conversations. As discourses shifted in 2013, I added semi-structured interviews to seize these changing narratives in more detail. I found this shift incredibly intriguing, especially since it happened very quickly. In early 2013, locals could go so far as to claim "not much" had changed, only to remember through the interview process the practices they had abandoned, the losses they had taken for granted. For example, an upper-middle class woman from San Pedro started a semi-structured interview stating that "not much" had changed. One recollection led to another and toward the end she stated, "I think that with this *recuento* (recollection), I've realized that things have changed a lot, for example, tonight . . . I'm wondering whether I should go with a friend or go on my own. Before, I was driving at three in the morning on my own."

One of my best interviews was with a member of the business elite, a direct descendant of the families that industrialized Monterrey. I met him through an acquaintance who designed social responsibility programs. This businessman had invited my acquaintance to tour his factory, and I tagged along. During our visit, I told this businessman about my study, and asked if I might be able to interview him to learn more about his perspective on how Monterrey had changed in recent years. "Let's have coffee," he said. Over coffee, he asked questions about my family and education to "get a sense" of me and what I was doing—*"te quiero agarrar la onda"*—and then agreed to an interview at a restaurant a week later. When I think about why this businessman agreed to talk to me, I think of some of the questions he asked during the visit to his factory. Like others I spoke to, this businessman wanted to know what he could do to improve his relationship with the

142 APPENDIX

workers residing around his factory out of security concerns—another example of fear deepening the criminalization of the working class, as discussed in Chapter 4. Should he build a school, a daycare, a park? "Raise their salaries," I answered. "Anything but that," was his reply.

The vetting conversation we had over coffee, which I counted as a conversational interview, was very rich. It touched on some of the topics I wanted to talk about in the semi-structured interview, since he asked me what I was interested in researching and shared some initial data with me. Semi-structured interviews, however, were better at seizing the narratives of how people understood the origins of the violence, the precautions that might keep them safe, and the new "after" period that I found so intriguing. "You get accustomed to it," is how this businessman put it toward the end of our semi-structured interview—"*te vas acostumbrando, aclimatando.*" He looked for a metaphor: "It's like the theory of the frog. If you drop a frog in boiling water it jumps. But if you gradually heat up the water, it stays there." "Until it's cooked?" I asked. "Well, I didn't want to get to that, but yes." As the interview unraveled the fear-binding strategies he had come to take for granted, this businessman recalled:

I loved going out of town. That's another thing, *ya hasta se me olvidó* [that I'd forgotten]. I liked going to the rivers and the mountains, to take the car out for a drive, to ride my bike, to walk, to climb . . . I stopped doing it, I do miss that. I do feel like they stole that from me. What do you know, it was so deeply hidden, *ya ni me acordaba* [I didn't even remember].

Listening to my informants reflect on the everyday losses they had taken for granted—including in idyllic forms—made me wonder what I was taking for granted as a researcher and as a local living through this period as fieldwork. In 2013, I wrote in my notes: What had I forgotten? What would it be like for me to "leave" or at least stop taking field notes? I could not have anticipated this then, but remembering, an essential component of any data coding process, proved to be the bigger challenge.

Time Is a Tool

This project had emotional hurdles that I did not experience in my first ethnography as a bus driver trainee and that required significant time to process. My main challenge to becoming a bus driver in this same metropolis, though at a less violent time, was gaining access to a new occupational world. A bus line owner said he would train me during an interview but turned me down when I tried to take him up on his offer a few months later. Had I not noticed that all his bus drivers were men? He was joking and thought I was, too. It was my luck that a new public-private school had just opened where I met a bus driver instructor that took me under his wing. Over the course of that project, I scribbled notes to trigger my memory on the backs of bus tickets and in bathroom breaks fleshed out into full field notes after long shifts or whenever possible. The experience of fieldwork blurred social divisions I had grown up with and profoundly transformed the way I understood the city. Nevertheless, I knew when I was inside and outside of the field. There were also clear lines separating informants—even those who became friends—from the rest of the people in my life. I stayed in touch with my bus driver instructor until his death, as well as the bus line secretary into this project, but I could leave.

APPENDIX   143

When I started fieldwork for this project, all was in flux. Despite my best efforts, my first field notes written during the summer of 2011 and early 2012 were shorter than the field notes I had written at the bus line—and the field notes I would write later. This was frustrating. I knew well that taking copious field notes in the beginning of an ethnographic project is essential, for one begins to take aspects of a world for granted that are more obvious at first. Yet this was a context in which the taken-for-granted was disrupted. I could not write about fear—others' or my own—while my own fears were unbound. Given the ubiquity of violence and fear, there was no stepping outside of its impact, and no break either—just as there was no stepping outside of disruption at the onset of the pandemic—which was emotionally challenging. Length came as I was able to re-create my own everyday, binding emotion through logistics of fear I described for others and observed in myself.

Even once I had settled into these new logistics, there could be delays between experience and writing—often the case in ethnography for many reasons ranging from time constraints to exhaustion. In my case, delays were necessary breaks from reliving emotionally charged moments. To write a field note is to relive a moment in slow motion. When field notes feature moments that are difficult to live through, it takes significant emotional labor to relive them slowly and dig into the details that help recreate an experience in writing. As Hochschild notes, emotional labor is invisible, and so is the experience of creating such difficult data.[2] As a simple example, I included a field note in chapter 5 where I describe driving home after a social gathering at night, when I saw a truck driving behind me and thought I was being followed. Though the threat in that moment was not real—the pick-up truck turned out to be a neighbor heading home— the adrenaline rush was. I wrote that note the morning after when I was calm. It's short, and it was a day's work to re-create the mundane experience of driving home after a social gathering in a context where others I spoke to had been followed. When I read it now, that field note does not prompt the emotion that it used to, but other field notes feel raw every time.

The field note at the beginning of Chapter 2 featuring the shoes of disappeared locals arranged as a 49—the number of dismembered bodies found on a nearby highway in March 2012—was also a day's work. Though short, that field note was not easy to write, and it is not easy to read, even a decade later. Every time I read that note and other notes like it, I cry. I heard Leticia Hidalgo Rea, also featured in the field note, share the story of her son Roy's abduction in public a dozen times and never asked for the details. That is an interview that I did not do. Spanish novelist Lolita Bosch did it with incredible tact and humanity in *Roy, desaparecido*.[3] She cried with Leticia Hidalgo Rea and left the tears in the text. I cried reading the transcript of their conversation and picking the details that went into the introduction of Chapter 2. If the reader cries too, it is a human response.

When difficult data include people and places you love, writing field notes and coding, the building blocks of an ethnography, take significant time. Conducting fieldwork amid war required binding emotion. Coding demanded unbinding emotion and experiencing difficult data anew. It was a different experience to live through this period and document it to the best of my ability than it was to look back on it and relive it in ethnographic detail. Both take significant time. Like Gould, I found myself "experiencing, virtually for the first time, the horrors of a recent past that I had lived through but on some affective level had refused"—in her case, the horrors of the AIDS epidemic.[4] The first lockdown of March 2020 re-created conditions of everyday logistical collapse that threw me back in time and

144 APPENDIX

plunged me deep into my notes. It was during that first lockdown that I was finally able to read and code all my fieldnotes and interview transcripts from start to finish. It took three hours a day for three months, but it really took seven years after most of the fieldwork was done to gain enough distance to dig into the details of the notes I had worked so hard to write. Through this experience, I learned that time is a tool. To ethnographers facing similar struggles I would say this: if you can give it time, time can give you distance.

Notes

Chapter 1

1. Caldeira and Holston (1999), Moser and McIlwaine (2004), Arias and Goldstein (2010), Imbusch, Misse, and Carrión (2011), O'Neill and Thomas (2011), Cruz (2016), Müller (2016), Zeiderman (2016), Arias (2017), Santamaría and Carey (2017), Bergman (2018), Durán-Martínez (2018).
2. Briceño-León (2007), Koonings and Krujit (2007), Menjívar (2011), Davis (2012), Valenzuela Aguilera (2013), Viterna (2013), Auyero and Berti (2015), Auyero et al. (2015), Denyer Willis (2015), Koonings and Krujit (2015), Larkins (2015), Zubillaga (2015), Capron (2016), Davis (2016), Rodgers (2016), Davis and Ruiz (2018), Fontes (2018), Zubillaga et al. (2019), Bell-Martin and Marston (2023), Fahlberg (2023).
3. Reguillo (2002, 2008), Rotker (2002), Carrión Mena and Núñez-Vega (2006), Briceño-León (2007), Kessler (2009), Vilalta (2011, 2016, 2010), Aquino Moreschi (2015), Valenzuela Aguilera (2016), Koury (2017), O'Hare and Bell (2020), Peeters (2021), Calonge Riello (2022), Sobalvarro and Luneke (2022), Villamizar-Santamaría (2022), de Lachica Huerta (2023), Jenss (2023).
4. Carrión (2008).
5. Schmitz and Eckert (2022).
6. Dammert and Malone (2003), Hale (1996), Lee (2001), Pain (2000), Stanko (2000).
7. On "cultures of fear," Furedi (2006), Glassner (2009); "liquid fear," Bauman (2006); "societies of fear," Bude (2018).
8. For prominent examples, see Katz (1999), Hochschild (1983), Mpondo-Dika (2019). For overviews, see Turner and Stets (2006), Ariza (2016, 2020).
9. Tavory (2016).
10. Barbalet (1998:81), drawing on James (1931). For more on macro approaches, see Turner (2010, 2014, 2015), Scheff and Retzinger (1991), Scheff (1994, 2000). For a longer theoretical discussion, see Villarreal (2022).
11. Elias ([1939] 1989:527), who wrote from experience having lived through war twice. On emotions and violence, see also Scheff (1994), Collins (2007), Göçek (2014), Luft (2023).
12. Elsewhere, I examine the social construction of *los malitos* (the bad guys) as a coping mechanism utilized in Monterrey at this time to minimize and to be able to talk about dangerous actors without endangering themselves. When applied to victims accused of having "done something," these codes produced symbolic security at victims' expense facilitating the domestication of danger. See Villarreal (2021). On the domesticating power of culture, Molnár (2016).
13. Patillo (1999, 2003).

146 NOTES

14. Caldeira (1996, 2000). For Mexico, see also Camus (2015), Capron (2015), Valenzuela-Aguilera (2007, 2016); for Argentina, see Janoschka (2002), Svampa (2001, 2004); for Chile, see Sabatini (2001); for Uruguay, see Álvarez-Rivadulla (2007); for Venezuela, see Rebotier (2011a,2011b); for the United States, see Blakely and Snyder (1999), Low (2001, 2004, 2006), Le Goix (2005), Vesselinov (2008), and Dinzey-Flores (2013); for the Phillipines, see Garrido (2019); for France, see Capron (2006).
15. Davis (2007), Müller (2016), Zamorano Villarreal (2019).
16. Capron (2019:17–22).
17. On policing and marginality, Denyer-Willis (2015), Sierra-Arévalo (2019), González (2020). For the United States, Stuart (2016), Vargas (2016), Rios (2017), Herring (2019).
18. Conger (2014), Basulto Yerena (2019), Ley and Guzmán (2019), Arzaluz Solano (2021), Buderath and Heath (2021). For more on the prominent role the private sector plays in the politics of urban violence in Latin America, see Moncada (2013, 2016).
19. Buderath and Heath (2021:172).
20. Ibid. (174).
21. On paramilitaries in San Pedro and northeastern Mexico, see Correa-Cabrera (2018) and Flores Pérez (2020).
22. Dorantes-Gilardi et al. (2020:10).
23. Suttles (1972). For localized orders among gangs, Moore (1991), Padilla (1992), Rodgers (2006), Sánchez-Jankowski (1991), Venkatesh (1997), Vigil (1988), Martínez (2016). On racial dimensions of defended neighborhoods in US cities, see Buell (1980), DeSena (1994), Grattet (2009), Kadowaki (2009).
24. On Santa Fe and elite enclaves, Valenzuela (2007), Wacquant (2010), Pinçon and Pinçon-Charlot (2007).
25. Marcuse (1997).
26. Rodgers (2004).
27. Suttles (1972:266) in conversation with Park (1967).
28. Camus (2015), Cerón-Anaya (2019), Ramos-Zayas (2020).
29. Durin (2013).
30. Hernández-León (2002). For the United States, see Anderson (2008).
31. Violence can stir numerous forms of civic engagement, particularly among victims of violence, who are more likely to organize. See Alvarado (2010), Bateson (2012), Davis (2012), Trelles and Carreras (2012), Gallagher (2013, 2022), Auyero (2014), Arjona (2017:764), Arias (2019), Ley (2018), Ley (2022), Zulver (2022, 2023).
32. Gonzalez and Mayka (2023). For a broader discussion of state categorization and inequality, see Menjívar (2023).
33. Ramírez Atilano (2019).
34. Pablo Ordaz, "En México no vamos a permitir que se pierda Monterrey," *El País*, February 21, 2011, retrieved March 17, 2023, https://elpais.com/diario/2011/02/21/internacional/1298242812_850215.html.
35. David Luhnow, "La violencia en Monterrey provoca un éxodo de extranjeros y mexicanos adinerados," *The Wall Street Journal*, September 12, 2010, retrieved March 17, 2023, https://www.wsj.com/articles/SB128415989195236683.

NOTES 147

36. Pablo Ordaz, "En México no vamos a permitir que se pierda Monterrey."
37. This origins story is also reiterated in the media, including in foreign media. For a recent example, see Schumpeter, "For business, water scarcity is where climate change hits home," *The Economist*, August 17, 2022, retrieved March 23, 2023, https://www.economist.com/business/2022/08/17/for-business-water-scarcity-is-where-climate-change-hits-home.
38. Cerutti (1993), Graf (1993), Mora-Torres (2001).
39. The governor of Nuevo León at the time was Santiago Vidaurri, a man with secession dreams of his own. He exploited this juncture to the fullest in the hopes of creating the Republic of the Sierra Madre. Confederate states wanted to funnel cotton through northeastern Mexico faster than it could be shipped. Vidaurri thus transformed Monterrey into a "free depot" where they could store an unlimited amount of cotton for up to a year in exchange for a dispatch fee (Cerutti 1993). Having annexed the state of Coahuila to the west, Vidaurri took miliary control of the state of Tamaulipas to the east, opened three new border towns, and took control of the small port of Matamoros, which became a de facto Confederate port at the time and one of the three busiest in the world (Delaney 1993; Tyler 1993). To disguise the trade from the disapproving Union and an impoverished Mexican federal government at war with the French—who wanted the cotton fees and needed the gunpowder—ship captains began to unload authorized goods during the day and war-related goods at night not registered by Mexican customs agents (Delaney 1993:110). Confederate boats disguised their cargo using both British and Mexican flags (Tyler 1993:113). Warehouses sprung up on both sides of the river to store goods discretely transported in smaller boats. Large-scale contraband along the US-Mexico border was born.
40. Delaney (1993:110).
41. Andreas (2014), Diaz (2015).
42. Correa-Cabrera (2017:269).
43. Osorno (2012), Correa-Cabrera (2017).
44. For rise of drug trafficking in northwestern Mexico, see Astorga (2005), Enciso (2015).
45. Durin (2019), Flores Pérez (2018), Sandoval Hernández (2018), Irazuzta (2017).
46. US Department of State Bureau of Consular Affairs. "Travel Warning- Mexico November 20, 2012." *Consulate General of the United States Citizen Services.* Retrieved April 21, 2015, http://monterrey.usconsulate.gov/acs_tw_11202012.html.
47. Browning and Feindt (1968), Puente Leyva (1969), Balán, Browning, and Jelin (1977), Montemayor Hernández (1972), Walton (1977), Zúñiga and Ribeiro (1990), Fouquet and Mercier (1994), López Estrada (2002), Cerutti (1992, 2000), Martínez Jazzo (1995), Vellinga (1988), Sandoval (2005), Vizcaya Canales (2006), Solís (2007), Palacios Hernández et al. (2010), Flores (2011), García Garza (2013), Davis et al. (2016).
48. García Ortega (2001).
49. José de Córdoba and Joel Millman, "Shootout Near School Shocks Mexico," *Wall Street Journal*, August 23, 2010, retrieved April 1, 2021, https://www.wsj.com/articles/SB10001424052748704504204575445970398254874.

148 NOTES

50. Burawoy (2003).
51. On Monterrey's metropolization, see Baby-Collin (2010), Jurado and Pereira (2010).
52. Walton (1977), Cerutti (1983), Saragoza (1988), Hassaine-Bau (2021).
53. On "studying up," Nader (1972), Pinçon-Charlot and Pinçon (2018), Cousin et al. (2018), Cerón-Anaya (2019), Mears (2020).
54. On legal cynicism, see Sampson and Bartusch (1998), Kirk and Papachristos (2011).

Chapter 2

1. Rizzo Reyes (2020), Gallagher (2022).
2. Ramírez Atilano (2014), FUNDENL (2019).
3. Amnesty International (2013), Human Rights Watch (2013), Valdez Cárdenas (2016), Polit Dueñas (2019).
4. For more, see Alberto Arnaut's (2018) documentary *Hasta los dientes* (Armed to the Teeth).
5. Guillermoprieto (2011), Hernández Castillo (2019).
6. Alejandra Guillén, Mago Torres, Marcela Turati, "El país de las 2 mil fosas," *Quinto Elemento Lab*, November 12, 2018, retrieved March 27, 2023, https://quintoelab.org/project/el-pais-de-las-2-mil-fosas.
7. Bosch (2015:44–45, 105).
8. Bosch (2015:48–58).
9. Daniela Rea, "ONU reconoce desaparición forzada de Roy Rivera, ordena a México investigar," *Pie de Página*, April 23, 2021, retrieved March 27, 2023, https://piedepagina.mx/onu-reconoce-desaparicion-forzada-de-roy-rivera-ordena-a-mexico-investigar/.
10. Bosch (2015:45).
11. Musto (1973), Astorga (1995, 2000, 2005), Gootenberg (2008), Enciso (2015b, 2015a), Smith (2021).
12. Bourgois (2003), Contreras (2013), Schoenfeld (2018), Simes (2021).
13. Idler and Garzón Vergara (2021).
14. Enciso (2015a).
15. Ackerman (2021).
16. Astorga (2005:31).
17. Enciso (2015b).
18. Astorga (2000), Villarreal (2002), Velasco (2005), Snyder and Durán-Martínez (2009), Knight (2012), Pansters (2012), Osorio (2015), Lessing (2017), Durán-Martínez (2018), Herrera (2019), Trejo and Ley (2020).
19. Durán-Martínez (2018:65).
20. Gootenberg (2008), Paley (2014).
21. Craig (1980b:558–65).
22. Craig (1980b, 1980a).
23. Cedillo (2021).
24. Craig (1980a:354).
25. Enciso (2015a).
26. Interview with Froylán Enciso, June 25, 2014.

NOTES   149

27. NSDD number 221. For full document, see http://fas.org/irp/offdocs/nsdd/23-2771a.gif.
28. Interview with Luis Astorga, May 31, 2015.
29. Astorga (2007), Moloeznik (2007), Reames (2007), Fondevila and Quintana-Navarrete (2015; 2013).
30. Enciso (2015a).
31. Midgette et al. (2019:xiv). The total amount US drug consumers spend on drugs has not changed dramatically. Rather, it is their preferences that have changed.
32. Gootenberg (2008).
33. They estimate a drop from around 3.8 million cocaine consumers in 2006 to 2.5 in 2010 to 2.3 in 2016. Retail expenditures on cocaine estimated at 58 billion in 2006 dropped to around 31 billion in 2010 and 24 billion in 2016. Measured in tons, around 384 tons of cocaine were consumed in the United States in 2006 compared to 143 tons in 2010 and 145 tons in 2016 with strong fluctuations between 2012 and 2015 meriting closer attention. See Midgette et al. (2019:xiv).
34. Kilmer (2016).
35. Gootenberg (2021).
36. UNODC (2023).
37. Gootenberg (2008).
38. Between 2006 and 2009, the net supply of Colombian cocaine fell from 522 to 200 metric tons, and the retail price of cocaine in the United States increased about 45% (Castillo, Mejía, and Restrepo 2020).
39. Jusionyte (2024).
40. Karla Zabludosky, "The Monterrey Massacre: A New Nadir in Mexico's Drug War," *The Guardian*, September 1, 2011, retrieved March 25, 2021, https://www.theguard ian.com/commentisfree/cifamerica/2011/sep/01/mexico-monterrey-drug-war.
41. Miguel Angel Gutierrez, "Mexico's Calderon Berates U.S. after Casino Attack," *Reuters*, August 25, 2011, retrieved March 25, 2021, https://www.reuters.com/article/ us-mexico-crime/mexicos-calderon-berates-u-s-after-casino-attack-idUSTRE77O 88V20110826.
42. On the importance of restoring the complexity of "violent events" most often flattened into death tolls in high-violence contexts, see De Lachica (2020); on what makes an event, see Wagner-Pacifici (2017).
43. Luciano Campos Garza, "Casino Royale: un año de impunidad y reclamos de justicia," *Proceso*, August 24, 2012, retrieved March 25, 2021, https://www.proceso.com.mx/ nacional/2012/8/24/casino-royale-un-ano-de-impunidad-reclamos-de-justicia-107 475.html.
44. Miguel Angel Gutierrez, "Mexico's Calderon Berates U.S. after Casino Attack."
45. Dorantes-Gilardi (2020:12).
46. Ibid. (10).
47. Wacquant (2008). On marginality and violence, see Auyero et al. (2015), Arias (2018).
48. The Spanish located the labor they needed close enough to exploit it but used the Santa Catarina River as a racial barrier to clearly set them apart. As García García (2003:237) notes, the river was the city's first racial and class boundary. For a broader theory of such forms of ethnoracial exploitation and enclosure, see Wacquant (2008, 2010).

150 NOTES

49. Casas (2010:19).
50. Palacios and Martínez (2010), García García (2010), King (2010:43), Zúñiga (2010:65).
51. Casas (2010:26–28).
52. Lipsitz (2011:56), Du Bois (1995), Drake and Cayton (1993), Wacquant (2010, 2012), Hunter et al. (2016).
53. Sandoval and Escamilla (2010).
54. Tracy Wilkinson, "Mexico Drug Cartels Buying Public Support," *Los Angeles Times*, March 13, 2009, retrieved November 20, 2022, https://www.latimes.com/world/la-fg-monterrey-drugs-recruits1-2009mar13-story.html.
55. For a timeline, see Hugo Maguey, "Narcobloqueos: 11 meses de miedo," *Animal Político*, February 5, 2011, retrieved November 20, 2022, https://www.animalpolitico.com/2011/02/narcobloqueos-11-meses-de-miedo/.
56. Journalists reported twenty to twenty-eight blockades. See Sanjuana Martínez, "Los *tapados*, ejército juvenil de los Zetas, se vengaron de una sociedad que los margina," *La Jornada*, June 10, 2010, retrieved November 20, 2022, https://www.jornada.com.mx/2010/06/10/politica/009n1pol; Juliana Rincón Parra, "Mexico: Drug Cartel-Led Protest Paralyzes Monterrey Metropolitan Area," *Global Voices*, June 11, 2010, retrieved November 20, 2022, https://globalvoices.org/2010/06/11/mexico-drug-car tel-led-protest-paralyzes-monterrey-metropolitan-area/.
57. For more on the coping code *los malitos*, see Villarreal (2021).
58. For more on extortion in Mexico, see Diaz-Cayeros et al. (2015), Magaloni et al. (2020), Moncada (2022).
59. Rizzo Reyes (2017, 2020).
60. Ansolabehere and Martos (2021:86).
61. Correa-Cabrera (2017), Magaloni et al. (2020).
62. Zepeda Lecuona (2004).
63. Corpovisionarios (2013: 35).
64. Sampson and Bartusch (1998), Kirk and Papachristos (2011).
65. Rea and Ferri (2019).
66. Nancy Gómez, "13 años sin justiciar para Jorge y Javier: No hay sentencia contra militares que mataron a los estudiantes del Tec de Monterrey," *sdpnoticias*, March 16, 2023, retrieved June 24, 2023, https://www.sdpnoticias.com/mexico/13-anos-sin-justicia-para-jorge-y-javier-no-hay-sentencia-contra-militares-que-mataron-a-los-estudiantes-del-tec-de-monterrey/.
67. Benito Jiménez, "Sube indemnización para familia de Otilio," p. 4 in *El Norte*, March 28, 2023.
68. Gallagher (2022).

Chapter 3

1. Andrea Menchaca, "Cambian hábitos por miedo," p. 1 in *El Norte*, November 21, 2010.
2. Dammert and Malone (2003), Hale (1996), Lee (2001), Pain (1997), Stanko (2000).
3. Cohen (2002).

NOTES 151

4. José Villasáez, "Dejan autos de lujo; eligen de bajo perfil," p.1 in *El Norte*, March 5, 2010.
5. María Dolores Ortega, "Sube inseguridad precio de autos pequeños," p. 5 in *El Norte*. February 12, 2011.
6. José Villasáez, "Dejan autos de lujo; eligen de bajo perfil.
7. For more on the rise of the term *secuestrable*, see Villarreal (2013).
8. Abraham Vázquez, "Cambia el crimen prácticas médicas," p. 1 in *El Norte*, August 2, 2010.
9. Ibid.
10. Ferniza-Quiroz and Soto-Canales (2021) find male bus passengers in Monterrey tend to take the back seats, while women tend to sit closer to the front rows and the driver (most often male) in the hopes that he might intervene in a violent scenario. Women who had experienced or witnessed violence were more likely to sit close to others and to the driver. These patterns illustrate the impact of violence on heightened gender segregation as women regroup within the bus to cope with fear of sexual violence.
11. José Villasáez and Alberto Rodríguez, "Libran paisanos las extorsiones al pasar por NL," p. 2 in *El Norte*, December 24, 2011.
12. Regarding dangers on northeastern Mexican highways at this time, a bus station supervisor in the border town of Reynosa, Tamaulipas explained, "Buses would leave with forty people, but only the driver would reach his destination . . . all those passengers gone missing . . . we know nothing about them." A journalist added that to travel alone "*es jugarse la vida*" (is to risk your life). See Arturo Angel, "Tamaulipas: viajar a la frontera de la mano de la policía," *Animal Político*, November 25, 2015, retrieved December 5, 2022, https://www.animalpolitico.com/vivirconelna rco/viajar-de-la-mano-de-la-policia.html.
13. Miguel Domínguez, "Regresan vacacionistas; congestionan aduanas," p. 4 in *El Norte*, April 25, 2011.
14. Encinas (1990), Hernández León (2002), Rodríguez Martínez (2003), Blanco Arboleda (2007), Cerda (2008).
15. Carrión (2012), Aguilar Avilés and Castillo Berthier (2013) and Rubio Campos et al. (2017).
16. Jésica Zermeño, "Pandillas, ¿cantera del narco en México?," October 25, 2012, retrieved March 7, 2023, https://www.chicagotribune.com/hoy/ct-hoy-8162894-pandillas-c2bfcantera-del-narco-en-mexico-story.html.
17. Ibid.
18. Aguilar Avilés and Castillo Berthier (2013:93).
19. Ibid. (94).
20. Rubio-Campos et al. (2017:94).
21. Aguilar Avilés and Castillo Berthier (2013:92).
22. Jésica Zermeño, "Pandillas, ¿cantera del narco en México?," *Chicago Tribune*, October 25, 2012, retrieved March 7, 2023, https://www.chicagotribune.com/hoy/ct-hoy-8162894-pandillas-c2bfcantera-del-narco-en-mexico-story.html.
23. Carrión (2012: 164).
24. Rubio-Campos et al. (2017:94).
25. Ibid. (97).
26. Watkins (2014).

152 NOTES

27. Bernardo Loyola and Stefan Ruiz, "The Cholombians," *Vice*, February 28, 2011, retrieved March 7, 2023, https://www.vice.com/en/article/gqdv84/the-cholombi ans-731-v18n3.
28. Pezard-Ramírez (2022:419–20).
29. For more on Twitter accounts set up for security, Ávila Loera (2010).

Chapter 4

1. Rossini et al. (2012).
2. See Pinçon and Pinçon-Charlot (2018:124). The mayor also sought to project time at the entrance of *La Milarca*, featuring eight generations of his ancestry depicted on a wall facing a thirteenth-century gothic arch. For pictures, see Nuria Díaz Masó, "Mauricio Fernández nos abre la *La Milarca*," *Quién*, March 2, 2010, retrieved November 28, 2021, https://www.quien.com/espectaculos/2010/03/02/mauricio-fernandez-nos-abre-la-milarca.
3. Violeta Montes de Oca, "Se cierran con todo," p. 1 in *El Norte*, October 18, 2009.
4. Pezard-Ramírez (2022), Ramírez Atilano (2019).
5. As an example, Óscar Omar Treviño, also known as the Z-42, was detained in his home in an exclusive neighborhood of San Pedro on March 6, 2015. See Osvaldo Robles, "Custodian casas del Z-42 en Olinalá y La herradura," p. 1 in *El Norte*, March 11, 2015.
6. Caldeira (2000), Low (2001), Svampa (2001, 2004), Sabatini (2003), Capron (2004, 2012; 2007), Garrido (2019).
7. Ley and Guzmán (2019:160-161).
8. Rizzo Reyes (2017:430-431).
9. For more on this group and "new paramilitaries" in northeastern Mexico, Correa-Cabrera (2018) and Flores Pérez (2020).
10. Dorantes-Gilardi et al. (2020:10).
11. Esther Herrera, "San Pedro, el municipio más seguro para vivir: Pulsómetro," *Milenio*, October 8, 2015, retrieved March 9, 2023, https://www.milenio.com/estados/san-pedro-municipio-seguro-vivir-pulsometro.
12. San Pedro Garza García, "3 años blindando San Pedro," *Sierra Madre,* October 19, 2012.
13. Alicia Díaz, "Regresan regios, pese a inseguridad," p. 3 in *El Norte*, September 29, 2011.
14. Ibid.
15. Francisco Cepeda, "Rentas de oficinas bajarán su precio," p. 1 in *El Norte*, April 10, 2011.
16. Francisco Cepeda, "Estiman que repunte mercado de oficinas," p. 2 in *El Norte*, July 15, 2012.
17. The priest and his missionaries confronted fear of strangers among the wealthy in San Pedro as well as in the marginalized neighborhoods where they worked. "When you start visiting a new community, first you see taxis, then you see vans, then they come," he said, referencing organized crime as a tacit "they." In one working-class

NOTES 153

neighborhood, it was the police who showed up to ask what they were up to. When they said "missions," the police wished them well and left.

18. Durin (2013:114–117).

19. Ibid.

20. Hernández-León (2008), Zúñiga (2010).

21. According to the Internal Displacement Monitoring Centre, at least 230,000 Mexicans were displaced by violence between 2007 and 2011, particularly along the states of Chihuahua, Tamaulipas, Nuevo León, Durango, Guerrero, Sinaloa, and Michoacán (IDMC 2011). Half of the displaced fled to the United States, while the other half relocated across the Mexican territory. For a nuanced, in-depth analysis of forced displacement in northeastern Mexico, see Durin (2012, 2019).

22. Jenalia Moreno, "The Woodlands: paraíso de empresarios Mexicanos," *Houston Chronicle*, August 26, 2011, retrieved April 6, 2021, https://www.chron.com/spanish/la-voz/article/The-Woodlands-para-so-de-empresarios-mexicanos-2143253.php.

23. Ibid.

24. Molly Hennessy-Fiske, "Wealthy, business-savvy Mexican immigrants transform Texas City," *Los Angeles Times*, March 24, 2013, retrieved March 10, 2023, https://www.latimes.com/nation/la-xpm-2013-mar-24-la-na-sonterrey-20130324-story.html. For more on Cubans in Miami, see Eckstein (2022).

25. Durin (2019:326).

26. Ibid (295-296).

27. Rubio-Campos et al. (2017:94).

28. Ibid (100).

29. Carrión (2012:173).

30. Similar pattern observed in other highly criminalized urban areas in Latin America. See Robb Larkins (2015). For more on gentrification, Brown-Saracino (2010, 2017), Lees et al. (2015, 2016).

31. Isabel Briseño, "'La Indepe' resiste contra el stigma y los megaproyectos en Nuevo León," *Pie de Página*, September 27, 2022, retrieved December 20, 2022, https://piedepagina.mx/la-indepe-resiste-contra-el-estigma-y-los-megaproyectos-en-nuevo-leon/.

Chapter 5

1. Laura Garza, "Barrio Antiguo: una herida al corazón de Monterrey," *Animal Político*, March 10, 2011, retrieved February 6, 2021, https://www.animalpolitico.com/2011/03/barrio-antiguouna-herida-en-el-corazon-de-monterrey/. For a list of attacks and death tolls at numerous bars, nightclubs, and strip clubs in downtown Monterrey in 2010, 2011, and 2012, see Luciano Campos Garza, "Monterrey muere de noche," *Proceso*, September 13, 2012, retrieved February 6, 2021, https://www.proceso.com.mx/reportajes/2012/9/13/monterrey-muere-de-noche-108297.html.

2. Campos Garza, "Monterrey muere de noche."

154 NOTES

3. Thump Mexico, "Clubes caídos por el narco en Monterrey," *Vice*, November 24, 2016, retrieved February 6, 2021, https://www.vice.com/es/article/mgndgp/clubes-caidos-monterrey-guerra-contra-el-narco.
4. Thump Mexico, "Clubes caídos por el narco en Monterrey."
5. Saucedo Villegas (2017).
6. Blanco Arboleda (2007a, 2007b), Olvera Gudiño (2010).
7. Olvera Gudiño (2010:140).
8. Blanco Arboleda (2007b:100).
9. Saucedo Villegas (2017:148–52).
10. Ibid. (148).
11. Ibid. (143–47).
12. Ibid. (146).
13. Miriam Canales, "Los jóvenes del norte perdieron la noche," *SinEmbargo*, January 11, 2013, retrieved March 10, 2023, https://www.sinembargo.mx/11-01-2013/486231.
14. Ibid.
15. Lindón (2000, 2007).
16. Torres Escalante (2014:11).
17. Such greetings are the core of the 2009 song *Cumbia de los saludos* (Greetings Cumbia) by Javier López y los Reyes Vallenatos. The song lists dozens and dozens of youth groups frequently greeting each other in the metropolis in the 2000s. The names often identify their neighborhood of origin. The song, like the practice of greeting each other, brought them together.
18. Blanco Arboleda (2008:209).
19. Torres Escalante (2014:98).
20. Thump Mexico, "Clubes caídos por el narco en Monterrey."
21. Ibid.
22. Pezard-Ramirez (2022:138).
23. Thump Mexico, "Clubes caídos por el narco en Monterrey."
24. Garza Villarreal (1999:576).

Chapter 6

1. For examples, see Caldeira (2000), Low (2004), Capron (2006), Alvarado (2010).
2. Montero (2017).
3. Auyero and Berti (2015).
4. For more on golf and its centrality for Mexican elites, Cerón-Anaya (2019).
5. Soto Canales (2018:103).
6. Torres Escalante (2014:89).
7. Mauss (2006).
8. Daniel de la Fuente, "Ahuyenta inseguridad a paseantes," *El Norte*, September 18, 2010, retrieved January 12, 2024, https://busquedas.gruporeforma.com/elnorte/BusquedasComs.aspx.

NOTES   155

9. Osorno (2012: 99-119) investigated the origins of his abduction. A few months earlier, the mayor decided to bring in the military to scrutinize his police forces. Two officers went missing; several others were detained or quit. Although the mayor's two guards reported directly to the military, days before his abduction they had a "strange accident" in their armored Grand Cherokee: one was killed by a wire crossing his chest despite wearing a bulletproof vest, while the other was sent to the hospital and accused of murdering his partner. Four days later, footage from hidden video cameras revealed the arrival of several trucks with strobe lights at the mayor's home. The local policeman who was guarding the mayor's home at the time seamlessly boarded one of the trucks. Moments later, the cameras taped the mayor walking toward one of the trucks with several men pointing guns at him. Fourteen men were involved in the abduction, including several of his local police agents. The mayor was shot twice in the head, once in the chest, and showed signs of torture.

10. The Mexican Ministry of Tourism designates funds to towns with unique cultural and historical heritage known as "magic towns."

11. Villarreal (2021).

12. I first consulted these reviews on Tripadvisor in 2015. The 2010 review cited in this paragraph was still available when I consulted the website again in early 2024, but not the 2012 reviews. See "Parque la Huasteca," Tripadvisor, retrieved January 12, 2024, https://www.tripadvisor.com/Attraction_Review-g150782-d184284-Reviews-or30-Parque_la_Huasteca-Monterrey_Northern_Mexico.html.

13. Monica Luna, "También en Nuevo León descubren fosas clandestinas," *Excelsior*, April 19, 2011, retrieved November 23, 2021, https://www.excelsior.com.mx/node/730860.

14. Jurado (2016) also found that as violence escalated in the city of Matamoros in the nearby state of Tamaulipas, social gatherings shifted indoors and among closer social circles of family and close friends.

15. For more on Consejo Cívico, see Conger (2014). The survey asked basic sociodemographic information (gender, birth year, municipality of residence, civil status, occupation), the number of people accompanying the respondent, and the following questions: 1) How often do you come here? (first time, occasionally, regularly); 2) How did you find out about this initiative? (social media, friends and/or family, saw it, media, advertising); 3) Would you invite your family and/or friends to come here? (yes, no, why?); 4) What activities do you engage in during your visit? (walking, socializing, meeting new people, cycling, walking dog, other); 5) Do you feel safe during your visit? (yes, no, why?); 6) Where do you meet up with your family and friends? (home, shopping mall, park, social or sports club, restaurant, other); 7) Where would you be if you were not here? (open answer); 8) How much do you trust your neighbors in the area where you live? (little, some, a lot, why?); 9) How much do you trust people here in this family space? (little, some, a lot, why?); 10) Have you reencountered old friendships and acquaintances here? (yes, no; if yes, who? and did you continue to see this person afterward?); 11) Suggestions (open answer).

156 NOTES

16. Out of 270 respondents, 101 resided in San Pedro, 89 in Monterrey, 11 in San Nicolás, 6 in Guadalupe, 3 in Apodaca, 1 in Santa Catarina, 1 in Villa de Santiago, and 4 were tourists not residing in the Monterrey Metropolitan Area.
17. Out of the San Pedro residents that were surveyed that summer day, two-thirds were regular attendees (66 out of 101) and nearly one-third occasional attendees (31 out of 101), with only 4 visiting the family walk for the first time.
18. Hinojosa and Aparicio (2014:12).
19. Drawing inspiration from similar programs in Colombia, Consejo Cívico launched a state accountability program called *Alcalde, cómo vamos?* (Mayor, how are we doing?) They used the media to pressure all candidates running for mayor in 2012 to commit to developing an open-streets program, among other initiatives, including increasing the number of police per one hundred thousand inhabitants. Once elected, the nine mayors of the metropolitan area (2013–2016) implemented an open-streets program, locally referred to as a *vía recreativa* (leisure avenue), that Consejo Cívico evaluated and ranked (stirring competition among municipalities).
20. Residente Staff (2012).
21. Marcela Cortés, "Arranca alcalde de Guadalupe proyecto 'Vive tu Ciudad,'" *Equidad,* March 11, 2013, retrieved January 12, 2024, http://revista-equidad.com/?p=9958
22. Pezard-Ramírez (2022:390).
23. Ibid. (402).
24. Samantha Gaillinar, "Sampetrinos alzan la voz," *Chic,* September 26, 2012, retrieved June 29, 2023, https://issuu.com/chic_monterrey/docs/chic_monterrey_308/119.

Chapter 7

1. Staff Sierra Madre, "Relatan su experiencia," p. 84 in *Sierra Madre,* March 19, 2020.
2. Isabella Cota, "Why wealthy Mexicans are getting vaccinated against Covid-19 in the US," *El Pais,* March 5, 2021, retrieved June 18, 2023, https://english.elp ais.com/usa/2021-03-05/why-wealthy-mexicans-are-getting-vaccinated-agai nst-covid-19-in-the-us.html.
3. Staff Sierra Madre, "Relatan su experiencia."
4. Soto Canales (2022:32).
5. El Norte Staff, "Dígale a su patron que no va a pasar," *El Norte,* April 25, 2020, retrieved June 20, 2023, http://busquedas.grupoforma.com/elnorte/BusquedasComs.aspx.
6. El Norte Staff, "Filtran accesos a San Pedro por Covid," *El Norte,* April 24, 2020, retrieved June 20, 2023, http://busquedas.grupoforma.com/elnorte/BusquedasC oms.aspx.
7. Hassaine-Bau (2021:324).
8. Multimedios Digital, "La 'Fase 4' en San Pedro desata los memes en redes sociales," *Multimedios,* April 25, 2020, retrieved June 18, 2023, https://www.multimedios.com/ television/la-fase-4-en-san-pedro-desata-los-memes-en-redes-sociales. For more, see Hassaine-Bau (2021).

NOTES   157

9. Kate Linthicum, Molly Hennessy-Fiske, "With Mexico's Vaccination Program Lagging, Wealthy Mexicans Are Flocking To The US," *Los Angeles Times*, March 31, 2021, retrieved June 18, 2023, https://www.latimes.com/world-nation/story/2021-03-31/with-mexicos-vaccination-program-lagging-wealthy-mexicans-are-flocking-to-the-u-s.

10. Leonardo González, "¿Cuál covid? Reviven antros", *El Norte*, May 29, 2021, retrieved June 20, 2023, p. 1.

11. José Villasáez, "Vuelve San Pedro de Pinta con aforo pre pandemia," p. 1 in *El Norte*, June 28, 2021, retrieved June 20, 2023.

12. César Cubero, "San Pedro, con la tasa más baja de muertes por covid-19 respecto a casos," *Milenio*, September 29, 2020, retrieved June 25, 2023, https://www.milenio.com/politica/comunidad/san-pedro-tasa-baja-muertes-covid-19-casos.

13. Milagros Berríos, Gianfranco Huamán, Dalila Sarabia, Ignacia Velasco, Javier Revetria, Natalia Arbeláez and Isaías Morales, "The Pandemic for the Rich and Poor: Spending Inequality in Latin America," *Redpalta*, 2022, retrieved June 25, 2023, https://redpalta.org/the-pandemic-for-the-rich-and-poor-spending-inequality-in-latin-america/.

14. INEGI (2023:3).

15. Gobierno de México, "San Pedro Garza García," *Data Mexico*, retrieved June 25, 2023, https://datamexico.org/en/profile/geo/san-pedro-garza-garcia.

16. Luis Chaparro, "'Debanhi's Death Killed Our Hope': Fear Over Missing Women," *Vice*, April 26, 2022, retrieved June 25, 2023, https://www.vice.com/en/article/v7dayb/debanhis-death-killed-our-hope-fear-over-missing-women.

17. Ibid.

18. Marcos Martínez Chacón, "Desaparecidos en México: impunidad marca lucha de una madre," *AP News*, November 5, 2021, retrieved June 26, 2023, https://apnews.com/article/9e06ad59070a535fcf75edcbdae0d947.

19. Gallagher (2017, 2022), Irazuzta (2017), Robledo Silvestre (2017), FUNDENL (2019), Hernández Castillo (2019).

20. Arias (2019).

21. On the impact of fear on elections and protests, see Ley (2018, 2022), Zulver (2023).

22. Sassen (2001).

23. Beckert (2001), Sherman (2017).

24. Sherman (2017).

25. Azi Paybarah, Matthew Block, Scott Reinhard, "Where New Yorkers Moved to Escape Coronavirus," *New York Times*, May 16, 2020, retrieved June 19, 2023, https://www.nytimes.com/interactive/2020/05/16/nyregion/nyc-coronavirus-moving-leaving.html.

26. Kevin Quealy, "The Richest Neighborhoods Emptied Out Most as Coronavirus Hit New York City," *New York Times*, May 15, 2020, retrieved June 19, 2023, https://www.nytimes.com/interactive/2020/05/15/upshot/who-left-new-york-coronavirus.html?action=click&module=Editors%20Picks&pgtype=Homepage.

27. Paul Berger, "New York City's Homeless Population Has High Covid-19 Mortality Rate," *Wall Street Journal*, June 9, 2020, retrieved June 19, 2023, https://www.wsj.com/

158 NOTES

articles/new-york-citys-homeless-population-has-high-covid-19-mortality-rate-11591735120?mod=article_inline.

28. New York City Department of Housing Preservation and Development (2023:18).

29. Kimmelman (2022).

30. Laura Meckler and Hannah Natanson, "For parents who can afford it, a solution for fall: Bring the teachers to them," *The Washington Post*, July 17, 2020, retrieved January 12, 2024, https://www.washingtonpost.com/education/fall-remote-private-teacher-pods/2020/07/17/9956ff28-c77f-11ea-8ffe-372be8d82298_story.html

31. Du Bois (1995), Wilson (1987).

32. Garrido et al. (2021), Go (2016). On rethinking case selection, Krauze (2021).

33. Pinçon and Pinçon (2018:116).

Appendix

1. Sherman (2017:255).

2. Hochschild (2012).

3. Bosch (2015).

4. Gould (2015:164).

Bibliography

Ackerman, Edwin. 2021. *Origins of the Mass Party: Disposession and the Party-Form in Mexico and Bolivia in Comparative Perspective*. New York: Oxford University Press.

Aguilar Avilés, Fernando and Héctor Castillo Berthier. 2013. "¿Existen pandillas en Monterrey?: Jóvenes entre la marginación y el estigma." *Revista Mexicana de Opinión Pública* 7:65–98.

Alvarado, Arturo. 2010. "Inseguridad pública, participación ciudadana y gobernanza: la Ciudad de México en la última década." *Estudios Sociológicos* 28(84):941–63.

Álvarez-Rivadulla, María José. 2007. "Golden Ghettos: Gated Communities and Class Residential Segregation in Montevideo, Uruguay." *Environment and Planning A: Economy and Space* 39(1):47–63.

Amnesty International. 2013. *Confronting a Nightmare: Disappearances in Mexico*. London, UK.

Anderson, Elijah. 2008. *Against the Wall: Poor, Young, Black, and Male*. Philadelphia, PA: University of Pennsylvania Press.

Andreas, Peter. 2014. *Smuggler Nation: How Illicit Trade Made America*. New York: Oxford University Press.

Ansolabehere, Karina and Alvaro Martos. 2021. "Disappearances in Mexico: An Analysis Based on the Northeast Region." Pp. 73–96 in *Disappearances in Post-Transition Era in Latin America*, edited by K. Ansolabehere, B. Frey, and L. Payne. New York: Oxford University Press.

Aquino Moreschi, Alejandra. 2015. "'Porque si llamas al miedo, el miedo te friega': La ilegalización de los trabajadores migrantes y sus efectos en las subjetividades." *Estudios Fronterizos* 16(32):75–98.

Arias, Desmond and Daniel Goldstein. 2010. *Violent Democracies in Latin America*. Durham, NC: Duke University Press.

Arias, Enrique Desmond. 2017. *Criminal Enterprises and Governance in Latin America and the Caribbean*. New York: Cambridge University Press.

Arias, Enrique Desmond. 2019. "Social Responses to Criminal Governance in Rio de Janeiro, Belo Horizonte, Kingston, and Medellín." *Latin American Research Review* 54(1):165–80.

Arias, Enrique Desmond and Ximena Tocornal Montt. 2018. "Social Disorganisation and Neighborhood Effects in Latin America: Insights and Limitations." Pp. 121–38 in *Social Theories of Urban Violence in the Global South: Towards Safe and Inclusive Cities*, edited by J. E. Salahub, M. Gottsbacher, and J. de Boer. Milton Park, UK: Routledge.

Arias Sobalvarro, Anya Mabel and Alejandra Luneke. 2022. "Inseguridad y producción del espacio: la paradoja de la prevención situacional del delito." *Revista de Urbanismo* (46):95–111.

Ariza, Marina (coord). 2016. *Emociones, afectos y sociología. Diálogos desde la investigación social y la interdisciplina*. Mexico City, MX: Universidad Nacional Autónoma de México, Instituto de Investigaciones Sociales.

160 BIBLIOGRAPHY

Ariza, Marina (coord). 2020. *Las emociones en la vida social: miradas sociológicas*. Mexico City, MX: Universidad Nacional Autónoma de México, Instituto de Investigaciones Sociales.

Arjona, Ana. 2017. "Civilian Cooperation and Non-Cooperation with Non-State Armed Groups: The Centrality of Obedience and Resistance." *Small Wars and Insurgencies* 28(4–5):755–78.

Arnaut Estrada, Alberto Saúl. 2018. *Armed to the Teeth*. Mexico City, MX: IMCINE-FOPROCINE.

Arzaluz Solano, María del Socorro. 2021. "¿Régimen urbano o gobernanza empresarial? Nuevo León en el siglo XXI." *Polis* 17(1):7–42.

Astorga, Luis. 1995. *Mitología del "narcotraficante" en México*. Mexico City, MX: Plaza y Valdés.

Astorga, Luis. 2002. "The Field of Drug Trafficking in Mexico." Pp. 6–20 in *Globalisation, Drugs and Criminalisation. Final Research Report on Brazil, China, India, and Mexico, Part I*, edited by Christian Geoffrey, Guilhem Fabre, and Michel Schiray. Paris, FR: United Nations Educational, Scientific and Cultural Organization.

Astorga, Luis. 2005. *El siglo de las drogas*. Mexico City, MX: Plaza & Janés.

Astorga, Luis. 2007. *Seguridad, traficantes y militares: El poder y la sombra*. Mexico City, MX: Tusquets.

Auyero, Javier and Maria Fernanda Berti. 2015. *In Harm's Way: The Dynamics of Urban Violence*. Princeton, NJ: Princeton University Press.

Auyero, Javier, Philippe Bourgois, and Nancy Scheper-Hughes. 2015. *Violence at the Urban Margins*. New York: Oxford University Press.

Auyero, Javier, Agustín Burbano de Lara, and María Fernanda Berti. 2014. "Violence and the State at the Urban Margins." *Journal of Contemporary Ethnography* 43(1):94–116.

Avila Loera, Adriana Melissa. 2010. "Perceptions of (Narco) Violence in Monterrey, Mexico." Master's thesis, University of Texas at Austin.

Baby-Collin, Virginie. 2010. "La metropolización de Monterrey: Un enfoque socioespacial." Pp. 19–46 in *Cuando México enfrenta la globalización. Permanencias y cambios en el área metropolitana de Monterrey*, edited by L. Palacios, C. Contreras, V. Zúñiga, T. Blöss, D. Mercier, V. Baby-Collin, and C. Sheridan. Monterrey, MX: UANL, COLEF, ITESM, UDEM, NMF, CIESAS.

Balán, Jorge, Harley L. Browning, and Elizabeth Jelin. 1977. *El hombre en una sociedad en desarrollo. Movilidad geográfica y social en Monterrey*. Mexico City, MX: Fondo de Cultura Económica.

Barbalet, Jack M. 1998. *Emotion, Social Theory, and Social Structure: A Macrosociological Approach*. Cambridge, UK: Cambridge University Press.

Basulto Yerna, Juan Enrique. 2019. "Jóvenes pobres del área metropolitana de Monterrey (AMM) y el grupo policial Fuerza Civil: una interacción compleja." Master's thesis, Universidad Autónoma de Nuevo León.

Bateson, Regina. 2012. "Crime Victimization and Political Participation." *American Political Science Review* 106(3):570–87.

Bauman, Zygmunt. 2006. *Liquid Fear*. Cambridge, UK: Polity.

Baverstock, Alasdair, Greg Dickinson, Brendon Griffin, Rebecca Hallett, and Rajesh Mishra. 2016. *The Rough Guide to Mexico*. London, UK: Rough Guides.

Beckert, Sven. 2001. *The Monied Metropolis: New York City and the Consolidation of the American Bourgeoisie, 1850–1896*. Cambridge, UK: Cambridge University Press.

BIBLIOGRAPHY   161

Bell-Martin, Rebecca and Jerome F. Marston. 2023. "Staying Power: Strategies for Weathering Criminal Violence in Marginal Neighborhoods of Medellín and Monterrey." *Latin American Research Review* 58(4):1–20.

Bergman, Marcelo. 2018. *More Money, More Crime. Prosperity and Rising Crime in Latin America*. New York: Oxford University Press.

Blakely, Edward J. and Mary Gayle Snyder. 1999. *Fortress America: Gated Communities in the United States*. Washington, D.C.: Brookings Institution Press.

Blanco Arboleda, Darío. 2007a. *La cumbia como matriz sonora de Latinoamérica: Los colombias en Monterrey-México. Interculturalidad, identidad, espacio y cuerpo (1960–2008)*. Mexico City, MX: FLACSO.

Blanco Arboleda, Darío. 2007b. "Mundos de frontera. Colombianos en la línea noreste de México y Estados Unidos." *Trayectorias* 9(25):89–105.

Blanco Arboleda, Darío. 2008. "La cumbia como matriz sonora de Latinoamérica. Los Colombias de Monterrey-México (1960–2008) Interculturalidad, Identidad, Espacio y Cuerpo." Doctoral dissertation, Colegio de México.

Du Bois, W. E. B. 1995. *The Philadelphia Negro: A Social Study*. Philadelphia, PA: University of Pennsylvania Press.

Bosch, Lolita. 2015. *Roy, desaparecido*. Mexico City, MX: Ediciones B.

Bourgois, Philippe. 2003. *In Search of Respect: Selling Crack in El Barrio*. Cambridge, UK: Cambridge University Press.

Briceño-León, Roberto. 2007. "Caracas." Pp. 86–100 in *Fractured Cities: Social Exclusion, Urban Violence and Contested Spaces in Latin America*, edited by K. Koonings and D. Krujit. London, UK: Zed Books.

Briceño León, Roberto. 2007. "Violencia urbana en América Latina: Un modelo sociológico de explicación." *Espacio Abierto* 16(3):541–74.

Brown-Saracino, Japonica. 2010. *The Gentrification Debates*. New York: Routledge.

Brown-Saracino, Japonica. 2017. "Explicating Divided Approaches to Gentrification and Growing Income Inequality." *Annual Review of Sociology* 43:515–39.

Browning, Harley and Waltraut Feindt. 1968. "Diferencias entre la población nativa y la migrante En Monterrey." *Demografía y Economía* 2(2):183–204.

Bude, Heinz. 2018. *Society of Fear*. Cambridge, UK: Polity.

Buderath, Markus and Matthew Heath. 2021. "Fuerza Civil: Capital Accumulation and Social Control in Nuevo León, Mexico." *Latin American Perspectives* 48(1):163–83.

Burawoy, Michael. 2003. "Revisits: An Outline of a Theory of Reflexive Ethnography." *American Sociological Review* 68(5):645–79.

Caldeira, Teresa. 1996. "Fortified Enclaves: The New Urban Segregation." *Public Culture* 8(2):303–28.

Caldeira, Teresa. 2000. *City of Walls: Crime, Segregation, and Citizenship in São Paulo*. Berkeley, CA: University of California Press.

Caldeira, Teresa and James Holston. 1999. "Democracy and Violence in Brazil." *Comparative Studies in Society* 41(4):691–729.

Calonge Riello, Fernando. 2022. "Estructuras del sentimiento de inseguridad. Posiciones ante la violencia y estratificación social en México." *Espiral* 29(83):149–86.

Camus, Manuela. 2015. *Vivir en el coto. Fraccionamientos cerrados, mujeres y colonialidad*. Guadalajara, MX: Universidad de Guadalajara.

Capron, Guénola. 2004. "Les Ensembles résidentiels sécurisés dans les Amériques: une lecture critique de la littérature." *L'Espace Géographique* 2(33):97–113.

162 BIBLIOGRAPHY

Capron, Guénola. 2006. *Quand la ville se ferme: quartiers résidentiels sécurisés*. Paris, FR: Bréal.

Capron, Guénola. 2012. "Sentiment d'insécurité et inconfort chez les classes moyennes et supérieures des banlieues résidentielles au Sud et au Nord." *Espaces et Sociétés* 2(150):129–47.

Capron, Guénola. 2016. "El otro como amenaza y la internalización de la diferencia en ámbitos residenciales cerrados suburbanos del Área Metropolitana de la Ciudad de México." *Sociológica* 31(89):45–68.

Capron, Guénola. 2019. "Coproducción de la seguridad pública en urbanizaciones cerradas del valle de México." *Nueva Antropología* 32(91):10–25.

Capron, Guénola, Mónica Lacarrieu, and Maria Florencia Girola. 2007. "L'urbanité périphérique latino-américaine. Lotissements résidentiels sécurisés et fermés." *Les Annales de la recherche urbaine* 102:78–87.

Capron, Guénola and Cristina Sánchez-Mejorada Fernández (Eds.). 2015. *La (in)seguridad en la metrópoli. Territorio, segurización y espacio público*. Mexico City, MX: Universidad Autónoma Metropolitana.

Carrión, Fernando. 2008. "Violencia urbana: un asunto de ciudad." *EURE* 34(103):111–30.

Carrión, Lydiette. 2012. "El barrio bajo acecho." Pp. 159–81 in *Entre las cenizas*, edited by E. Baltazar, L. Carrión, T. Gómez Durán, J. Gibler, L. G. Hernández, V. Job, A. Nájar, D. Pastrana, D. Rea Gómez, and M. Turati. Oaxaca City, MX: Sur+ Ediciones.

Carrión Mena, Fernando and Jorge Núñez-Vega. 2006. "La inseguridad en la ciudad: hacia una comprensión de la producción social del miedo." *EURE* 32(97):5–16.

Casas, Juan Manuel. 2010. "Del barrio San Luisito a la colonia Independencia." Pp. 17–32 in *Ecos y colores de la colonia Independencia*, edited by C. Contreras. Monterrey, MX: COLEF and Municipio de Monterrey.

Castillo, Juan Camilo, Daniel Mejía, and Pascual Restrepo. 2020. "Scarcity without Leviathan: The Violent Effects of Cocaine Supply Shortages in the Mexican Drug War." *Review of Economics and Statistics* 102(2):269–86.

Cedillo, Adela. 2021. *Operation Condor, the War on Drugs, and Counterinsurgency in the Golden Triangle (1977–1983)*. Notre Dame, IN: Kellogg Institute for International Studies.

Cerda Pérez, Patricia. 2008. *Violencia y familia*. Monterrey, MX: Universidad Autónoma de Nuevo León.

Cerón-Anaya, Hugo. 2019. *Privilege at Play: Class, Race, Gender, and Golf in Mexico*. New York: Oxford University Press.

Cerutti, Mario. 1983. *Burguesía y capitalismo en Monterrey (1850–1910)*. Mexico City, MX: Claves Latinoamericanas.

Cerutti, Mario. 1992. *Burguesía, capital e industria en el norte de México. Monterrey y su ámbito regional (1850–1910)*. Mexico City, MX: Alianza Editorial-UANL.

Cerutti, Mario. 1993. "Estudio introductorio." Pp. 7–25 in *Frontera e historia económica. Texas y el norte de México (1850–1865)*, edited by M. Cerutti and M. A. González Quiroga. Mexico City, MX: Instituto de Investigaciones Dr. Mora/UAM.

Cerutti, Mario. 2000. *Propietarios, empresarios y empresas en el norte de México*. Mexico City, MX: Siglo XXI.

Cohen, Stanley. 2002. *Folk Devils and Moral Panics: The Creation of the Mods and Rockers*. London, UK: Routledge.

Collins, Randall. 2007. *Violence: A Micro-Sociological Theory*. Princeton, NJ: Princeton University Press.

BIBLIOGRAPHY 163

Conger, Lucy. 2014. "The Private Sector and Public Security: The Cases of Ciudad Juárez and Monterrey." Pp. 173–209 in *Building Resilient Communities in Mexico: Civic Responses to Crime and Violence*, edited by D. A. Shirk, D. Wood, and E. L. Olson. Washington, D.C.: Woodrow Wilson International Center for Scholars; University of San Diego Justice in Mexico Project.

Consejo Nacional de Población. 2018. *Indicadores demográficos básicos*. Mexico City, MX.

Contreras, Randol. 2013. *The Stickup Kids: Race, Drugs, Violence, and the American Dream*. Berkeley, CA: University of California Press.

Corpovisionarios. 2013. *La cultura ciudadana en Monterrey: resultados medición 2010-2012*. Bogotá, CO.

Correa-Cabrera, Guadalupe. 2017. *Los Zetas Inc: Criminal Corporations, Energy, and Civil War in Mexico*. Austin, TX: University of Texas Press.

Correa-Cabrera, Guadalupe. 2018. "Una política de seguridad no convencional y el nuevo paramilitarismo en México." Pp. 94–115 in *La crisis de seguridad y violencia en México: causas, efectos y dimensiones del problema*, edited by C. A. Flores Pérez. Mexico City, MX: Centro de Investigaciones y Estudios Superiores en Antropología Social.

Cousin, Bruno, Shamus Khan, and Ashley Mears. 2018. "Theoretical and Methodological Pathways for Research on Elites." *Socio-Economic Review* 16(2):225–49.

Craig, Richard. 1980a. "Operation Condor: Mexico's Antidrug Campaign Enters a New Era." *Journal of Interamerican Studies and World Affairs* 22(3):345–63.

Craig, Richard. 1980b. "Operation Intercept: The International Politics of Pressure." *The Review of Politics* 42(4):556–80.

Cruz, José Miguel. 2016. "State and Criminal Violence in Latin America." *Crime, Law and Social Change* 66(4):375–96.

Dammert, L. and M. Malone. 2003. "Fear of Crime or Fear of Life? Public Insecurities in Chile." *Bulletin of Latin America Research* 22(1):79–101.

Davis, Diane E. 2007. "El factor Giuliani: delincuencia, la 'cero tolerancia' en el trabajo policiaco y la transformación de la esfera pública en el centro de la Ciudad de México." *Estudios Sociológicos* 25(75):639–81.

Davis, Diane. 2012. *Urban Resilience in Situations of Chronic Violence*. Cambridge, MA: Massachusetts Institute of Technology and USAID.

Davis, Diane. 2016. "The Production of Space and Violence in Cities of the Global South: Evidence from Latin America." *Nóesis. Revista de Ciencias Sociales y Humanidades* 25(49–1):1–15.

Davis, Diane E. 2012. "Urban Violence, Quality of Life, and the Future of Latin American Cities: The Dismal Record So Far and the Search for New Analytical Frameworks to Sustain the Bias towards Hope." Pp. 37–59 in *Latin American Urban Development into the 21st Century*, edited by D. Rodgers, R. Kanbur, and J. Beall. London, UK: Palgrave Macmillan.

Davis, Diane, Nélida Escobedo, Fernando Granados, Francisco Lara, David Schoen, and Margaret Scott. 2016. *Case Study Compendium: Understanding the Barriers and Enablers to Densification at the Metropolitan Level. Qualitative Evidence from Seven Mexican Cities*. Cambridge, MA: Harvard University Graduate School of Design.

Davis, Diane and Guillermo Ruiz. 2018. "El reajuste espacial de estrategias de seguridad: tácticas de estado y respuestas ciudadanas a la violencia en la Ciudad de México." Pp. 131–60 in *Gobernando la Ciudad de México. Lo que se gobierna y lo que no se gobierna en una gran metrópoli*, edited by P. Le Galès and V. Ugalde. Mexico City, MX: El Colegio de México.

164 BIBLIOGRAPHY

Delaney, Robert W. 1993. "Matamoros, puerto de Texas durante la Guerra de Secesión." Pp. 97–111 in *Frontera e historia económica. Texas y el norte de México (1850–1865)*, edited by M. Cerutti and M. A. González Quiroga. Mexico City, MX: Instituto de Investigaciones Dr. Mora/UAM.

Denyer Willis, Graham. 2015. *The Killing Consensus: Police, Organized Crime, and the Regulation of Life and Death in Urban Brazil.* Berkeley, CA: University of California Press.

Diaz-Cayeros, Alberto, Beatriz Magaloni, and Vidal Romero. 2015. "Caught in the Crossfire: The Geography of Extortion and Police Corruption in Mexico." Pp. 252–74 in *Greed, Corruption, and the Modern State*, edited by S. Rose-Ackerman and P. Lagunes. Cheltenham, UK: Edward Elgar Publishing.

Diaz, George T. 2015. *Border Contraband: A History of Smuggling Across the Rio Grande.* Austin, TX: University of Texas Press.

Dinzey-Flores, Zaire Zenit. 2013. *Locked in, Locked out: Gated Communities in a Puerto Rican City.* Philadelphia, PA: University of Pennsylvania Press.

Dorantes-Gilardi, Rodrigo, Diana García-Cortés, Hiram Hernández-Ramos, and Jesús Espinal-Enríquez. 2020. "Eight years of homicide evolution in Monterrey, Mexico: a network approach." *Scientific Reports* 10(1):21564.

Drake, St. Clair and Horace R. Cayton. 1993. *Black Metropolis: A Study of Negro Life in a Northern City.* Chicago, IL: University of Chicago Press.

Durán-Martínez, Angélica. 2018. *The Politics of Drug Violence: Criminals, Cops and Politicians in Colombia and Mexico.* New York: Oxford University Press.

Durin, Séverine. 2012. "Los que la guerra desplazó: familias del noreste de México en el exilio." *Desacatos* 38:29–42.

Durin, Séverine. 2013. "Servicio doméstico de planta y discriminación en el Área Metropolitana de Monterrey." *Relaciones. Estudios de historia y sociedad* 34(134):93–129.

Durin, Séverine. 2019. *Sálvese quien pueda! Violencia generalizada y desplazamiento forzado en el noreste de México.* Mexico City, MX: Centro de Investigaciones y Estudios Superiores en Antropología Social.

Eckstein, Susan. 2022. *Cuban Privilege: The Making of Immigrant Inequality in America.* Cambridge, UK: Cambridge University Press.

Elias, Norbert. 1994. *Reflections on a Life.* Oxford, UK: Polity Press.

Elias, Norbert. 2000. *The Civilizing Process.* Malden, MA: Blackwell Publishing.

Encinas Garza, José. 1990. "Los reyes del barrio FZ: Etnografía de una banda juvenil de Monterrey." Bachelor's thesis, Universidad Autónoma de Nuevo León.

Enciso, Froylán. 2015a. *Nuestra historia narcótica: pasajes para (re)legalizar las drogas en México.* Mexico City, MX: Debate.

Enciso, Froylán. 2015b. "The Origin of Contemporary Drug Contraband: A Global Interpretation From Sinaloa." Doctoral Dissertation, State University of New York at Stony Brook.

Ferniza-Quiroz, Sheila and Karina Soto-Canales. 2021. "Imaginarios urbanos y violencia de género en la movilidad cotidiana en transporte público urbano. Zona Metropolitana de Monterrey." *Quivera* 23(2):89–109.

Flores, Óscar. 2011. *Industria, comercio, banca y finanzas en Monterrey 1890–2000.* Monterrey, MX: Centro de Estudios Históricos UDEM.

BIBLIOGRAPHY 165

Flores Pérez, Carlos Antonio. 2018. *La crisis de la seguridad y violencia en México: causas, efectos y dimensiones del problema*. Mexico City, MX: Centro de Investigaciones y Estudios Superiores en Antropología Social.

Flores Pérez, Carlos Antonio. 2020. *Negocios de sombras: red de poder hegemónica, contrabando, tráfico de drogas y lavado de dinero en Nuevo León*. Mexico City, MX: Centro de Investigaciones y Estudios Superiores en Antropología Social.

Fondevila, Gustavo and Miguel Quintana-Navarrete. 2015. "War Hypotheses: Drug Trafficking, Sovereignty and the Armed Forces in Mexico." *Bulletin of Latin America Research* 34(4):517–33.

Fondevila, Gustavo and Miguel Quintana Navarrete. 2013. "Juego de palabras: los discursos presidenciales sobre el crimen." *Estudios Sociológicos* 9(1):721–54.

Fouquet, Anne and Delphine Mercier. 1994. *La industria maquiladora de exportación en la Zona Metropolitana de Monterrey*. Monterrey, MX: Colegio de la Frontera Norte.

Fuerzas Unidas por Nuestros Desaparecidos en Nuevo León. 2019. *Un sentido de vida: la experiencia de búsqueda de Fuerzas Unidas Por Nuestros Desaparecidos en Nuevo León, 2012-2019*. Mexico City, MX: Universidad Iberoamericana Ciudad de México.

Furedi, Frank. 2006. *Culture of Fear Revisited: Risk-Taking and the Morality of Low-Expectation*. London, UK: Continuum.

Gallagher, Janice. 2013. "Mobilization in Mexico 2012: The Movement for Peace and the Struggle for Justice." Pp. 1235–60 in *Anuario del Conflicto Social 2012 / 2012 Social Conflict Yearbook*. Barcelona: Universitat de Barcelona.

Gallagher, Janice. 2022. *Bootstrap Justice: The Search for Mexico's Disappeared*. New York: Oxford University Press.

García García, Alejandro. 2003. "Territorialidad y violencia en la colonia Independencia de Monterrey." In *Aedificare 2003: Anuario de Investigaciones de la Facultad de Arquitectura*, edited by A. Narváez Tijerina. Monterrey, MX: Universidad Autónoma de Nuevo León.

García García, Alejandro. 2010. "Paisajes, querencias y apegos." Pp. 31–42 in *Colores y ecos de la colonia Independencia*, edited by C. Contreras. Monterrey, MX: COLEF and Municipio de Monterrey.

García Garza, Domingo. 2013. "Aportaciones para el análisis de la cultura empresarial en la universidad Mexicana: el caso del Tec de Monterrey." *Revista Mexicana de Investigación Educativa* 18(56):191–221.

García Ortega, Roberto. 2001. "Asentamientos irregulares en Monterrey, 1970-2000. Divorcio entre planeación y gestión urbana." *Frontera Norte* 13(2):119–55.

Garrido, Marco. 2019. *The Patchwork City: Class, Space and Politics in Metro Manila*. Chicago, IL: University of Chicago Press.

Garza Villarreal, Gustavo. 1999. "La estructura socioespacial de Monterrey, 1970-1990." *Estudios Demográficos y Urbanos* 14(3):545–98.

Glassner, Barry. 2009. *The Culture of Fear: Why Americans Are Afraid of the Wrong Things*. New York: Basic Books.

Göçek, Fatma Müge. 2014. *Denial of Violence: Ottoman Past, Turkish Present, and Collective Violence against the Armenians, 1789-2009*. New York: Oxford University Press.

Le Goix, Renaud. 2005. "La Dimension territoriale des *gated communities* aux États-Unis: La clôture par contrat." *Cercles* 13:97–121.

González, Yanilda. 2020. *Authoritarian Police in Democracy: Contested Security in Latin America*. Cambridge, UK: Cambridge University Press.

166 BIBLIOGRAPHY

González, Yanilda and Lindsay Mayka. 2023. "Policing, Democratic Participation, and the Reproduction of Asymmetric Citizenship." *American Political Science Review* 117(1):263–79.

Gootenberg, Paul. 2008. *Andean Cocaine: The Making of a Global Drug.* Chapel Hill, NC: University of North Carolina Press.

Gootenberg, Paul. 2021. "Shifting South: Cocaine's Historical Present and the Changing Politics of Drug War, 1975–2015." Pp. 287–3216 in *Cocaine: From Coca Fields to the Streets,* edited by E. D. Arias and T. Grisaffi. Durham, NC: Duke University Press.

Gould, Deborah. 2015. "When Your Data Make You Cry." Pp. 163–71 in *Methods of Exploring Emotions,* edited by H. Flam and J. Kleres. London, UK: Routledge.

Graf, Le Roy. 1993. "Historia económica del bajo río Grande (1820–1875)." Pp. 28–41 in *Frontera e historia económica. Texas y el norte de México (1850--1865),* edited by M. Cerutti and M. González Quiroga. Mexico City, MX: Instituto de Investigaciones Dr. Mora/UAM.

Guillermoprieto, Alma. 2011. *72 Migrantes.* Oaxaca de Juárez, MX: Almadía.

Hale, C. 1996. "Fear of Crime: A Review of the Literature." *International Review of Victimology* 4(2):79–150.

Hassaine Bau, Leïly. 2021. "L'elite en ses territoires: financiarisation, privatisation et projets urbains (Monterrey, Mexique)." Doctoral dissertation, Aix-Marseille Université.

Hernández-León, Rubén. 2008. *Metropolitan Migrants: The Migration of Urban Mexicans to the United States.* Berkeley, CA: University of California Press.

Hernández León, Rubén. 2002. "Cholos, carniceros, reos y cobras (definición de la situación y lógicas de acción en tres pandillas de barrios marginados en Monterrey)." Pp. 243–86 in *La marginación urbana en Monterrey,* edited by V. Zúñiga and M. Ribeiro. Monterrey, MX: Universidad Autónoma de Nuevo León.

Herrera, Joel S. 2019. "Cultivating Violence: Trade Liberalization, Illicit Labor, and the Mexican Drug Trade." *Latin American Politics and Society* 61(3):129–53.

Herring, Chris. 2019. "Complaint-Oriented Policing: Regulating Homelessness in Public Space." *American Sociological Review* 84(5):769–800.

Hinojosa, Karen and Carlos Aparicio. 2014. "Passer de la violence à la solidarité à Monterrey." *Kaléidoscope: le développement collectif dans tous ses états* 2(2):11–13.

Hochschild, Arlie. 2012. *The Managed Heart: Commercialization of Human Feeling.* Berkeley, CA: University of California Press.

Human Rights Watch. 2013. *Mexico's Disappeared: The Enduring Costs of a Crisis Ignored.* New York.

Hunter, Marcus Anthony, Mary Pattillo, Zandria F. Robinson, and Keeanga-Yamahtta Taylor. 2016. "Black Placemaking: Celebration, Play, and Poetry." *Theory, Culture & Society* 33(7–8):31–56.

Idler, Annette and Juan Carlos Garzón Vergara. 2021. *Transforming the War on Drugs: Warriors, Victims and Vulnerable Regions.* Oxford: Oxford University Press.

IDMC. 2011. *Mexico: Displacement Due to Criminal and Communal Violence.* Geneva, CH.

Imbusch, Peter, Michel Misse, and Fernando Carrión. 2011. "Violence Research in Latin America and the Caribbean: A Literature Review." *International Journal of Conflict and Violence* 5(1):87–154.

Instituto Nacional de Estadística y Geografía. 2018. "Estadísticas de Mortalidad." *INEGI.* Retrieved (http://www.beta.inegi.org.mx/proyectos/registros/vitales/mortalidad/).

BIBLIOGRAPHY 167

Instituto Nacional de Estadística y Geografía. 2023. *Encuesta nacional de seguridad pública urbana primer trimestre 2023*. Mexico City, MX.

James, William. 1931. *The Principles of Psychology, Vol. II*. New York: Henry Holt.

Janoschka, Michael. 2002. "El nuevo modelo de la ciudad latinoamericana: fragmentación y privatización." *EURE* 28(85):11–29.

Jenss, Alke. 2023. *Selective Security in the War on Drugs: The Coloniality of State Power in Colombia and Mexico*. London: Rowman & Littlefield.

Jurado, Mario and Kevin Pereira. 2010. "La gestión del servicio de transporte público. El caso del municipio de García y su relación con la movilidad geográfica laboral metropolitana." Pp. 89–110 in *Cuando México enfrenta la globalización: permanencias y cambios en el area metropolitana de Monterrey*, edited by L. Palacios, C. Contreras, V. Zúñiga, T. Blöss, D. Mercier, V. Baby-Collin, and C. Sheridan. Monterrey, MX: UANL, COLEF, ITESM, UDEM, NMF, CIESAS.

Jurado Montelongo, Mario Alberto. 2016. "Espacios de convivencia primaria e inseguridad en Matamoros, Tamaulipas." *Estudios Fronterizos* 17(34):41–63.

Jusionyte, Ieva. 2024. *Exit Wounds:How America's Guns Fuel Violence across the Border*. Berkeley, CA: University of California Press.

Katz, Jack. 1999. *How Emotions Work*. Chicago, IL: University of Chicago Press.

Kessler, Gabriel. 2009. *El sentimiento de inseguridad: sociología del temor al delito*. Buenos Aires, AR: Siglo XXI.

Kilmer, Beau. 2016. "Uncle Sam's Cocaine Nosedive: A Brief Exploration of a Dozen Hypotheses." Pp. 67–75 in *After the Drug Wars: Report of the LSE Expert Group on the Economics of Drug Policy*, edited by J. Collins. London, UK: The London School of Economics and Political Science.

Kimmelman, Michael. 2022. *The Intimate City: Walking New York*. New York: Penguin Press.

King, Jimmie L. 2010. "Arquitectura sin arquitectos: imagen, forma y vida en la evolución de su entorno urbano y espacios de integración social." Pp. 43–51 in *Ecos y colores de la colonia Independencia*, edited by C. Contreras. Monterrey, MX: COLEF and Municipio de Monterrey.

Kirk, David S. and Andrew V. Papachristos. 2011. "Cultural Mechanisms and the Persistence of Neighborhood Violence." *American Journal of Sociology* 116(4):1190–1233.

Knight, Alan. 2012. "Narco-Violence and the State in Modern Mexico." Pp. 115–34 in *Violence, Coercion and State-Making in Mexico: The Other Half of the Centaur*, edited by W.G. Pansters. Palo Alto, CA: Stanford University Press.

Koonings, Kees and Dirk Krujit. 2007. *Fractured Cities: Social Exclusion, Urban Violence and Contested Spaces in Latin America*. London, UK: Zed Books.

Koonings, Kees and Dirk Krujit. 2015. *Violence and Resilience in Latin American Cities*. London, UK: Zed Books.

Koury, Mauro Guilherme Pinheiro. 2017. "A cidade de João Pessoa revisitada: cultura emotiva e sentimentos de medo na cidade." *Revista Brasileira de Sociologia Da Emoção* 16(47):155–72.

de Lachica Huerta, Fabiola. 2020. "Shattering the Everyday. Rearranging the Ordinary. The Categories, Temporalities, and Spatial Dimensions of an Acute Event: The Case of the Villas de Salvarcar Massacre." Doctoral dissertation, The New School for Social Research.

168 BIBLIOGRAPHY

de Lachica Huerta, Fabiola. 2023. "Lugares violentados. Modificaciones a los usos y significados de espacios cotidianos en contextos de violencia." *Revista Colombiana de Sociología* 46(2): 343–63.

Larkins, Erika Mary Robb. 2015. *The Spectacular Favela: Violence in Modern Brazil.* Oakland, CA: University of California Press.

Lee, M. 2001. "The Genesis of 'Fear of Crime.'" *Theoretical Criminology* 5(4):467–85.

Lees, Loretta, Hyun Bang Shin, and Ernesto López-Morales. 2015. *Global Gentrifications: Uneven Development and Displacement.* Bristol, UK: Policy Press.

Lees, Loretta, Hyun Bang Shin, and Ernesto López-Morales. 2016. *Planetary Gentrification.* Cambridge, UK: Polity Press.

Lessing, Benjamin. 2017. *Making Peace in Drug Wars: Crackdowns and Cartels in Latin America.* Cambridge, UK: Cambridge University Press.

Ley, Sandra. 2018. "To Vote or Not to Vote: How Criminal Violence Shapes Electoral Participation." *Journal of Conflict Resolution* 62(9):1963–90.

Ley, Sandra. 2022. "High-Risk Participation: Demanding Peace and Justice amid Criminal Violence." *Journal of Peace Research* 59(6):794–809.

Ley, Sandra and Magdalena Guzmán. 2019. "Doing Business amid Criminal Violence. Companies and Civil Action in Mexico." Pp. 147–77 in *Civil Action and the Dynamics of Violence,* edited by D. Avant, M. Berry, E. Chenoweth, R. Epstein, C. Hendrix, O. Kaplan, and T. Sisk. Oxford: Oxford University Press.

Lindón, Alicia. 2000. *La vida cotidiana y su espacio-temporalidad.* Mexico City, MX: El Colegio Mexiquense; Universidad Autónoma Nacional de México; Anthropos Editorial.

Lindón, Alicia. 2007. "La construcción social de los paisajes invisibles del miedo." Pp. 219–42 in *La construcción social del paisaje,* edited by J. Nogué. Madrid, ES: Biblioteca Nueva.

Lipsitz, George. 2011. *How Racism Takes Place.* Philadelphia, PA: Temple University Press.

López Estrada, Raúl Eduardo (Ed.). 2002. *La pobreza en Monterrey: los recursos económicos de las unidades domésticas.* Monterrey, MX: Universidad Autónoma de Nuevo León.

Low, Setha. 2001. "The Edge and the Center: Gated Communities and the Discourse of Urban Fear." *American Anthropologist* 103(1):45–58.

Low, Setha. 2004. *Behind the Gates: Life, Security, and the Pursuit of Happiness in Fortress America.* New York: Routledge.

Low, Setha. 2006. "Unlocking the Gated Community: Moral Minimalism and Social (Dis) Order in Gated Communities in the United States and Mexico." Pp. 43–60 in *Private Cities: Global and Local Perspectives,* edited by G. Glasze, C. Webster, and K. Frantz. New York: Routledge.

Luft, Aliza. 2023. "The Moral Career of the Genocide Perpetrator: Cognition, Emotions, and Dehumanization as a Consequence, Not a Cause of Violence." *Sociological Theory* 41(4):324–51.

Magaloni, Beatriz, Gustavo Robles, Aila M. Matanock, Alberto Diaz-Cayeros, and Vidal Romero. 2020. "Living in Fear: The Dynamics of Extortion in Mexico's Drug War." *Comparative Political Studies* 53(7):1124–74.

Marcuse, Peter. 1997. "The Enclave, the Citadel, and the Ghetto: What has Changed in the Post-Fordist U.S. City." *Urban Affairs Review* 33(2):228–64.

Martinez, Cid. 2016. *The Neighborhood Has Its Own Rules: Latinos and African Americans in South Los Angeles.* New York: New York University Press.

Martínez Jazzo, Irma. 1995. *La distribución del ingreso en Monterrey.* Monterrey, MX: UANL, Mimeo.

BIBLIOGRAPHY 169

Mauss, Marcel. 2006. *Sociologie et anthropologie*. Paris, FR: Presses Universitaires de France.

Menjívar, Cecilia. 2023. "State Categories, Bureaucracies of Displacement, and Possibilities from the Margins." *American Sociological Review* 88(1):1–23.

Midgette, Gregory, Steven Davenport, Jonathan P. Caulkins, and Beau Kilmer. 2019. *What America's Users Spend on Illegal Drugs, 2006-2016*. Santa Monica, CA: RAND Corporation.

Molnár, Virág. 2016. "The Power of Things: Material Culture as Political Resource." *Qualitative Sociology* 39(2):205–10.

Moloeznik, Marcos Pablo. 2007. "Balance de la función de seguridad pública en México." In *Aproximaciones empíricas al estudio de la inseguridad: Once estudios en materia de seguridad ciudadana en México*, edited by L. González Placencia, J. L. Arce Aguilar, and M. Álvarez. Mexico City, MX: Miguel Ángel Porrúa.

Moncada, Eduardo. 2013. "Business and the Politics of Urban Violence in Colombia." *Studies in Comparative International Development* 48(3):308–30.

Moncada, Eduardo. 2016. *Cities, Business, and the Politics of Urban Violence in Latin America*. Palo Alto, CA: Stanford University Press.

Moncada, Eduardo. 2022. *Resisting Extortion: Victims, Criminals, and States in Latin America*. Cambridge, UK: Cambridge University Press.

Montemayor Hernández, Andrés. 1972. *Historia de Monterrey*. Monterrey, MX: Asociación de Editores y Libreros de Monterrey.

Montero, Sergio. 2017. "Worlding Bogota's Ciclovia: From Urban Experiment to International 'Best Practice.'" *Latin American Perspectives* 44(2):111–31.

Moore, Joan. 1991. *Going Down to the Barrio: Homeboys and Homegirls in Change*. Philadelphia, PA: Temple University Press.

Mora-Torres, Juan. 2001. *The Making of the Mexican Border: The State, Capitalism, and Society in Nuevo León, 1848-1910*. Austin, TX: University of Texas Press.

Moser, Caroline and Cathy McIlwaine. 2004. *Encounters with Violence in Latin America*. New York: Taylor & Francis.

Müller, Markus-Michael. 2016. *The Punitive City: Privatised Policing and Protection in Neoliberal Mexico*. London, UK: Zed Books.

Musto, David F. 1973. *The American Disease: Origins of Narcotic Control*. New Haven, CT: Yale University Press.

Nader, Laura. 1972. "Up the Anthropologist- Perspectives Gained From Studying Up." Pp. 284–311 in *Reinventing Anthropology*, edited by D. Hymes. New York: Vintage Books.

New York City Department of Housing Preservation and Development. 2023. *Essential Every Day: The Lives of NYC's Essential Workforce During Covid-19*. New York: Center for Research on Home; NYC Department of Housing Preservation and Development.

O'Hare, Patrick and Lucy Bell. 2020. "Cultural Responses to the War on Drugs: Writing, Occupying, and 'Public-ing' in the Mexican City." *City & Society* 32(1):203–27.

O'Neill, Kevin Lewis and Kedron Thomas (Eds.). 2011. *Securing the City: Neoliberalism, Space, and Insecurity in Postwar Guatemala*. Durham, NC: Duke University Press.

Olvera Gudiño, José Juan. 2010. "Los caminos de la vida son de migración y diversidad... ademas de la 'Colombia.'" Pp. 135–50 in *Colores y ecos de la colonia Independencia*, edited by C. Contreras. Monterrey, MX: COLEF and Municipio de Monterrey.

Osorio, Javier. 2015. "The Contagion of Drug Violence: Spatiotemporal Dynamics of the Mexican War on Drugs." *Journal of Conflict Resolution* 59(8): 1403–32.

170 BIBLIOGRAPHY

Osorno, Diego Enrique. 2012. *La guerra de los Zetas: viaje por la frontera de la necropolítica*. Mexico City, MX: Grijalbo.

Padilla, Felix. 1992. *The Gang as an American Enterprise*. New Brunswick, NJ: Rutgers University Press.

Pain, Rachel. 1997. "Social Geographies of Women's Fear of Crime." *Transactions of the Institute of British Geographers* 22(3):231–44.

Pain, Rachel. 2000. "Place, Social Relations and the Fear of Crime: A Review." *Progress in Human Geography* 24(3):365–87.

Palacios Hernández, Lylia, Camilo Contreras Delgado, Víctor Zúñiga, and Thierry Blöss (Eds.). 2010. *Cuando México enfrenta la globalización: permanencias y cambios en el área metropolitana de Monterrey*. Monterrey, MX: UANL, COLEF, ITESM, UDEM, NMF, CIESAS.

Palacios, Lylia and Eleocadio Martínez. 2010. "El corazón del oficio zapatero en Monterrey." Pp. 117–30 in *Ecos y colores de la colonia Independencia*, edited by C. Contreras. Monterrey, MX: COLEF and Municipio de Monterrey.

Paley, Dawn. 2014. *Drug War Capitalism*. Oakland, CA: AK Press.

Pansters, Wil G. 2012. "Zones of State-Making: Violence, Coercion, and Hegemony in Twentieth-Century Mexico." Pp. 3–42 in *Violence, Coercion and State-Making in Mexico: The Other Half of the Centaur*, edited by W. G. Pansters. Palo Alto, CA: Stanford University Press.

Park, Robert Ezra, Ernest W. Burgess, and Roderick Duncan McKenzie. 1967. *The City: Suggestions for Investigation of Human Behavior in the Urban Environment*. Chicago, IL: University of Chicago Press.

Patillo-McCoy, Mary. 1999. *Black Picket Fences: Privilege and Peril among the Black Middle Class*. Chicago, IL: University of Chicago Press.

Patillo, Mary. 2003. "Extending the Boundaries and Definition of the Ghetto." *Ethnic and Racial Studies* 26(6):1046–57.

Peeters, Timo. 2021. *The Unseen: Withdrawal and the Social Order of Violence in Guatemala City*. Rotterdam, NL: Erasmus University Rotterdam.

Pezard-Ramirez, Edna. 2022. "City of Fear: Feelings of Insecurity, Daily Practices, and Public Space in Monterrey, Mexico." Doctoral dissertation, Université de Paris.

Pinçon-Charlot, Monique and Michel Pinçon. 2018. "Social Power and Power Over Space: How the Bourgeoisie Reproduces itself in the City." *International Journal of Urban and Regional Research* 42(1):115–25.

Pinçon, Michel and Monique Pinçon-Charlot. 2007. *Les Ghettos du Gotha: comment la bourgeoisie défend ses espaces*. Paris, FR: Éditions du Seuil.

Polit Dueñas, Gabriela. 2019. *Unwanted Witnesses: Journalists and Conflict in Contemporary Latin America*. Pittsburgh, PA: University of Pittsburgh Press.

Puente Leyva, Jesús. 1969. *Distribución del ingreso en un área urbana*. Mexico City, MX: Siglo XXI Editores.

Ramírez Atilano, Dairee Alejandra. 2014. "Fuerzas Unidas por Nuestros Desaparecidos en Nuevo León (FUNDENL): la acción colectiva en busca de las personas desaparecidas en Monterrey." Bachelor's thesis, Universidad de Monterrey.

Ramírez Atilano, Dairee Alejandra. 2019. "Hacia una isla urbana segura y participativa: efectos socio-espaciales en el proyecto de regeneración urbana Distrito Tec, Monterrey." Master's thesis, Colegio de México.

Ramos-Zayas, Ana. 2020. *Parenting Empires: Class, Whiteness, and the Moral Economy of Privilege in Latin America*. Durham, NC: Duke University Press.

BIBLIOGRAPHY   171

Rea, Daniela and Pablo Ferri. 2019. *La tropa: por qué mata un soldado*. Mexico City, MX: Penguin Random House.

Reames, Benjamin. 2007. "A Profile of Police Forces in Mexico." Pp. 117–32 in *Reforming the Administration of Justice in Mexico*, edited by W. A. Cornelius and D. A. Shirk. Notre Dame, IN: University of Notre Dame Press.

Rebotier, Julien. 2011a. "Politicizing Fear of Crime and Insecurity in Caracas." *Emotion, Space and Society* 4(2):104–12.

Rebotier, Julien. 2011b. "La fábrica de la inseguridad en Caracas. Entre leyenda urbana y necesidad de gestión." *Tempo Social* 22(2): 143–63.

Reguillo, Rossana. 2002. "The Social Construction of Fear: Urban Narratives and Practices." Pp. 187–206 in *Citizens of Fear: Urban Violence in Latin America*, edited by S. Rotker. New Brunswick, NJ: Rutgers University Press.

Reguillo, Rossana. 2008. "Sociabilidad, inseguridad y miedos. Una trilogía para pensar la ciudad contemporánea." *Alteridades* 18(36):63–74.

Residente Staff. 2012. "Visiones de ciudad." *Residente Monterrey. Acciones para una ciudad mejor,* October issue, 10–11.

Rios, Victor M. 2017. *Human Targets: Schools, Police, and the Criminalization of Latino Youth*. Chicago, IL: University of Chicago Press.

Rizzo Reyes, Cordelia. 2017. "La nostalgia de la invulnerabilidad: violencia y cultura de paz en Nuevo León." Pp. 427–54 in *Violencia y paz. Diagnósticos y propuestas para México,* edited by F. Enciso. Mexico City, MX: Colegio de México, Instituto Belisario Domínguez, CNDH.

Rizzo Reyes, Cordelia. 2020. "Modos de recordar que sanan: el derecho a la memoria y políticas de reparación del daño." Pp. 25–42 in *Formas de resistencia: siete experiencias de escucha y denuncia en las prácticas artísticas,* edited by L. M. Sánchez Cardona and S.-C. A. Paula. Mexico City, MX: UAM Lerma.

Rodgers, Dennis. 2006. "Living in the Shadow of Death: Gangs, Violence and the Social Order in Urban Nicaragua, 1996-2002." *Journal of Latin American Studies* 38(2):267–92.

Rodgers, Dennis. 2016. "Critique of Urban Violence: Bismarckian Transformations in Managua, Nicaragua." *Theory, Culture & Society* 33(7–8):85–109.

Rodríguez Hernández, Rogelio. 2003. "Atribuciones causales a la violencia en adolescentes miembros de las pandillas: un análisis desde la teoría de la identidad social." Master's thesis, Universidad Autónoma de Nuevo León.

Rossini, Carlos, Emiliano Altuna, and Diego Enrique Osorno. 2012. *El Alcalde.* Mexico: Bambú Audiovisual/IMCINE-FOPROCINE.

Rotker, Susana. 2002. *Citizens of Fear: Urban Violence in Latin America*. New Brunswick, NJ: Rutgers University Press.

Rubio-Campos, Jesús, Mónica Chávez-Elorza, and Héctor Rodríguez-Ramírez. 2017. "Significados, causas y efectos de la violencia social entre la juventud en Monterrey, Nuevo León, México." *Sociedad y Economía* 32:85–106.

Sabatini, Francisco. 2003. *La segregación social del espacio en las ciudades de América Latina*. Pp. 1–41 in *Serie Azul,* 35. Washington, D.C.: Inter-American Development Bank.

Sabatini, Francisco, Gonzalo Cáceres, and Jorge Cerda. 2001. "Segregación residencial en las principales ciudades chilenas: Tendencias de las tres últimas décadas y posibles cursos de acción." *EURE* 27(81):21–42.

172 BIBLIOGRAPHY

Sampson, Robert J. and Dawn Jeglum Bartusch. 1998. "Legal Cynicism and (Subcultural?) Tolerance of Deviance: The Neighborhood Context of Racial Differences." *Law & Society Review* 32(4):777–804.

Sánchez-Jankowski, Martin. 1991. *Islands in the Street: Gangs and American Urban Society*. Berkeley, CA: University of California Press.

Sandoval, Efrén. 2005. "Pobreza, marginación y desigualdad en Monterrey: puntos de partida." *Frontera Norte* 17(33):133–41.

Sandoval Hernández, Efrén. 2018. *Violentar la vida en el norte de México. Estado, tráficos y migraciones en la frontera con Texas*. Mexico City, MX: Centro de Investigaciones y Estudios Superiores en Antropología Social; Plaza y Valdés.

Sandoval Hernández, Efrén and Rodrigo Escamilla. 2010. "La historia de una colonia, un puente y un mercado: La Pulga del Puente del Papa en Monterrey." *Estudios Fronterizos* 11(22):157–84.

Santamaría, Gema and David Carey. 2017. *Violence and Crime in Latin America: Representations and Politics*. Norman, OK: University of Oklahoma Press.

Saragoza, Alex M. 1988. *The Monterrey Elite and the Mexican State, 1880-1940*. Austin, TX: University of Texas Press.

Sassen, Saskia. 2001. *The Global City: New York, London, Tokyo*. Princeton, NJ: Princeton University Press.

Saucedo Villegas, Alma Leticia. 2017. "Imaginarios urbanos de la violencia en el espacio público de Monterrey." Doctoral dissertation, Universidad Autónoma de Nuevo León.

Scheff, Thomas J. 1994. *Bloody Revenge: Emotions, Nationalism and War*. Boulder, CO: Westview Press.

Scheff, Thomas J. 2000. "Shame and the Social Bond: A Sociological Theory." *Sociological Theory* 18(1):84–99.

Scheff, Thomas J. and Suzanne M. Retzinger. 1991. *Emotions and Violence: Shame and Rage in Destructive Conflicts*. Lexington, MA: Lexington Books.

Schmitz, Andreas and Judith Eckert. 2022. "Towards a General Sociology of Fear: A Programmatic Answer to Crucial Deficits of the Contemporary Fear Discourse." *Emotions and Society* 4(3):275–89.

Schoenfeld, Heather. 2018. *Building the Prison State: Race and the Politics of Mass Incarceration*. Chicago, IL: University of Chicago Press.

Sherman, Rachel. 2017. *Uneasy Street: The Anxieties of Affluence*. Princeton, NJ: Princeton University Press.

Sierra-Arévalo, Michael. 2019. "Police and Legitimacy in Mexico City." *Contexts* 18(4):34–43.

Simes, Jessica. 2021. *Punishing Places: The Geography of Mass Imprisonment*. Berkeley, CA: University of California Press.

Smith, Benjamin. 2021. *The Dope: The Real History of the Mexican Drug Trade*. New York: W.W. Norton & Company.

Snyder, Richard and Angélica Durán-Martínez. 2009. "Does Illegality Breed Violence? Drug Trafficking and State-Sponsored Protection Rackets." *Crime, Law and Social Change* 52(3):253–73.

Solís, Patricio. 2007. *Inequidad y movimiento social en Monterrey*. Mexico City, MX: Colegio de México.

Soto Canales, Karina. 2018. "Imaginarios urbanos de segregación en espacios estigmatizados del Área Metropolitana De Monterrey." *TOPOFILIA* 16:91–109.

BIBLIOGRAPHY 173

Soto Canales, Karina. 2022. "Movilidad cotidiana en tiempos pandémicos. Entre la necesidad y el miedo." Pp. 15–39 in *Urbanismo y arquitectura: 11 aproximaciones*, edited by G. Carmona Ochoa. Saltillo, MX: Editorial Labyrinthos; Universidad Autónoma de Coahuila.

Stanko, Elizabeth A. 2000. "Victims R US: The Life History of 'Fear of Crime' and the Politicisation of Violence." Pp. 13–30 in *Crime, Risk and Insecurity: Law and Order in Everyday Life and Political Discourse*. London, UK: Routledge.

Stuart, Forrest. 2016. *Down, Out, and Under Arrest: Policing and Everyday Life in Skid Row*. Chicago, IL: University of Chicago Press.

Suttles, Gerald D. 1972. *The Social Construction of Communities*. Chicago, IL: University of Chicago Press.

Svampa, Maristella. 2001. *Los que ganaron. La vida en los countries y barrios privados*. Buenos Aires, AR: Biblos.

Svampa, Maristella. 2004. *La brecha urbana. Countries y barrios privados en Argentina*. Buenos Aires, AR: Capital Intelectual SA.

Tavory, Iddo. 2016. *Summoned: Identification and Religious Life in a Jewish Neighborhood*. Chicago, IL: University of Chicago Press.

Torres Escalante, Benito. 2014. "Sentimiento vallenato: permanencia y cambios en el estilo de vida de los jóvenes colombias de Monterrey, 1990–2014." Master's thesis, Universidad Autónoma de Nuevo León.

Trejo, Guillermo and Sandra Ley. 2020. *Votes, Drugs, and Violence. The Political Logic of Criminal Wars in Mexico*. Cambridge, UK: Cambridge University Press.

Trelles, Alejandro and Miguel Carreras. 2012. "Bullets and Votes: Violence and Electoral Participation in Mexico." *Journal of Politics in Latin America* 4(2):89–123.

Turner, Jonathan H. 2010. "The Stratification of Emotions: Some Preliminary Generalizations." *Sociological Inquiry* 80(2):168–99.

Turner, Jonathan H. 2014. "Emotions and Societal Stratification." Pp. 179–97 in *Handbook of the Sociology of Emotions: Volume II*, edited by J. E. Stets and J. H. Turner. New York: Springer.

Turner, Jonathan H. 2015. *Revolt From the Middle: Emotional Stratification and Change in Post-Industrial Societies*. New Brunswick, N.J.: Transaction Publishers.

Turner, Jonathan H. and Jan E. Stets. 2006. "Sociological Theories of Human Emotions." *Annual Review of Sociology* 32:25–52.

Tyler, Ronnie C. 1993. "Santiago Vidaurri y la Confederación." Pp. 112–30 in *Frontera e historia económica. Texas y el norte de México (1850-1865)*, edited by M. Cerutti and M. A. González Quiroga. Mexico City, MX: Instituto de Investigaciones Dr. Mora/UAM.

United Nations Office on Drugs and Crime. 2023. *Global Report on Cocaine 2023: Local Dynamics, Global Challenges*. Vienna, AU.

Valdez Cárdenas, Javier. 2016. *Narcoperiodismo: la prensa en medio del crimen y la denuncia*. Mexico City, MX: Penguin Random House.

Valenzuela Aguilera, Alfonso. 2013. "Urban Surges: Power, Territory, and the Social Control of Space in Latin America." *Latin American Perspectives* 40(2):21–34.

Valenzuela Aguilera, Alfonso. 2016. *La construcción espacial del miedo*. Cuernavaca, MX: Universidad Autónoma del Estado de Morelos; Juan Pablos Editor.

Valenzuela, Alfonso. 2007. "Santa Fe (México): Megaproyectos para una ciudad dividida." *Cuadernos Geográficos* 40(1):53–66.

Vargas, Robert. 2016. *Wounded City: Violent Turf Wars in a Chicago Barrio*. New York: Oxford University Press.

174   BIBLIOGRAPHY

Velasco, José Luis. 2005. *Insurgency, Authoritarianism, and Drug Trafficking in Mexico's "Democratization."* New York: Routledge.

Vellinga, Menno. 1988. *Desigualdad, poder y cambio social en Monterrey*. Mexico City, MX: Siglo XXI.

Venkatesh, Sudhir Alladi. 1997. "The Social Organization of Street Gang Activity in an Urban Ghetto." *American Journal of Sociology* 103(1):82–111.

Vesselinov, Elena. 2008. "Members Only: Gated Communities and Residential Segregation in the Metropolitan United States." *Sociological Forum* 23(3):536–55.

Vigil, James Diego. 1988. *Barrio Gangs: Street Life and Identity in Southern California*. Austin, TX: University of Texas Press.

Vilalta, Carlos J. 2011. "Fear of Crime in Gated Communities and Apartment Buildings: A Comparison of Housing Types and a Test of Theories." *Journal of Housing and the Built Environment* 26:107–21.

Vilalta, Carlos J. 2016. "Does the Mexican War on Organized Crime Mediate the Impact of Fear of Crime on Daily Routines?" *Crime & Delinquency* 62(11):1448–64.

Vilalta Perdomo, Carlos J. 2010. "El miedo al crimen en México: estructura lógica, bases empíricas y recomendaciones iniciales de política pública." *Gestión y Política Urbana* 19(1):3–36.

Villamizar-Santamaría, Sebastián. 2022. "Eyes on the Screen: Digital Interclass Coalitions Against Crime in a Gentrifying Rural Town." *City & Community* 21(1):62–81.

Villarreal, Ana. 2013. "Kidnappable: On the Normalization of Violence in Urban Mexico." *Global Dialogue* 3(3): 23–24.

Villarreal, Ana. 2021. "Domesticating Danger: Coping Codes and Symbolic Security amid Violent Organized Crime in Mexico." *Sociological Theory* 39(4):225–44.

Villarreal, Ana. 2022. "The Logistics of Fear: Violence and the Stratifying Power of Emotion." *Emotions and Society* 4(3):290–306.

Villarreal, Andres. 2002. "Political Competition and Violence in Mexico: Hierarchical Social Control in Local Patronage Structures." *American Sociological Review* 67(4):477–98.

Vizcaya, Isidro. 2006. *Los orígenes de la industrialización de Monterrey: una historia económica y social desde la caída del Segundo Imperio hasta el fin de la Revolución (1867-1920)*. Monterrey, MX: Fondo Editorial Nuevo León, ITESM.

Wacquant, Loïc. 2004. "Decivilizing and Demonizing: The Remaking of the Black American Ghetto." Pp. 95–121 in *The Sociology of Norbert Elias*, edited by S. Loyal and S. Quilley. Cambridge, UK: Cambridge University Press.

Wacquant, Loïc. 2008. *Urban Outcasts: A Comparative Sociology of Advanced Marginality*. Cambridge, UK: Polity Press.

Wacquant, Loïc. 2010. "Designing Urban Seclusion in the Twenty-First Century." *Perspecta, The Yale Architectural Journal* 43: 164–75.

Wacquant, Loïc. 2012. "A Janus-Faced Institution of Ethnoracial Enclosure: A Sociological Specification of the Ghetto." Pp. 1–32 in *The Ghetto: Contemporary Global Issues and Controversies*, edited by R. Hutchinson and B. D. Haynes. Boulder, CO: Westview Press.

Wagner-Pacifici, Robin. 2017. *What Is an Event?* Chicago, IL: University of Chicago.

Walton, John. 1977. *Elites and Economic Development*. Austin, TX: The University of Texas at Austin.

Watkins, Amanda. 2014. *Cholombianos*. Monterrey, MX: Trilce Ediciones.

Zamorano Villarreal, Claudia Carolina. 2019. "¿Qué tan pública es la seguridad pública en México?" *Revista Mexicana de Sociología* 81(3):479–507.

BIBLIOGRAPHY 175

Zeiderman, Austin. 2016. *Endangered City: The Politics of Security and Risk in Bogotá.* Durham, NC: Duke University Press.

Zepeda Lecuona, Guillermo. 2004. *Crimen sin castigo. Procuración de justicia penal y ministerio público.* Mexico City, MX: Fondo de Cultura Económica.

Zubillaga, Verónica, Manuel Llorens, and John Souto. 2015. "Chismosas and Alcahuetas: Being the Mother of an Empistolado within the Everyday Armed Violence of a Caracas Barrio." Pp. 162–88 in *Violence at the Urban Margins*, edited by J. Auyero, P. Bourgois, and N. Scheper-Hughes. New York: Oxford University Press.

Zulver, Julia. 2022. *High-Risk Feminism in Colombia: Women's Mobilization in Violent Contexts.* Rutgers, NJ: Rutgers University Press.

Zulver, Julia. 2023. "Complex Gendered Agency in Mexico: How Women Negotiate Hierarchies of Fear to Search for the Disappeared." *European Journal of Politics and Gender* 1(aop):1–17.

Zúñiga, Víctor. 2010. "La puerta de Monterrey: la historia de Simona y las dos Julietas." Pp. 55–65 in *Ecos y colores de la colonia Independencia*, edited by C. Contreras. Monterrey, MX: COLEF and Municipio de Monterrey.

Zúñiga, Víctor and Manuel Ribeiro (Eds.). 1990. *La marginación urbana en Monterrey.* Monterrey, MX: Universidad Autónoma de Nuevo León.

Index

For the benefit of digital users, indexed terms that span two pages (e.g., 52–53) may, on occasion, appear on only one of those pages.

Figures are indicated by *f* following the page number

acquaintances (*conocidos*)
  fear of strangers, 1, 9–10, 97–98
  increased in-network socializing, 9–10,
    69–74, 98
Arellanes, Margarita, 119–20
Arias, Desmond, 130
Astorga, Luis, 30, 31–32

Barrio Antiguo, 83–84
  gunned down, 17, 19–20, 85–90
  as metropolitan nightlife center, 85–87
  new daytime businesses, 87–88
  shifting acoustics, 86–87
  upper class not returning, 71, 85, 100
  See also Café Iguana
beer
  in daily life, 51, 56, 89, 94, 107–
    8, 110–11
  factory downtown, 36–37
  in Monterrey's industrial history, 11–12
bus line, adaptations to fear, 16–17
business elite, 20–21, 48
  calls to defend metropolis, 11, 14–22
  revamping state police, 8–9, 63–64
  spatial concentration, 65–69, 129
  taking office (*see* Fernández, Mauricio)
  targeted, killed, 17, 40–41

Cadereyta
  country homes, 107–9
  massacre, 49 dismembered bodies, 26–28
Café Iguana, 83–84, 85–86, 100, 128
Calderón, Felipe
  contested presidential election, 31–32
  launching "War on drug trafficking,"
    11, 12

narratives criminalizing victims, 27
  response to Casino Royale
    Attack, 33–34
caravanning and carpooling for
  safety, 52–54
  buses on highways, 53–54
  moms at school, 52
  motorcyclists and "power of the
    pack," 52–53
  scheduled convoys for work, 53
  spontaneous on highways, 53
Casino Royale Attack, 33–35, 86–87
Centrito, El, 85, 95–96, 128
  "the same" partying for some, 95–96
checkpoints, 125–26, 127
civic engagement
  classed, 10–11, 130
  in San Pedro de Pinta, 113
  See also Caravan for Peace;
    Embroidering peace
classism, exacerbated, 10–19, 23, 69–74
  See also domestic workers: increasingly
    surveilled
Colombian dances, 87–90, 99–100
  See also La Fe Music Hall
consumption, shifts in, 47–52
  discrete dress codes, 50–51
  downgrading cars, 47–50
Covid-19 pandemic, 128, 131–34
  first case detected in San Pedro, 125
  flying to Texas for vaccine, 127–28
  heightened seclusion, 125–26
  lowest mortality rate in Mexico, 128
crime. *See* violent crime
crime stories, 45–47, 58
crises, 125–34

178 INDEX

defended city, 8–11
disappeared, the
  organized family collectives, 130
  origins, 12, 27, 31–32
  protesting disappearances in public
    space, 26–27, 35f, 38–39
  See also *Fuerzas Unidas por Nuestros*
    Desaparecidos en Nuevo León;
    Hidalgo Rea, Leticia; Rivera
    Hidalgo, Roy
  domestic workers, 10, 15, 19–20, 52,
    64–65, 66, 79, 123–24
  conversations with employers, 76–77
  getting around the city, 16, 70, 126
  increasingly surveilled, 75–77
drugs, and violence, 29–34
  binational (US-Mexico) antidrug
    campaigns, 30–31
  cocaine, 12–13, 22–23, 29–30, 32–33,
    41–42
  drug trafficking, 13–14, 30–31
  prohibition, 12–13, 22–23, 29–30
  war on drugs, 30–32
Durin, Séverine, 10, 76–77, 78–79

employment, fear and
  decreased opportunities for working
    class, 69, 75, 80–81
  increased opportunities for business
    within San Pedro, 68–69
  See also domestic workers: increasingly
    surveilled
Enciso, Froylán, 29–31
Escobar, Debanhi, 129–30
extortion (*cobro de piso*)
  becoming widespread, 37–38
  in middle-class neighborhoods, 51, 122
  police extortion, 23, 55, 89–90
  prompting job reconversion, 51
  prompting relocation abroad, 51
  prompting strategies to "lower one's
    profile," 45
  responses to fear of extortion (*see*
    logistics of fear)
  small business, 51–52, 122
  in upper-class neighborhoods, 40–41,
    51–52
  in working-class neighborhoods, 51

fear, as a problem, 3, 131
fear of crime, 5, 8, 44, 128–29
Fernández, Mauricio, 60–62, 64, 127–28
Fuerza Civil (Civic Force), 8–9, 63–
  64, 80–81
Fuerzas Unidas por Nuestros Desaparecidos
  en Nuevo León (United Forces for
  our Disappeared in Nuevo
  León), 38–39
  See also Hidalgo Rea, Leticia

gated communities, proliferating
  abroad, in Texas, 78
  first built in San Pedro, 65–69
  moving into new office buildings
    within, 68
  weighing advantages against
    disadvantages, 66
gating neighborhoods
  in Guadalupe, 62
  in San Nicolás, 62
  in San Pedro Garza García, 19–20, 70
gender, 5, 111
  reinforced male protective role, 2–3,
    6–7, 44, 67, 79
  violence against women (*see* Escobar,
    Debanhi)
Guadalupe
  bus line ethnography, 16–17
  open-streets program, 106, 120–21
  police raids, 55
  a public schoolteacher's story, 1–3
gunfights, 2, 37, 86
guns, proliferation of, 12

Hidalgo Rea, Leticia, 26, 28–29, 38–39,
  130, 139–40
Huasteca, la, 109–12, 123
  increased security, 110
  rock-climbing, 110–11
human rights groups, 27, 33–34, 38–39
  See also *Fuerzas Unidas por Nuestros*
    Desaparecidos en Nuevo León

impunity, 27–30, 41–42, 129–30
Independencia, la, 2–3, 19–20, 50, 55–56,
  69
  brief history, 35–36

Colombiano fashion and hairstyle, 56,
57*f*, 137
gentrification attempts, 81–82
tapados (the covered ones), 36

kidnappings, widespread, 37–38,
67, 108–9
among medical personnel, 50–51
casa de seguridad (safety house), 1, 94
everyday responses (*see* logistics of fear)
kidnappable, 49–51
middle-class, 28, 46, 47, 49–50
most concerning crime, 65
underreported, 40–41
upper-class, 41, 45–46, 61, 66–67
working-class, 1, 50

La Fe Music Hall, 87–90, 94, 96–
97, 99–100
legal cynicism, 22–23, 42
leisure, shifts in
abandoned and ravaged country
homes, 106–9
decreased outdoor activities, 106–12
moving family gatherings
indoors, 104–5
See also Huasteca, la; Santiago, villa de:
plummeted tourism
logistics of fear, 6–7, 15, 18, 23, 44–
59, 131–34

Macro Plaza, 38–39, 84, 119–20
Heroes Esplanade, 26–27, 38–39
marginalized youth, 54–57
dancing, large metropolitan
gatherings, 88–89
fashion, 56–57
forcibly recruited into organized
crime, 35–37
gangs, 55–56
greeting each other on the radio, 94–95
harassed and extorted in public
space, 105
music, *cumbia*, 88
See also La Fe Music Hall
memorials, victims of violence, 33–
34, 83–84
memory, and violence

forgetting violence, 24, 117–18
recalling violence, 36–37, 64–65
migrants, classed
industrial migrants, 12, 27–28, 35–36
music, *cumbia*, 88
wealthy Mexican immigrants in
Texas, 61–78
military forces
calling on them (or not), 28
checkpoints, 107–8
debriefing privileged residents, 40–41
deployed during bi-national
operations, 30–31
dwindling trust, 42
human rights abuses, 42–43
interactions with working class, 2, 56
patrolling streets, 64, 96, 105, 106, 107
replacing local police, 122
staged "protests" against their
deployment, 36
surveilling peace protests, 38
Monterrey Metropolitan Area, 11–
15, 19–20
urbanization, 11–12
See also Guadalupe; San Nicolás de los
Garza; San Pedro Garza García

New York City, logistics of fear in a global
pandemic, 131–34
fear isolates and regroups, 133
fear relocates, 131–32
fear reschedules, 132–33
fear reveals and widens the
gaps, 133–34
nightlife, shifts in
carne asada as social refuge, 49, 84–85,
90, 91–93
new curfews, 2–3, 6–7, 14–15, 44, 45,
47, 59
partying closer to home, 90–95
sleepovers for safety, 83, 93, 94, 96
See also Barrio Antiguo; Centrito, El; La
Fe Music Hall
Norte, El, newspaper, 48, 53–54, 62, 106,
125, 126, 128

open-streets programs, 119–22
See also San Pedro de Pinta

180 INDEX

organized crime, 22–23, 30, 34, 36–38, 48, 54, 56–57, 61, 107–8
  forced recruitment into, 15, 35–36, 55–56
  Gulf Cartel, 13
  relations with Mexican State, 30
  Zetas, 13–14, 33–34, 36, 37–38, 75
  See also Casino Royale Attack

pandemic. *See* Covid-19
paramilitary forces, 8–9, 64
parenting, fear and
  becoming a helicopter mom, 75–76
  fathers sending family somewhere safer, 66–67
  losing sight of child in crowd, 118
  not sharing fears with daughters, 2–3
Partido de Acción Nacional, 31–32, 61
Partido Revolucionario Institucional, 30
pedestrians
  class differences, 18, 113–14
  decreased accessibility, 19, 24, 126
pick-up trucks
  association with organized crime, 50, 92–93, 110–12
  warnings against driving them, 46, 48, 50
police, 3, 4, 26, 36, 53–54, 84, 87, 106
  calling police, 118
  colluded with organized crime, 28, 105, 106, 108–9, 122
  extorting marginalized youth, 54–55, 56–57, 80–81, 89–90
  federal police, 33–34, 38, 106, 110–11
  guarding public officials, 60, 119–20
  late to respond (or did not respond), 36, 84
  low trust in police, 42, 65
  private use of public security, 8–9, 63–64, 102–3, 125–26
  surveilling protests, 38
  See also *Fuerza Civil*
private security
  harassing marginalized youth, 89–90
  protecting privileged residents, 66–68, 96–97, 126–27
protests, peace
  caravan for peace, 38
  embroidering peace, 38–39, 40*f*

public space, violence and
  decreased use of parks in San Bernabé, 105
  decreased use of parks in San Nicolás, 104–5
  See also disappeared, the: protesting disappearances in public space; San Pedro de Pinta

racism, exacerbated, 5, 6–7, 10, 19, 54–57, 69–74
Rivera Hidalgo, Roy, 26, 28–29
  See also Hidalgo Rea, Leticia

Sabino Gordo, el, 86–87
San Nicolás de los Garza, 39, 50, 52, 94, 113, 115–16
  armoring neighborhoods program, 62
  aspirational status markers, shifts in, 49
  extorted businesses, 51
  gating of parks, 104–5
  individual safety precautions, 62, 93–94
  open-streets program, 121–22
  San Nicolás police, 28, 89–90
  See also La Fe Music Hall; Roy Rivera Hidalgo
San Pedro Garza García, 4, 8–9
  "Armoring" narrative, 60–62
  brief history of urbanization, 61
  Calzada del Valle, 102–3, 112, 119
  heightened suspicion among residents, 69–77
  likening its border to US-Mexico border, 127
  lower crime rates, 34–35
  as new nightlife center, 95–99
  organizing everyday life within, 14–15
  organized crime residents, 61
  spatial regrouping of urban wealth, 21, 65–69
  See also Centrito, El; defended city; Fernández, Mauricio; San Pedro de Pinta
San Pedro de Pinta, 101–4, 105–6, 112
  attendee characteristics and activities, 115–19
  comparison to other open-street programs, 119–22

INDEX   181

during the Covid-19 pandemic, 128
origins and regulation, 112–15
Santa Catarina, 64, 93, 115
open-streets program, 19–20, 106, 120,
121, 127
Santa Catarina police, 106
Santa Catarina River, 16, 19–20
Santiago, Villa de
murdered mayor, 106
plummeted tourism, 106–7
Saucedo Villegas, Leticia, 87–90, 94, 96–97
shootings, 7, 17, 37–38, 44, 61, 83, 104–
5, 115–16
at bars and clubs, 84, 85–90
caught in crossfire, 37
checking Twitter for shootings, 58
distinguishing gunshots from
fireworks, 2, 64
hearing shootings nearby, 64–65, 78–79,
85–86, 87, 107–8
military shooting civilians, 27–28, 42–43
shooting range, 110, 111–12
surviving a shooting, 1–2
See also Café Iguana
Sicario (killer), 10, 17, 27–28, 54–55
Sierra Madre (socialite magazine), 21,
65, 125
Sierra Madre Mountains, 60, 67, 70
Chipinque natural reserve, 102–3
exclusive neighborhoods, 18–21, 67–68
reduced access to pedestrians, 126
reduced access to trails, 19–20
space, fear and
perception of widened distances, 91
relocating work and leisure closer to
home, 3, 7, 62–63, 68, 90–99
socializing with those living nearby,
102, 121, 133
status, and fear
weighing security and status
concerns, 47–52
strangers. *See* acquaintances
symbolic security, 7, 46, 50, 58, 107–8, 118
binding fear through everyday
logistics, 5–7

constructing home as safer than
elsewhere, 64–65, 94
criminalizing the dead, 78–79

Texas, fleeing violence
attempts to recreate privilege
abroad, 78–79
navigating Hispanic identity, 78
new classed spatial enclaves, 78
returning, 80
when breadwinner stays in
Mexico, 79–80

urban segregation
unequal urban planning, 15, 119, 120
widening disparities, 63–65, 95–99,
112–19
See also defended city

victimization, widespread and
unequal, 34–41
and civic engagement, 130
in close social networks, 41, 45–47, 96
links to deepened racism, 74
violence, gruesome, 2, 37–38, 108
See also Cadereyta: Mass murder,
49 dismembered bodies; Escobar,
Debanhi; Rivera Hidalgo, Roy
violent crime
blockades, road, 36–38
burglaries, 28, 46, 66, 76–77
carjackings, 36–37, 46, 48
car theft, 52, 65
homicides, 4, 8–9, 13, 27, 32–33, 34–35,
63–64, 65–66, 103
stopped or held at gunpoint, 28, 36–
37, 80–81
violence against women, 129–30
See also disappeared, the; extortion;
kidnappings; shootings

walls
raised and reinforced, 62
stripped of family pictures, 17
unnecessary at San Pedro de Pinta, 114